Corona SDK Mobile Game Development

Beginner's Guide

Beginner's Guide

Create monetized games for iOS and Android with minimum cost and code

Michelle M. Fernandez

BIRMINGHAM - MUMBAI

Corona SDK Mobile Game Development
Beginner's Guide

First published: April 2012

Production Reference: 1170412

Published by Packt Publishing Ltd.
Livery Place
35 Livery Street
Birmingham B3 2PB, UK.

ISBN 978-1-84969-188-8

www.packtpub.com

Cover Image by Raphael Pudlowski (r.pudlowski@gmail.com)

Credits

Author

Michelle M. Fernandez

Reviewers

Mitch Allen

Nicholas C. Golden

Alan Grace

Clement Ho

Steve Hoffman

Predrag Pedja Končar

Walter Luh

Edgar Miranda

Jordan Schuetz

Jayant Varma

Acquisition Editor

Robin de Jongh

Lead Technical Editor

Chris Rodrigues

Technical Editors

Manasi Poonthottam

Manali Mehta

Ankita Shashi

Manmeet Singh Vasir

Copy Editor

Laxmi Subramanian

Project Coordinator

Alka Nayak

Proofreader

Lisa Brady

Indexer

Rekha Nair

Production Coordinator

Prachali Bhiwandkar

Cover Work

Prachali Bhiwandkar

About the Author

Michelle M. Fernandez is a mobile game developer for iOS/Android devices and co-founder of MobiDojo (http://www.mobidojo.com). She is also a mentor for aspiring artists and programmers trying to break into the game industry. After experimenting with several game engines over the years, she was introduced to Corona SDK in late 2010 and has been an avid user of the program ever since. She enjoys creating tutorials and new game frameworks for others to learn from. When Michelle is not developing games, she is spending time with friends and family, playing video games, basketball, singing, or baking delicious pastries.

I would like to thank first and foremost my family and friends for their love and encouragement throughout the production of this book. To my dear friend and partner, Ed Ho, thanks for introducing me to Corona SDK. You have genuinely been my support throughout this project and always challenged and pushed me to succeed. To April Quileza and Yanglyn Ou, you guys have always been there for me to help review my work and become my personal cheerleaders when things got hectic. I would like to acknowledge the founders of Ansca Mobile, Carlos Icaza and Walter Luh for giving Corona developers an amazing platform to work with. Big thanks to David Barnes, Robin de Jongh, Chris Rodrigues, Alka Nayak, Manasi Poonthottam, Steven Wilding, the reviewers, and the rest of the Packt staff for giving me this opportunity to share my love and knowledge of mobile game development in this book.

About the Reviewers

Mitch Allen has worked on software projects for Lotus, IBM, Dragon, Nuance, Yahoo, and Intuit. He specializes in everything from Enterprise Web Apps to Mobile. He currently lives and works in Silicon Valley. For more information, please visit his website at: http://mitchallen.com.

Nicholas Golden can be found coding furiously away working on dozens of games and applications simultaneously. He is also heavily involved with helping others out and will go out of his way to assist. He is an accomplished professional with a *jack of all trades, master of a few* approach in key areas such as music composition and games, specifically game development. His thinking is extremely eccentric but focused, abstract but concentrated which results in approaching problem solving in non-standard ways while avoiding the status quo.

Nicholas Golden runs an indie development studio, information regarding his adventures can be found at: www.NicholasGolden.com and www.AngryCarrot.com.

I would like to thank my wife Michelle and my baby boy Ryan (3 months old at the time of writing), for putting up with my ramblings and late-night reviewing while being overly excited about the material. I am always pitching insane ideas at least dozens of times a day which amounts to me having so much work to do, it would literally take me 30 lifetimes to finish!

I would also like to of course thank Michelle Fernandez who let me in on this Corona SDK book in the first place. What started out as a curiosity on the Anscamobile.com forums, turned into an opportunity to communicate with a talented writer and review this fantastic book. I am sure you, the reader will enjoy this book as much as I did reviewing it!1!!11!11! (The 1s are on purpose and signify importance to a statement, ZoMg don't you know this?)

I would also like to give a shout out to CARLOS THE MAN over at Anscamobile.com for the Corona SDK! Without that, there would be no book! Carlos is FTW!

Alan Grace is a co-founder of Pixel Wolf Studios, an Indie game development studio based in Dublin, Ireland. Having worked for a number of years in Web and graphic design running his own company Alpha Solutions, Alan has a vast area of expertise across multimedia and game design. He recently completed his MSc in Digital Games and set up Pixel Wolf Studios moving his focus into game development for the iOS and Google Play Store.

Pixel Wolf Studios was established in 2011 and currently has three titles in development for the iOS and Google Play Store. All three are due for release in 2012 and will be developed using Corona SDK. For more information visit www.pixelwolfstudios.com.

Clement Ho is currently pursuing an undergraduate degree in Computer Science from Abilene Christian University. He has a strong passion for mobile and web development which has led him to pursue multiple freelance and independent projects. He has developed for the iOS and BlackBerry platform using Corona SDK, xCode and Adobe Air technologies.

Steve Hoffman (also known as Captain Hoff) is a high tech serial entrepreneur. He's currently involved in Playkast, a stealth startup that will be launching a new type of entertainment platform later this year.

Hoffman is a founding member of the Academy of Television's Interactive Media Group and was the Chairman and Founder of the San Francisco Chapter of the Producers Guild. He is also as serving on the Board of Governors for the New Media Council.Hoffman and co-founded LavaMind, which publishes Founders Space, as well as numerous websites, games and mobile applications.

In 2007, Hoffman founded RocketOn, a social media and virtual world startup. Prior to this, Hoffman was the COO of Tap11 (formerly Zannel), a venture-funded startup that provides businesses with advanced analytics and CRM for Twitter.

Before that, Hoffman was the North American Studio Head for Infospace, where he ran the US mobile games publishing and development group. While in Los Angeles, Hoff was the Chairman and CEO of Spiderdance, Hollywood's leading interactive television studio, whose customers included NBC, Viacom, Time Warner, TBS, GSN and A&E. He also consulted for R/GA Interactive, designing projects for Kodak, Disney, Intel, AdAge, and the Children's Television Workshop.

In Japan, Hoffman worked as a game designer for Sega, generating new concepts and designs for games and amusement rides. Prior to Sega, he was a Hollywood development executive at Fries Entertainment, where he managed TV development. He graduated from the University of California with a BS in Electrical Computer Engineering and went on to earn a Masters in Film and Television from USC. He is also the co-author of the first-edition of *Game Design Workshop* published by CMP.

Predrag is a renaissance man who is interested in a number of different subjects. His primary areas of interest are programming and digital and traditional art. He also likes to spend his free time painting and exploring robotics and interactive design. In the last 12 years, Predrag has worked as a Technical and Art Director on many interactive projects, published over 40 online games, and has participated in a production of several iPhone projects. He has a strong background in ActionScript, MEL script, and Lua. Predrag is a member of MENSA International and has a number of professional certificates in different areas.

Walter is the creator of Corona SDK.

In a former life, he led the Adobe Flash Lite engineering team as lead architect. He has a track record of shipping successful products from mobile runtimes like Flash Lite to industry-standard desktop products such as Adobe Illustrator and Apple's Final Cut Pro.

Walter holds an undergraduate degree in Physics from Swarthmore College, and a master's degree in computer science from Stanford University.

Edgar Miranda has been developing games since 2006, everything from simple action games, multiplayer turn base games, social games to mobile games. He's had several years of experience as a consultant working with technologies like Flash, Flex, and Corona SDK. He is the founder and owner of Pie Hammer Games (`www.piehammer.com`), which is focused on building mobile games for iOS and Android. You can check out his blog at: `www.edgarmiranda.net`.

> I'd like to thank my parents for always supporting my dream of making games for a living and all the people out there who support me by playing my games.

Jordan Schuetz is currently a 17 year old high school student who will be attending college in the fall of 2012. Jordan has been developing with Corona from the age of 16 and has had success with the development software ever since.

He is the founder of Ninja Pig Studios which creates games and applications for mobile cellular devices. Ninja Pig Studios has released some very successful applications on iPhone, Android, Nook, and Kindle. Their most popular application is called *Gun App* which reached the fourth spot in the Entertainment category on Nook. *Annoying Pig Game* was another hit which reached spot 34 in the Top New Free Games on the Google Play Store. The game is currently available for iPhone, Android, Nook, and Kindle.

In addition to owning his own company, Jordan has also been a great contributor to the Ansca Mobile community. He has become a Corona Ambassador and has been featured as a Case Study on the Ansca Mobile website.

Jordan has also developed a mobile application for an online shopping website called *WeirdStuff* which is a computer electronics store in the Silicon Valley. Jordan will be studying Computer Engineering in college and will continue working on application development throughout his college career.

Jayant Varma has been the IT Manager for BMW and Nissan dealership in Asia and the Middle East, an Academic lecturer in Australia before being a Technopreneur. With his diverse knowledge in the industry, he has founded OZ Apps a consultancy, specializing in mobile development, training and consulting services globally. He has a master's degree in Business and IT and is well versed with and has developed a wide range of languages including Assemble, dBase, Clipper, Pascal, C, C++, Obj-C, java, Visual Basic, and Lua to name a few. He has run workshops and has been a speaker for the AUC (Apple University Consortium), ACS (Australian Computer Society), and other organizations. He runs a blog, `howto.oz-apps.com`, that helps developers with tutorials on using lua-based frameworks for mobile development and review `me.oz-apps.com` that reviews software. He has to his credit over a dozen apps on the app store both personal and contractual that have been in the charts.

www.PacktPub.com

Support files, eBooks, discount offers, and more

You might want to visit www.PacktPub.com for support files and downloads related to your book.

Did you know that Packt offers eBook versions of every book published, with PDF and ePub files available? You can upgrade to the eBook version at www.PacktPub.com and as a print book customer, you are entitled to a discount on the eBook copy. Get in touch with us at service@packtpub.com for more details.

At www.PacktPub.com, you can also read a collection of free technical articles, sign up for a range of free newsletters and receive exclusive discounts and offers on Packt books and eBooks.

 PACKTLiB®

http://PacktLib.PacktPub.com

Do you need instant solutions to your IT questions? PacktLib is Packt's online digital book library. Here, you can access, read and search across Packt's entire library of books.

Why Subscribe?

- ◆ Fully searchable across every book published by Packt
- ◆ Copy and paste, print and bookmark content
- ◆ On demand and accessible via web browser

Free Access for Packt account holders

If you have an account with Packt at www.PacktPub.com, you can use this to access PacktLib today and view nine entirely free books. Simply use your login credentials for immediate access.

Table of Contents

Preface

This book is designed to introduce you to the basic standards of using the Corona SDK across iOS and Android platforms. You will enhance your learning experience by building three unique games in easy-to-follow steps. Apart from developing games, you will also dive into learning about social network integration, In-App Purchasing, monetizing, and shipping your applications to the App Store and/or Google Play Store.

What this book covers

Chapter 1, *Getting Started With Corona SDK*, begins by teaching users how to install Corona SDK on both Mac OSX and Windows operating systems. You will learn how to create your first program in just two lines of code. Lastly, we'll go through the process of building and loading an application to an iOS or Android device.

Chapter 2, *Lua Crash Course and the Corona Framework*, dives into the Lua programming language that is used to develop in Corona SDK. We'll go over the basics of variables, functions, and data structures in Lua. This chapter will also introduce how to implement a variety of display objects within the Corona framework.

Chapter 3, *Building our First Game: Breakout*, discusses the first half of building your first game, Breakout. We'll learn how to structure game files in a Corona project and create game objects that will display on screen.

Chapter 4, *Game Controls*, continues on with the last half of building your first game, Breakout. We'll cover game object movement as well as collision detection between objects in the scene. You will also learn how to create a score system that will implement win and lose conditions of the game.

Chapter 5, *Animating our Game*, explains how to animate a game using movie clips and sprite sheets. This chapter will go in depth with managing motion and transitions while creating a new game framework.

Chapter 6, Playing Sounds and Music, provides information on how to apply sound effects and music to your applications. It is vital to include some type of audio to enhance the sensory experience of our game's development. You will learn how to incorporate audio through loading, executing, and looping techniques with the Corona Audio System.

Chapter 7, Physics: Falling Objects, covers how to implement the Box2D engine in Corona SDK using display objects. You will be able to customize body construction and work with physical behaviors of falling objects. In this chapter, we'll apply the uses of dynamic/static bodies and explain the purpose of post-collisions.

Chapter 8, Operation Storyboard, discusses how to manage all your game scenes with Storyboard API. We'll also go into detail on menu design, such as creating a pause menu and main menu. In addition, you'll learn how to save high scores within your game.

Chapter 9, Handling Multiple Devices and Networking your Apps, provides information about integrating your applications with social networks such as Twitter or Facebook. Other social capabilities that will be discussed are incorporating achievements and leaderboards with OpenFeint. This will enable your app to reach a bigger audience globally.

Chapter 10, Optimizing, Testing, and Shipping your Games, explains the application submission process for both iOS and Android devices. This chapter will guide you on how to set up a Distribution Provisioning Profile for the App Store and manage your app information in iTunes Connect. Android developers will learn how to sign their applications for publication so it can be submitted to the Google Play Store.

Chapter 11, Implementing In-App Purchases, covers monetization of your game by creating consumable, non-consumable, or subscription purchases. You will apply In-App Purchases in the App Store using Corona's store module. We'll take a look at testing purchases on a device to see if transactions have been applied using the Sandbox environment.

What you need for this book

You will need the following items before you can start developing games with Corona SDK for Mac:

- ◆ If you are installing Corona for Mac OS X, be sure that your system is as follows:
  - ❑ Mac OS® X 10.6 or later
  - ❑ Intel-based system that runs Snow Leopard or Lion
  - ❑ 64-bit CPU (Core 2 Duo)
  - ❑ OpenGL 1.4 or higher graphics system

- ◆ You must be enrolled in the Apple Developer Program
- ◆ XCode
- ◆ A text editor such as TextWrangler, BBEdit, or TextMate

You will need the following items before you can start developing games with Corona SDK for Windows:

- ◆ If you are running Microsoft Windows, be sure that your system is as follows:
    - ❑ Windows 7, Vista, or XP operating system
    - ❑ 1 GHZ processor (recommended)
    - ❑ 38 MB of disk space (minimum)
    - ❑ 1 GB of RAM (minimum)
    - ❑ OpenGL 1.3 or higher graphics system (available in most modern Windows systems)
- ◆ Java 6 SDK
- ◆ A text editor such as Notepad++ or Crimson Editor

You must be enrolled as an Google Play developer if you want to submit and publish apps for Android devices.

The game tutorials require resource files that are available with this book and can be downloaded from the Packt website.

Lastly, you will need the latest stable build of Corona SDK: Version 2011.704. This is applicable for test drivers and subscribers.

Who this book is for

This book is for anyone who wants to have a go at creating commercially successful games for Android and iOS. You don't need game development or programming experience.

Conventions

In this book, you will find several headings appearing frequently.

To give clear instructions of how to complete a procedure or task, we use:

Time for action – heading

1. Action 1

2. Action 2

3. Action 3

Instructions often need some extra explanation so that they make sense, so they are followed with:

What just happened?

This heading explains the working of tasks or instructions that you have just completed.

You will also find some other learning aids in the book, including:

Pop quiz – heading

These are short multiple choice questions intended to help you test your own understanding.

Have a go hero – heading

These set practical challenges and give you ideas for experimenting with what you have learned.

You will also find a number of styles of text that distinguish between different kinds of information. Here are some examples of these styles, and an explanation of their meaning.

Code words in text are shown as follows: "Continue changing values of the current display object, `textObject`."

A block of code is set as follows:

```
Hello World/    name of your project folder
Icon.png         required for iPhone/iPod/iPad
Icon@2x.png       required for iPhone/iPod with Retina display
main.lua
```

When we wish to draw your attention to a particular part of a code block, the relevant lines or items are set in bold:

```
textObject = display.newText( "Hello World!", 50, 40, native.
systemFont, 36 )
textObject:setTextColor( 124,252,0 )
```

Any command-line input or output is written as follows:

```
--This is number 4
   --This is number 5
```

New terms and **important words** are shown in bold. Words that you see on the screen, in menus or dialog boxes for example, appear in the text like this: "Once you have done so, under the **Corona Simulator** menu bar, select **Window | View As | iPhone 4**".

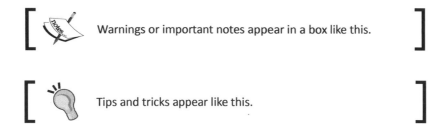

> Warnings or important notes appear in a box like this.

> Tips and tricks appear like this.

Reader feedback

Feedback from our readers is always welcome. Let us know what you think about this book—what you liked or may have disliked. Reader feedback is important for us to develop titles that you really get the most out of.

To send us general feedback, simply send an e-mail to feedback@packtpub.com, and mention the book title via the subject of your message.

If there is a book that you need and would like to see us publish, please send us a note in the **SUGGEST A TITLE** form on www.packtpub.com or e-mail suggest@packtpub.com.

If there is a topic that you have expertise in and you are interested in either writing or contributing to a book, see our author guide on www.packtpub.com/authors.

Customer support

Now that you are the proud owner of a Packt book, we have a number of things to help you to get the most from your purchase.

Downloading the example code

You can download the example code files for all Packt books you have purchased from your account at http://www.PacktPub.com. If you purchased this book elsewhere, you can visit http://www.PacktPub.com/support and register to have the files e-mailed directly to you.

Errata

Although we have taken every care to ensure the accuracy of our content, mistakes do happen. If you find a mistake in one of our books—maybe a mistake in the text or the code—we would be grateful if you would report this to us. By doing so, you can save other readers from frustration and help us improve subsequent versions of this book. If you find any errata, please report them by visiting http://www.packtpub.com/support, selecting your book, clicking on the **errata submission form** link, and entering the details of your errata. Once your errata are verified, your submission will be accepted and the errata will be uploaded on our website, or added to any list of existing errata, under the Errata section of that title. Any existing errata can be viewed by selecting your title from http://www.packtpub.com/support.

Piracy

Piracy of copyright material on the Internet is an ongoing problem across all media. At Packt, we take the protection of our copyright and licenses very seriously. If you come across any illegal copies of our works, in any form, on the Internet, please provide us with the location address or website name immediately so that we can pursue a remedy.

Please contact us at copyright@packtpub.com with a link to the suspected pirated material.

We appreciate your help in protecting our authors, and our ability to bring you valuable content.

Questions

You can contact us at questions@packtpub.com if you are having a problem with any aspect of the book, and we will do our best to address it.

1
Getting Started With Corona SDK

Before we jump right into coding some simple games, we need to install and run the necessary programs that will make our applications come to life. **Corona SDK** *is primarily a 2D development engine. If you've had experience developing for iOS or Android, you will find the experience working with Corona refreshing and simple to use. In no time you'll be creating finished products to distribute on the iPhone App Store and Google Play Store.*

In this chapter, we will:

- ◆ Set up Corona SDK on Mac OS X and Windows
- ◆ Install Xcode for Mac OS X
- ◆ Create a Hello World program in two lines
- ◆ Add devices in the iOS Provisioning Portal
- ◆ Load an application to an iOS device
- ◆ Load an application to an Android device

Downloading and installing Corona

You have the option of choosing the Mac OS X or Microsoft Windows operating system to develop on. Keep in mind the following system requirements required to run the program.

If you are installing Corona for Mac OS X, be sure that your system is as follows:

◆ Mac OS® X 10.6 or later

◆ An Intel-based system that runs Snow Leopard or Lion

◆ 64-bit CPU (Core 2 Duo)

◆ An OpenGL 1.4 or higher graphics system

If you are running Microsoft Windows, be sure that your system is as follows:

◆ Windows 7, Vista, or XP operating system

◆ 1 GHZ processor (recommended)

◆ 38 MB of disk space (minimum)

◆ 1 GB of RAM (minimum)

◆ OpenGL 1.3 or higher graphics system (available in most modern Windows systems)

Time for action – setting up and activating Corona on Mac OS X

Let's begin by setting up Corona SDK on our desktop.

1. If you haven't downloaded the SDK, please do so at: `http://www.anscamobile.com/corona/`. You will have to register as a user before you can access the SDK.

2. The file extension for any Mac program should end in `.dmg`, otherwise known as an **Apple disk image**. Once you've downloaded the disk image, double-click on the disk image file to mount it. The name should be similar to `CoronaSDK.dmg`.

Once it is loaded, you should see the mounted disk image folder as shown in the following screenshot:

3. Next, drag the CoronaSDK folder into the Applications folder. This will copy the contents of the Corona folder into /Applications. You will be prompted to enter an administrator password if you are not the main administrator of the account. You will be able to see the CoronaSDK folder in /Applications once it has been successfully installed.

For easy access to the folder's contents, create an alias by dragging the `CoronaSDK` folder to the Dock of your Mac desktop.

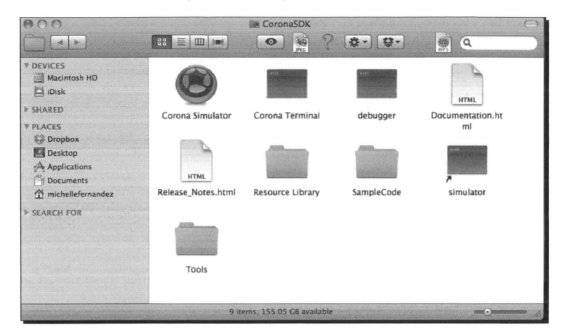

First time Corona SDK users will have to perform a quick and easy one-time authorization process before it can be accessible.

 You must be connected to the Internet to complete the authorization process.

4. Launch the Corona Simulator in the SDK folder.

5. Assuming this is your first time, you will be presented with an End-user License Agreement (EULA). Once you have accepted the agreement, enter the e-mail you used to register for Corona and password to activate the SDK. Otherwise, click **Register** to create an account.

If you register with Corona as a trial user, there is no fee to develop on iOS and/or Android devices. Developers that would like to publish their applications on the App Store or Google Play need to purchase the Corona SDK subscription on the website in order to do so at: `http://www.anscamobile.com/corona/`.

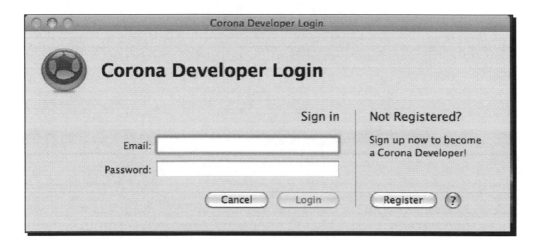

6. Upon successful login, you will get a confirmation dialog to show that the SDK is ready to use as shown in the following screenshot:

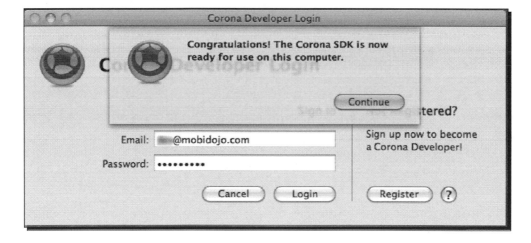

7. Click on the **Continue** button and you'll be presented with the **Welcome to Corona** screen as shown in the following screenshot:

What just happened?

Setting up Corona SDK on your Mac operating system is as simple as installing any other dedicated Mac program. After you have authorized the SDK on your machine and logged in with your e-mail and password it will be ready for use. From here on out, every time you launch Corona, it will automatically log in to your account. You will notice that you are greeted with a **Corona SDK** screen when this happens.

Time for action – setting up and activating Corona on Windows

Let's set up Corona SDK on our desktop.

1. Download Corona SDK from the following URL: `http://www.anscamobile.com/corona/`. You will have to register as a user before you can access the SDK.

2. The file extension for the Windows version of Corona should end in `.msi`, otherwise known as a **Windows Installer**, a component of Windows made for installing programs by Microsoft. Double-click on the file. The filename should be similar to `CoronaSDK.msi`.

3. Follow the onscreen directions for installation.

4. Corona will install directly to your `Programs` folder by default. On Microsoft Windows, select **Corona** from the list of **Programs** in your **Start** menu or double-click the Corona icon on the desktop. Upon successful activation, you should be greeted with the following screen:

> The process to activate the SDK should be the same as that of the Mac procedure once you launch Corona for the very first time.

> If you run into issues with images not displaying properly, check to see if you're using an up-to-date OpenGL graphics driver that is 1.3 or higher.

> Be aware that Corona SDK on Windows can only build for Android devices, not for iOS devices (iPhone, iPad, or iPod Touch). A Mac can only build for iOS devices in Corona but can also build applications for Android.

5. To create device builds, Java 6 SDK needs to be installed on your PC. You will need to go to the JDK download page: `http://jdk6.java.net/download.html` and click the **Download** button under the **Java SE 6** option.

6. On the next page, select the **Accept License Agreement** radio button and then click on the **Windows x86** link to download the installer. You will be asked to log in or create a user account on the Oracle website if you don't already have one.

7. As soon as the JDK is downloaded, run the installer. Once installed, you'll be able to create device builds for Android on your PC.

What just happened?

Installing the SDK on Windows has a different setup to that of the Mac OS X. While executing the installer file, Windows will automatically present a designated location to install the application such as the `Programs` folder so you won't have to manually choose a destination. Upon a successful installation you will see the Corona SDK icon on your desktop for easy access or highlighted in the **Programs** list in the **Start** menu, assuming you're accessing it for the first time. When you authorize Corona on your machine and sign in with your login information, it is ready for you to use and will log in automatically every time it is launched.

Using the simulator on Mac and Windows

On Mac OS X, launch Corona SDK by either selecting `Corona Terminal` or `Corona Simulator` from the `Applications Directory`. Both selections will access the SDK. The `Corona Simulator` will only open the simulator. The `Corona Terminal` will open both the simulator and terminal window. The terminal is helpful for debugging your programs and displays simulator errors/warnings and `print()` messages.

On Microsoft Windows, select the `Corona SDK` folder and click on **Corona Simulator** from the list of **Programs** in your **Start** menu or double-click the Corona icon on the desktop. (The simulator and terminal are always opened together if you are using Windows).

Let's go over the useful contents contained in the `Corona SDK` folder (located in `Applications/Corona SDK` on Mac and `Start/All Programs/Corona SDK` on Windows:

- **Debugger** (Mac)/**Corona Debugger** (Windows)—Tool for finding and isolating issues in your code.

- **Corona Simulator**—The environment used to launch your application for testing. It simulates the mobile device you're developing on your local computer. (On Windows, it will open both the simulator and terminal).

- ◆ **Corona Terminal**—Launches the **Corona Simulator** and opens a **Terminal** window to display error/warning messages and `print()` statements. It is very helpful for debugging your code (only on Mac).

- ◆ **Simulator**—Has the same properties as `Corona Terminal`, but called from the command line (only on Mac).

- ◆ **SampleCode**—A set of sample applications to get you started with Corona. Contains code and art assets to work with.

The **Corona SDK** window opens by default when you launch the simulator. You can open a Corona project in the simulator, create a device build for testing or distribution, and view some example games and apps to get you familiar with the SDK.

Time for action – viewing a sample project in the simulator

Let's take a look at the `HelloPhysics` sample project in the simulator:

1. Click on **Simulator** in the **Corona SDK** window.

2. In the **Open** dialog that appears, navigate to `Applications/CoronaSDK/ SampleCode/Physics/HelloPhysics` **(Mac)** or `C:\Program Files\Ansca\ Corona SDK\Sample Code\Physics\HelloPhysics` **(Windows)**. On Mac, click **Open** and it will automatically open `main.lua`. On Windows, double-click on `main.lua` to open the file. The `HelloPhysics` application opens and runs in the **Simulator**.

What just happened?

Accessing the SDK through the `Corona Terminal` or `Corona Simulator` depends on your preference of action. Many Mac users prefer to use the `Corona Terminal` so they can track messages outputted in the terminal, especially for debugging purposes. When you launch the SDK through the `Corona Simulator`, the simulator will display, but not the terminal window. When Windows users launch the **Corona Simulator**, it will display both the simulator and terminal windows. This is nice to use when you want to play around with any of the example applications that are provided by Corona.

The `main.lua` file is a special filename that tells Corona where to start in a project folder. This file can also load other code files or other program resources such as sounds or graphics.

When you launch the `HelloPhysics` application in Corona, you will observe a box object fall from top of the screen in the simulator and collide with a ground object. The transition from launching the `main.lua` file to viewing the results in the simulator are almost immediate.

Have a go hero – use a different device shell

As you start getting familiar with the `Corona Simulator`, whether you're in Windows or Mac OSX, a default device is always used when you launch an application. Windows uses the Droid as the default device, while the Mac OS X uses the regular iPhone. Try launching the sample code on a different device shell to view the difference in screen resolution in all the devices the simulator has available.

When porting builds to more than one platform, you'll have to consider the variety of screen resolutions in both iOS and Android devices. A **build** is a compiled version of all your source code converted into one file. Having your game build configured for multiple platforms broadens the audience reach for your application.

Choosing a text editor

Corona does not have a designated program editor to code in so you will have to find one that suits your needs.

For Mac OS, **TextWrangler** is a good one and free too! You can download it at `http://www.barebones.com/products/textwrangler/download.html`. Other text editors such as **BBEdit** at `http://www.barebones.com/thedeck` and **TextMate** at `http://macromates.com/` are great, but you will need to purchase those in order to use them. TextMate is also compatible with the Corona TextMate Bundle: `http://www.ludicroussoftware.com/corona-textmate-bundle/index.html`.

For Microsoft Windows **Notepad++** is recommended and can be downloaded at `http://notepad-plus-plus.org/` or **Crimson Editor** at `http://www.crimsoneditor.com/`. Both editors are free.

Any text editor, such as TextEdit for Mac or Notepad for Windows, that is already included in each operating system works as well, but it'll be easier to work with one that is designed for programming. For Corona, using an editor that supports Lua syntax highlighting will work the best when coding. Syntax highlighting adds formatting attributes to keywords and punctuation in a way that makes it easier for the reader to separate code from text.

Developing on devices

Apple's developer kit **Xcode** or the **Android SDK** is not necessary to download if you only want to use the Corona Simulator. In order to build and test your code on an iOS device (iPhone, iPod Touch and iPad), you will need to sign up as an Apple Developer and create and download provisioning profiles. If you want to develop on Android, you don't need to download the Android SDK unless you want to use the ADB tool to help with installing builds and viewing debug messages.

The trial version of Corona Simulator allows building Adhoc (for iOS) and Debug builds (Android) for testing on your own devices. The builds will contain a **Trial User** message box when the app runs on the device. You will need to purchase a Corona Subscription if you want to build for Apple's App Store or Android's Google Play Store. Corona Subscribers also get the benefit of subscriber-only features such as access to Daily Builds, **Subscribers Only** areas on the Corona forums and LaunchPad.

Time for action – downloading and installing Xcode

In order to develop any iOS application you will need to enroll in the Apple Developer Program, which costs $99 a year, and create an account on the Apple website `http://developer.apple.com/programs/ios/`.

1. Click on the **Enroll Now** button and follow Apple's instructions to complete the process.

2. When you have completed your enrollment, click on the iOS link under the section marked **Dev Centers.**

3. If you are using Snow Leopard, scroll down to the **Downloads** section and download the current Xcode. If you are using Lion, you can download Xcode in the Mac App Store.

4. Once you have fully downloaded Xcode, double-click on the `.mpkg` Installer package (icon is an open brown box). By default, Xcode will install in the folder `/Developer`. You will be asked to authenticate as an administrative user.

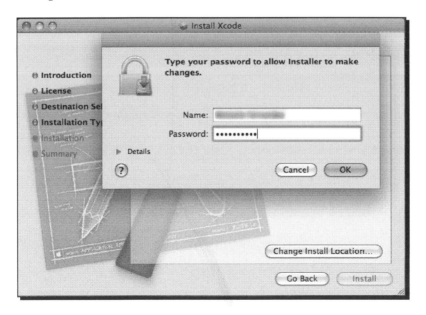

5. After you have entered your credentials, click on the **OK** button to complete the installation.

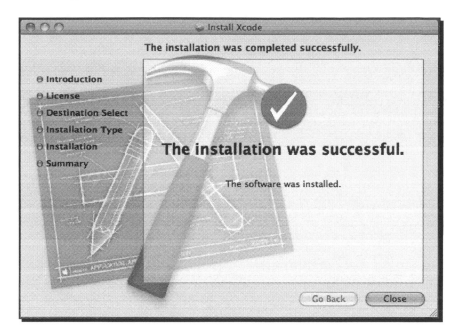

6. When you have installed the Xcode developer tools, you can access the documentation by launching Xcode and choosing any of the items in the **Help** menu. Developer applications such as Xcode and Instruments are installed in /Developer/Applications. You can drag those following app icons to your Dock for convenient accessibility.

What just happened?

We just went through the steps of how to install Xcode to Mac OS X. By enrolling in the Apple Developer Program, you will have access to up-to-date development tools on the website. Remember that to continue being an Apple Developer you have to pay a fee of $99 annually to keep your subscription.

The Xcode file is quite large so it will take a bit of time to download depending on how fast your Internet connection is. When your installation is complete, Xcode will be ready to go.

Time for action – creating a Hello World application in two lines of code

Now that we have the simulator and text editors set up, let's start making our very first Corona program! The first program we will be making is called **Hello World**. It is a traditional program that many people learn when starting a new programming language.

1. Open your preferred text editor and type the following lines:

```
textObject = display.newText( "Hello World!", 50, 40, native.
systemFont, 36 )
textObject:setTextColor( 255,255,255)
```

2. Next, create a folder on your desktop called `Hello World`. Save the preceding text as a file named `main.lua` to the location of your project folder.

3. Launch Corona. You will be greeted with the **Corona SDK** screen. Click on **Simulator** and navigate to the `Hello World` folder you just created. You should see your `main.lua` file in this folder as shown in the following screenshot:

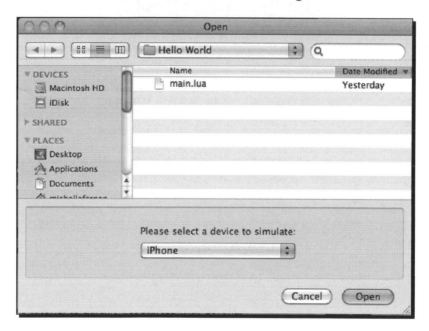

4. On Mac, click on the **Open** button. On Windows, select the `main.lua` file and click the **Open** button. You'll see your new program running in the Corona Simulator:

Time for action – modifying our application

Before we dive into more complex examples, let's alter some minor things in your program.

1. Let's alter the second line of `main.lua` to display as follows:

```
textObject = display.newText( "Hello World!", 50, 40, native.
systemFont, 36 )
textObject:setTextColor( 124,252,0 )
```

2. Save your file and go back to the **Corona Simulator**. The simulator will detect a change from your file and automatically re-launch with the new changes. If the simulator doesn't re-launch automatically upon saving your file, press *Command + R* (Mac)/*Ctrl + R* (Windows).

 As you continue learning more Corona functions, you'll notice that some of the text values will be optional. In this case, we need to use all five values.

Time for action – applying a new font name to your application

Now let's play around with the font name.

1. Change the first line to the following code:

```
textObject = display.newText( "Hello World!", 50, 40, "Times New
Roman", 36 )
```

2. Be sure to save your `main.lua` file after making any alterations, then press *Command+R* (Mac)/*Ctrl+R* (Windows) in Corona to re-launch the simulator to view the new font. If you're using a Mac, usually the simulator automatically re-launches after saving your file or it may ask you if you want to re-launch the program.

What just happened?

You have now made your first complete mobile application! What's even more amazing is that this is a completed iPhone, iPad, and Android application. This two-line program will actually install and run on your iOS/Android device if you were to create a build. You have now seen what the basic workflow in Corona is like.

If you take a look at line 2 in your `main.lua` file you will notice that `setTextColor` alters the color of the text for **Hello World!**.

Colors are made up of three sets of **RGB** numbers representing the amount of red, green, and blue contained within a color. They are displayed with three numbers with values ranging from 0 to 255. For example, the color black would be (0,0,0), blue would be (0,0,255), and the color white (255,255,255).

Continue playing around with different color values to see the different results. You can see the alterations to the code in the simulator when you save your `main.lua` file and re-launch Corona.

When you view the first line from the `main.lua` file you will notice that `newText()` is called by `textObject`, a name that is then used to reference the display text. The `newText()` function returns an object that will represent the text on the screen. `newText` is part of the display library.

When you want to access the display property of `newText`, type in `display.newText`. The two numbers after `Hello World!` control the horizontal and vertical positions of the text on the screen in pixels. The next item specifies the font. We used the name `native.systemFont`, which by default refers to the standard font on the current device. For example, the iPhone's default font is Helvetica. You can use any standard font name such as `Times New Roman` (used in the preceding example). The last number used is the font size.

Have a go hero – adding more text objects

Now that you're starting to get a taste of coding, try applying the following in your current project file:

♦ Create a new display object using a different font and text color. Display it below the **Hello World!** text. Hint: Make sure your new text object has a different object name.

♦ Continue changing values of the current display object, `textObject`. Alter the x and y, the coordinates, the string text, the font name, and even the font size.

♦ While the object `setTextColor( r,g,b)` sets the color of the text, there is an optional parameter you can add that controls the opacity of the text. Try using the object `setTextColor( r, g, b [, a])`. The values available for a also range between 0 to 255 (255 is opaque, which is the default value). Observe the results of your text color.

Testing our application on an iOS device

If you are only interested in testing the application on an Android device, please skip past this section of the chapter to *Testing Our Application on an Android Device*. Before we can upload our first Hello World application on an iOS device, we need to log in to our Apple Developer account so we can create and install our signing certificates on our development machine. If you haven't created a Developer account yet, please do so at `http://developer.apple.com/programs/ios/`. Remember that there is a fee of $99 a year to become an Apple Developer.

The Apple Developer account is only applied to users developing on Mac OS X. Make sure your version of Xcode is the same as or newer than the version of the OS on your phone. For example, if you have version 5.0 of the iPhone OS installed you will need Xcode that is bundled with the iOS SDK version 5.0 or later.

Time for action – obtaining the iOS developer certificate

Make sure that you're signed up for the developer program; you will need to use the **Keychain Access** tool located in `/Applications/Utilities` so you can create a certificate request. A valid certificate must sign all iOS applications before they can be run on an Apple device in order to do any kind of testing.

1. Open **Keychain Access | Certificate Assistant | Request a Certificate From a Certificate Authority**.

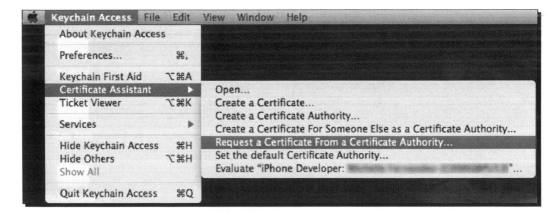

2. In the **User Email Address** field, type in the e-mail address you used when you registered as an iOS developer. For **Common Name**, enter your name or team name. Make sure that the name entered matches the information that was submitted when you registered as an iOS developer. The **CA Email Address** field does not need to be filled in so you can leave it blank. We are not e-mailing the certificate to a Certificate Authority (CA). Check **Saved to disk** and **Let me specify key pair information**. When you click **Continue**, you will be asked to choose a save location. Save your file at a destination where you can locate it easily such as your desktop.

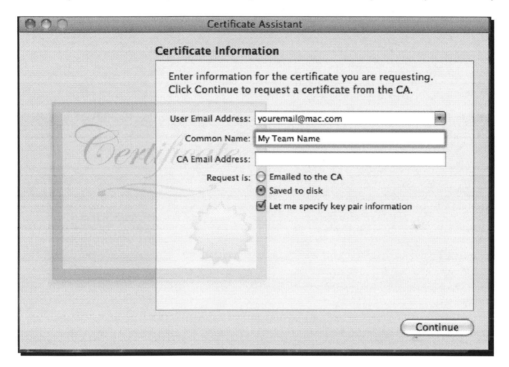

3. In the following window, make sure that **2048 bits** is selected for the **Key Size** and
RSA for the **Algorithm**, and then click **Continue**. This will generate the key and save
it to the location you specified. Click **Done** in the next window.

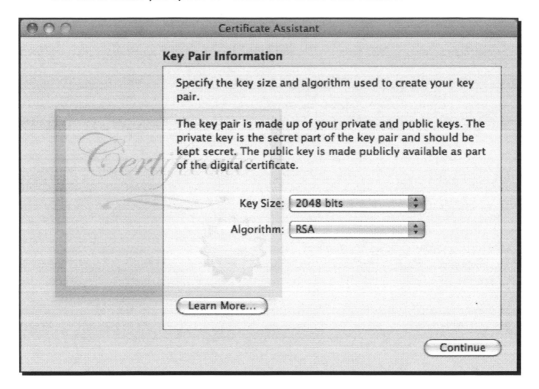

4. Next, go to the Apple Developer website: `http://developer.apple.com/`, click
on **iOS Dev Center**, and log in to your developer account. Select the **iOS Provisioning**
Portal tab and navigate to **Certificates** on the left-hand column. Click on the
Development tab if it's not already selected and then select the **Add Certificate**
button on the right side of the page.

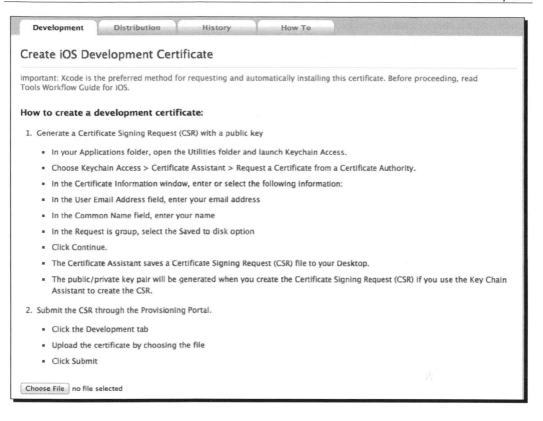

5. Click on the **Choose File** button, locate your certificate file that you saved to your desktop, and click on the **Submit** button.

6. Upon pressing the **Submit** button, you will get an e-mail notification you specified in the **Certificate Authority (CA)** request form from Keychain Access. The person who created the certificate will receive this e-mail and can approve the request by pressing the **Approve** button. You can download the certificate once it has been approved.

7. Click on the **Download** button and save the certificate to a location that is easy to find. Once this is completed, double-click on the file and you will see the following dialog:

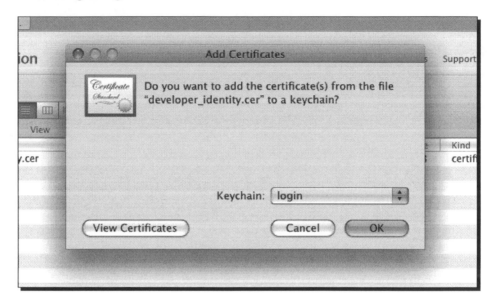

8. Click **OK**. This will install your iPhone Development Certificate in your Keychain.

What just happened?

We now have a valid certificate for iOS devices. The iOS Development Certificate is used for development purposes only and is valid for about a year. The key pair is made up of your public and private keys. The private key is what allows Xcode to sign iOS applications. Private keys are available only to the key-pair creator and are stored in the system keychain of the creator's machine. The following are other websites you can refer to to create valid certificates:

◆ Building for devices on the Ansca website: http://developer.anscamobile.com/content/building-devices-iphoneipad

◆ iPhone provisioning setup and App Store submission (created by an Ansca engineer): http://www.authorstream.com/Presentation/anscamobile-509082-iphone-provisioning-setup-and-app-store-submission/

◆ The AppCode blog: http://www.theappcodeblog.com/2011/04/28/getting-an-apple-developer-certificate/

Adding iOS devices

You are allowed to assign up to 100 devices for development and testing purposes in the iPhone Developer program. To register a device, you will need the **Unique Device Identification (UDID)** number. You can find this in iTunes and Xcode.

Xcode

To find out your device's UDID, connect your device to your Mac and open Xcode. In Xcode, navigate to the menu bar and select **Window** and click on **Organizer**. The 40 hex character string in the **Identifier** field is your device's UDID. Once the **Organizer** window is open, you should see the name of your device in the **Devices** list on the left. Click on it and select the identifier with your mouse, copying it to the clipboard:

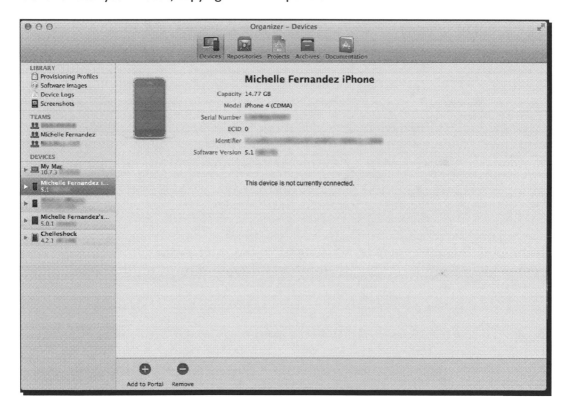

Usually when you connect a device to the **Organizer** for the first time, you'll receive a button notification that says **Use for Development**. Select it and Xcode will do most of the provisioning work for your device in the iOS Provisioning Portal.

iTunes

With your device connected, open **iTunes** and click on your device in the device list. Select the **Summary** tab. Click on the **Serial Number** label to show the **Identifier** field and the 40 character UDID. Press *Command + C* to copy the UDID to your clipboard.

Time for action – adding/registering your iOS device

To add a device to use for development/testing:

1. Select **Devices** in the iOS Provisioning Portal and click on **Add Devices**.

2. Create a name for your device in the **Device Name** field and put your UDID in the **Device ID** by pressing *Command + V* to paste the number you have saved on the clipboard.

3. Click **Submit** when you are done.

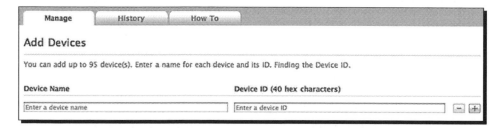

Time for action – creating an App ID

Now that you have added a device to the portal, you will need to create an **App ID**. An App ID has a unique 10-character **Bundle Seed ID** prefix generated by Apple and a **Bundle Identifier** suffix that is created by the Team Admin in the Provisioning Portal. An App ID could look similar to the following example: `7R456G1254.com.companyname. YourApplication.` To create a new App ID follow these steps:

1. Click on the **New App ID** button in the **App ID** section of the portal.

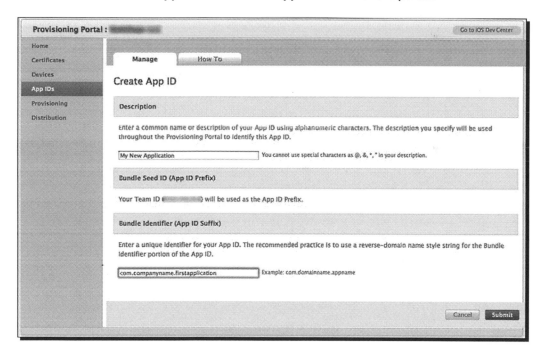

2. Fill out the **Description** field with the name of your application.

3. You are already assigned a Bundle Seed ID (also known as **Team ID**).

4. In the **Bundle Identifier (App ID Suffix)** field, specify a unique identifier for your app. It is up to you as to how you want to identify your app, but it is recommended that you use the reverse-domain style string, that is `com.domainname.appname`.

> You can create a wildcard character in the **Bundle Identifier** that you can share among a suite of applications using the same Keychain access. To do this, simply create a single App ID with an asterisk (*) at the end. You would place this in the field for the **Bundle Identifier** either by itself or at the end of your string: `com.domainname.*`. More information on this topic can be found in the App IDs section of the iOS Provisioning Portal: https://developer.apple.com/ios/manage/bundles/howto.action.

What just happened?

All UDIDs are unique on every device and we can locate them in Xcode and iTunes. When we added a device in the iOS Provisioning Portal we took the UDID, which consists of 40 hex characters and made sure we created a device name so we can identify what we're using for development.

We now have an App ID for applications we want to install on a device. An **App ID** is a unique identifier that iOS uses to allow your application to connect to the Apple Push Notification service, share keychain data between applications, and communicate with external hardware accessories that you wish to pair your iOS application with.

Provisioning Profiles

A **Provisioning Profile** is a collection of digital entities that uniquely ties developers and devices to an authorized iOS development team and enables a device to be used for testing. These profiles tie your devices to your development team for testing and distribution.

Time for action – creating a Provisioning Profile

To create a **Provisioning Profile**, go to the **Provisioning** section of the iOS Provisioning Portal and click **New Profile** on the **Development** tab.

1. Enter a name for the Provisioning Profile. It could be the same name as your application.

2. Check the box next to **Certificates**.

3. Select the **App ID** that you created for your application in the pull-down menu.

4. Check the devices you wish to authorize for this profile.

5. Click on the **Submit** button when you are done.

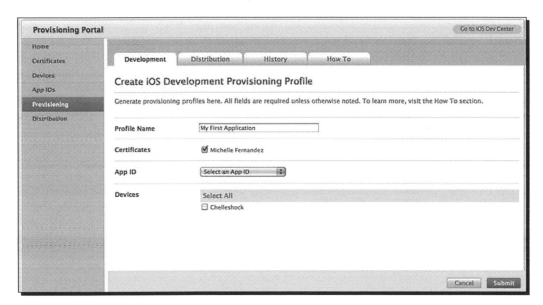

6. You will be returned to the **Development** tab where the status will most likely say **Pending**. Click **Refresh** on your browser and it should show that your profile's status says **Active**.

7. Click the **Download** button. While the file is downloading, launch Xcode if it's not already open and press *Shift + Command + 2* on the keyboard to open **Organizer**.

8. Under **Library**, select the **Provisioning Profiles** section. Drag the downloaded .mobileprovision file to the **Organizer** window. This will automatically copy the .mobileprovision file to the proper directory.

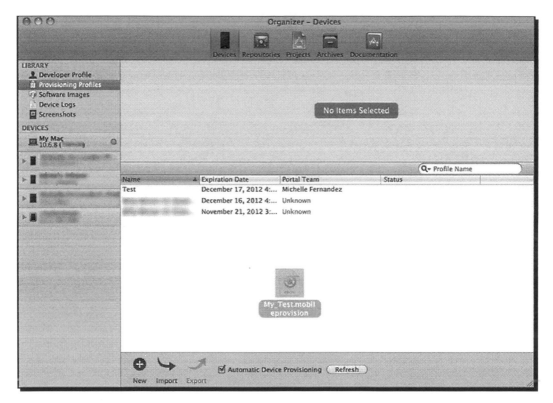

What just happened?

Devices that have permission within the **Provisioning Profile** can be used for testing as long as the certificates are included in the profile. One device can have multiple provisioning profiles installed.

Application icon

Currently our app has no icon image to display on the device. By default, if there is no icon image set for the application you will see a light gray box displayed along with your application name below it once the build has been loaded to your device. So launch your preferred creative developmental tool and let's create a simple image.

The application icon for iPhone/iTouch should be a 57 x 57 PNG image file or 72 x 72 for iPad. The image should always be saved as `Icon.png` and must be located in your current project folder. For iPhone / iPod touch devices that support **Retina** display, we need an additional high-resolution 114 x 114 icon named `Icon@2x.png`.

The contents of your current project folder will look like this:

```
Hello World/      name of your project folder
Icon.png            required for iPhone/iPod/iPad
Icon@2x.png          required for iPhone/iPod with Retina display
main.lua
```

In order to distribute your app, the App Store requires a 512 x 512 pixel version of the icon. It is best to create your icon at a higher resolution first. Please refer to the **Apple iOS Human Interface Guidelines** for the latest official App Store requirements:

```
http://developer.apple.com/library/ios/#documentation/userexperience/
conceptual/mobilehig/Introduction/Introduction.html
```

Creating an application icon is a visual representation of your application name. You will be able to view the icon on your device once you compile a build together. The icon is also the image that launches your application.

Creating the Hello World build for iOS

We are now set to build our Hello World application for our device. Since we have our provisioning profiles in place, the build process from here on is pretty simple. Make sure that you are connected to the Internet before creating a device build. You can build your application for testing in the **Xcode Simulator** or on a device.

Time for action – creating an iOS build

Follow these steps to creating a new iOS build in Corona SDK:

1. Open the Corona Simulator and select **Simulator**.

2. Navigate to your Hello World application and select your `main.lua` file.

3. Once the application is launched on the simulator, go to the Corona Simulator menu bar and select **File | Build | iOS** or press *Command + B* on your keyboard. The following dialog box appears:

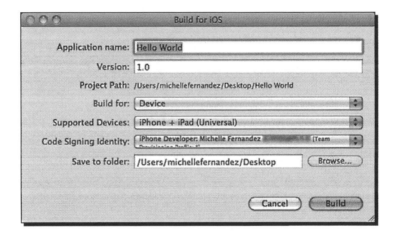

4. Create a name for your app in the **Application Name** field. We can keep the same name **Hello World.** In the **Version** field, keep the number at **1.0.** In order to test the app in the Xcode Simulator, select **Xcode Simulator** from the **Build For** drop-down menu. If you want to build for the device, choose **Device** to build an app bundle. Next, select the target device (iPhone or iPad) from the **Supported Devices** drop-down menu. Under the **Code Signing Identity** drop-down menu, choose the provisioning file you created for the specified devices you are building for. It is the same name as the **Profile Name** in the iOS Provisioning Portal on the Apple Developer website. In the **Save to folder** section, click **Browse** and choose where you would like your application to save in.

5. If all the information has been confirmed in the dialog box, click on the **Build** button.

It is more convenient to set your application to save on the `Desktop`; that way it is easy to find.

What just happened?

Congratulations! You now have created your first iOS application file that can be uploaded to your device. As you start developing apps for distribution, you will want to create new versions of your application so you can keep track of the changes in every new build you make. All the information from your **Provisioning Profile** was created in the iOS Provisioning Portal and applied to the build. Once Corona has finished compiling the build, the application should be located in your preferred folder you saved it under.

Time for action – loading an app on your iOS device

Select the Hello World build that you created and choose either of the following to load your app onto your iOS device. iTunes, Xcode, or the iPhone Configuration Utility can be used to transfer the application file.

If using iTunes, drag your build into your iTunes library and then synch your device normally.

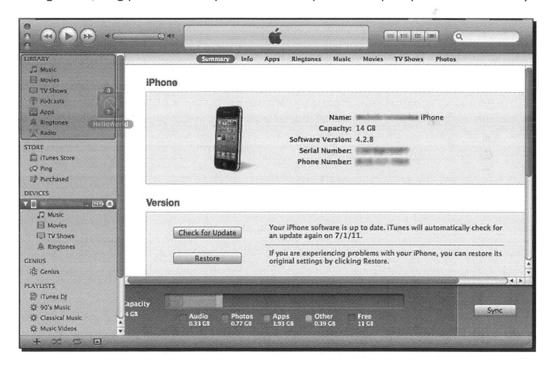

Another way to install your app onto your device is to use Xcode since it provides a convenient method for installing iOS device applications.

1. With the device connected, open Xcode's **Organizer** from the menu bar, **Window | Organizer**, and navigate to your connected device under the **Devices** list on the left.

2. If a proper connection is established, you will see a green indicator. If it is yellow after a couple minutes, try powering the device off and on again or disconnect the device and connect it again. This will usually establish a proper connection.

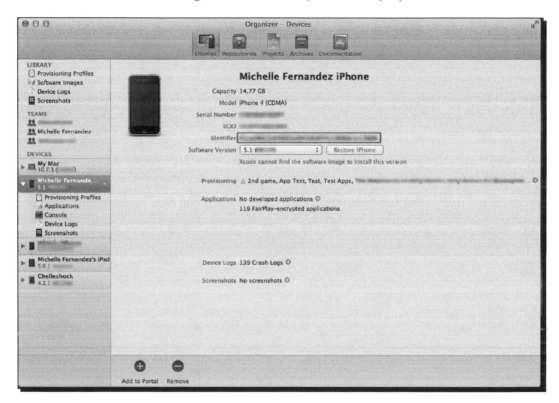

3. Simply drag your build file and drop it in the **Applications** area of the **Organizer** window and it will automatically install on your device.

Lastly, you can use the iPhone Configuration Utility that is available as a separate download from the Apple website under the **Support** tab: http://www.apple.com/support/iphone/enterprise/. It allows you to manage your configuration profiles, track and install provisioning profiles and authorized applications, and capture device information including console logs.

4. Click on the **Download** button and follow the directions on how to install the program.

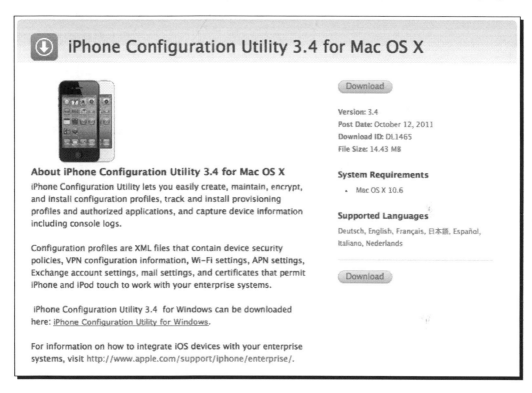

5. Make sure that your device is connected to your computer, launch the iPhone Configuration Utility, and then click the **Add** button at the top left of the box. Navigate to your Hello World build on your desktop or wherever you saved it and then click **Open**.

6. When your device is recognized, select your device under the **Devices** section. You will see a list of applications that are currently installed or yet to be installed. Click on the **Install** button next to your Hello World app you added to the utility.

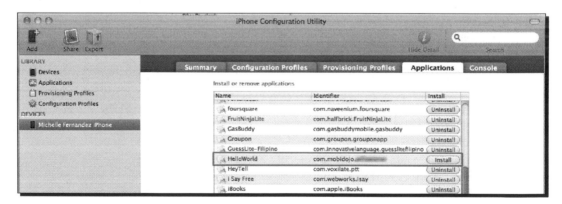

If you are testing the same version number of the same application repeatedly, make sure to delete the previous versions of your application from the device before a new install to remove any cached or associated data. Or use different version numbers in the build options.

What just happened?

We just learned three different ways using iTunes, Xcode, and the iPhone Configuration Utility to load an application build to an iOS device.

Using iTunes provides a simple drag-and-drop feature into your **Library** and then allows you to transfer the build as long as your device is synced up.

The Xcode method is probably the easiest and most common way to load a build to a device. As long as your device is connected properly and ready to use in the **Organizer**, drag-and-drop the build to **Applications** and it loads automatically.

Finally, the iPhone Configuration Utility is a step-by-step tool where you can easily differentiate which applications have been installed on your device. When you load your build within the main **Library**, the **Devices** area will pull up a list of applications you want to install or uninstall. After you locate your build, all you have to do is click the **Install** button and the file is loaded.

Testing our application on an Android device

Creating and testing our builds on an Android device does not require a developer account like how Apple does for iOS devices. The only tools you need to build for Android is a PC or Mac, Corona SDK, a JDK6 installation, and an Android device. If you plan on submitting an app to the Google Play Store, you'll need to sign up as an Google Play Developer at: `http://play.google.com/apps/publish`. There is a one-time $25 registration fee you have to pay if you want to publish software on the Google Play Store.

Creating the Hello World build for Android

Building our Hello World application is fairly simple since we do not have to create a unique **Keystore** or **Key Alias** for debug builds. When you're ready to submit an application to the Google Play Store, you'll need to create a release build and generate your own private key to sign your app. We'll discuss release builds and private keys in more detail later on in this book.

Time for action – creating an Android build

Follow these steps to create a new Android build in Corona SDK:

1. Launch the Corona Simulator and select **Simulator**.

2. Navigate to your Hello World application and select your `main.lua` file.

3. Once your application is running on the simulator, go to the **Corona Simulator** menu bar and select **File | Build For | Android** (Windows)/*Shift + Command + B* on your keyboard (Mac). The following dialog box appears:

4. Create a name for your app in the **Application name** field. We can keep the same name Hello World. In the **Version Code** field, set the number to 1 if that is not already the default number. This specific field must always be an integer and is not visible to users. In the **Version Name** field, keep the number at 1.0. This attribute is the string shown to users. In the **Package** field, you will need to specify a name that uses the traditional Java scheme, which is basically the reverse format of your domain name. For example, com.mycompany.app.helloworld would work as a package name. The **Project Path** shows the location of where your project folder is. **Target OS Compatibility** currently supports Android 2.2 and newer devices running the ArmV7 processor. In the **Keystore** field, you will be signing your build with the Debug Keystore that is already provided in Corona. In the **Key Alias** field, select androiddebugkey from the pull-down menu if it's not selected. In the **Save to folder** section, click **Browse** and choose where you'd like your application to save in.

5. If all the information has been confirmed in the dialog box, click on the **Build** button.

 For more information about Java package names, see the section on **Unique Package Names** in the Java documentation at: http://java.sun.com/docs/books/jls/ third_edition/html/packages.html#40169.

What just happened?

You have created your very first Android build! See how simple that was? Since Corona SDK already provides the Debug Keystore and androiddebugkey Key Alias within the engine, most of the signing work is already done for you. The only requirement from you is to fill out the build information for your application and click on the **Build** button to make a debug build. Your Hello World application will save as an .apk file at the location you designated. The file name will appear as Hello World.apk.

Time for action – loading an app on your Android device

There are several ways to load your Hello World build to your Android device that don't require you to download the Android SDK. Here are some simple methods:

The most fundamental method to upload an `.apk` file onto your device is to transfer it to the SD Card via the USB interface. If your device doesn't come with some kind of file manager application, a great one you can download from the Google Play Store is ASTRO File Manager at: `https://play.google.com/store/apps/details?id=com.metago.astro`. There are many other installers like AppInstaller at: `https://play.google.com/store/apps/details?id=com.funtrigger.appinstaller`. AppInstaller allows you to install `.apk` files from your SD card. You can always do a normal search for the preceding apps on the Google Play Store app on your device.

1. Under your device's **Settings**, select **Applications** and then select **Development**. Tap on **USB Debugging** if the mode is not active.

2. Go back a couple of screens to the **Applications** section. Enable **Unknown Sources** if it is not already active. This will allow you to install any non-market application (that is, debug builds). Select the home button on your device when done.

3. Connect the device to your computer with a USB cable. You will see a new notification that a new drive has connected to your PC or Mac. Access the SD drive and create a new folder. Name the folder something that you can identify easily for your Android builds. Drag-and-drop your `Hello World.apk` file from the desktop to the folder.

4. Eject the drive from your desktop and disconnect your device from the USB cable. Launch ASTRO File Manager or AppInstaller, whichever app you decided to download from the Google Play Store. In ASTRO, select **File Manager**, search for the folder you added on your SD card and select it. In AppInstaller, search for your newly named folder and select it. In both apps, you will see your `Hello World.apk` file. Select the file and a prompt will appear asking you to install it. Select the **Install** button and you should see your Hello World application appear in the **Apps** folder of your device.

A convenient method is through Dropbox. You can create an account at: `https://www.dropbox.com/`. Dropbox is a free service that lets you upload/download your files on your PC/Mac and mobile devices.

5. Download the Dropbox installer and install it on your computer. Also, download the mobile app from the Google Play Store (which is also free) on to your device and install it.

6. Log in to your Dropbox account on your computer and mobile device. From your computer, upload your `Hello World.apk` file.

7. Once it has finished uploading, go to the Dropbox app on your device and select your `Hello World.apk` file. You will be greeted with a screen that will ask you if you want to install the application. Select the **Install** button. Assuming that it installs correctly, another screen will appear saying **Application installed** and you can launch your Hello World app by pressing the **Open** button that is available.

One of the easiest methods is through Gmail. If you don't already have a Gmail account, create one at: `https://mail.google.com/`.

8. Log in to your account, compose a new e-mail and attach your `Hello World.apk` file to the message.

9. Address the recipient of the message to your own e-mail address and send it.

10. On your Android device, make sure you have your e-mail account linked on there as well. As soon as you receive the message, open the e-mail, and you will be given the option to install the application to your device. There will be an **Install** button or something similar displayed.

What just happened?

We just learned several ways on how to load a `.apk` file to an Android device. The preceding methods are some of the easiest ways to load an application quickly without running into any problems.

Using the file manager method allows you to access your `.apk` files easily without requiring any carrier data or Wi-Fi connection. By using a USB cable that is compatible with your device and connecting it to your computer, it's a simple drag-and-drop procedure.

The Dropbox method is the most convenient method of... once you have it set up on your computer and your mobile devices. All you have to do is drag-and-drop your `.apk` file to your account folder and it's instantly accessible to any device with the Dropbox app installed. You can also share your files through a download link—another great feature provided by Dropbox.

Setting up a Gmail account and sending your `.apk` files as attachments to yourself is a simple process if you don't want to download any file managers and other programs to your device and computer. The only thing you have to remember is that you can't e-mail an attachment over the size of 25 MB in Gmail.

Pop quiz – understanding Corona

1. When using Corona, which of the following statements is true?

    a. You need a `main.lua` file to launch your application.

    b. Corona SDK only runs on Mac OSX.

    c. The Corona Terminal doesn't launch the simulator.

    d. None of the above.

2. How many iOS devices can you use for development in the iPhone Developer Program?

    a. 50.

    b. 75.

    c. 5.

    d. 100.

3. What does the Version Code have to be when building for Android in Corona SDK?

    a. A string.

    b. An integer.

    c. Has to follow the Java scheme format.

    d. None of the above.

Summary

In this chapter, we covered some of the necessary tools needed to start developing applications for Corona SDK. Whether you are working on a Mac OS X or Microsoft Windows, you will notice the similarities on how to work on both operating systems and how simple it is to run Corona SDK.

To familiarize yourself with Corona better, try doing the following:

◆ Take the time to look into the sample code provided by Corona to view the capabilities of the SDK

◆ Feel free to alter any of the sample code to your liking to get a better understanding of programming in Lua

- ◆ Whether you're working on iOS (if you're a registered Apple Developer) or Android, try installing any of the sample code to your device to see how the applications work outside the simulator environment

- ◆ Take a look at the Ansca forums at `http://developer.anscamobile.com/forum/` and browse through the latest discussions on Corona development by fellow Corona SDK developers and personnel

Now that you understand the process of displaying objects in Corona, we'll be able to dive into other functions that will help create an operational mobile game.

In the next chapter, we'll be going into more depth on Lua programming language and learning simple coding techniques that are similar to the sample code in Corona. You will get a better understanding of the Lua syntax and notice how fast and easy it is to learn compared to other programming languages. So let's get started!

2

Lua Crash Course and the Corona Framework

Lua is the programming language used to develop the Corona SDK. Up until now, we have learned how to use the major resources to run the SDK and other development tools to create an application for mobile devices. Now that we have dabbled into creating a couple of lines of code that make a program work, let's jump into the fundamentals that will give you a better understanding of what Lua is capable of.

In this chapter, you will learn how to:

- ◆ Apply variables to a script
- ◆ Use data structures to form tables
- ◆ Work with display objects
- ◆ Implement functions using object methods and arguments
- ◆ Optimize your workflow

So let's get right to it.

Lua to the rescue

Lua is the industry standard for game programming. It is similar to JavaScript and Flash's ActionScript. Anyone who's done any scripting in these languages will make the transition to Lua almost immediately.

Lua has been useful in creating various applications and games. Many game programmers have found Lua to be a convenient scripting language due to how easy it is to embed, its fast execution, and its small learning curve. It is ubiquitous in World of Warcraft. It is also used by Electronic Arts, Rovio, ngmoco, and Tapulous in games such as Angry Birds, Tap Tap Revenge, Diner Dash, and so on.

For more information on Lua, refer to `http://www.lua.org`.

Valuable variables

Like in many scripting languages, Lua has variables. You can think of it as something that stores values. When you apply a value to a variable, you can refer to it using the same variable.

An application consists of statements and variables. **Statements** provide instructions on what operations and computations need to be done. **Variables** store the values of these computations. Setting a value into a variable is called an **assignment**.

Lua uses three kinds of variables: **global**, **local**, and **table fields**.

Global variables

A **global variable** can be accessed in every scope and can be modified from anywhere. The term scope is used to describe the area in which a set of variables live. You don't have to declare a global variable. It is created as soon as you assign a value to it.

```
myVariable = 10
print( myVariable )  -- prints the number 10
```

Local variables

A **local variable** is accessed from a local scope and usually called from a **function** or block of code. When we create a block, we are creating a scope in which variables can live or a list of statements, which are executed sequentially. When referencing a variable, Lua must find the variable. Localizing variables helps speed up the look-up process and improves the performance of your code. By using the local statement, it declares a local variable.

```
local i = 5  -- local variable
```

The following is how to declare a local variable in a block:

```
x = 10    -- global 'x' variable
local i = 1
```

```
while i <= 10 do
   local x = i * 2    -- a local 'x' variable for the while block
   print( x )         -- 2, 4, 6, 8, 10 ... 20
   i = i + 1
end

print( x )   -- prints 10 from global x
```

Table fields (properties)

Table fields are elements of the table themselves. Arrays can be indexed with numbers and strings or any value pertaining to Lua except nil. You index into the array to assign the values to a field using integers. When the index is a string, the field is known as a **property**. All properties can be accessed using the dot operator (x.y) or a string (x["y"]) to index into a table. The result is the same.

```
x = { y="Monday" }   -- create table
print( x.y )   -- "Monday"
z = "Tuesday"      -- assign a new value to property "Tuesday"
print( z )   -- "Tuesday"
x.z = 20   -- create a new property
print( x.z )   -- 20
print( x["z"] )   -- 20
```

More information relating to tables will be discussed later in the section called *Tables*.

You may have noticed the additional text on certain lines of code in the preceding examples. Those are what you call comments. Comments begin anywhere with a double hyphen -- , except inside a string. They run until the end of the line. Block comments are available as well. A common trick to comment out a block is to surround it with -- [[.

Here is how to comment one line:

```
a = 2
--print(a)      -- 2
```

The following is a block comment:

```
--[[
k = 50
print(k)      -- 50
]]--
```

Assignment conventions

There are rules for variable names. A variable starts with a letter or an underscore. It can't contain anything other than letters, underscores, or digits. It also can't be one of the following words reserved by Lua:

- which
- are
- and
- break
- do
- else
- elseif
- end
- false
- for
- function
- if
- in
- local
- nil
- not
- or
- repeat
- return
- then
- true
- until
- while

The following are valid variables:

- x
- X
- ABC

- `_abc`
- `test_01`
- `myGroup`

The following are invalid variables:

- `function`
- `my-variable`
- `123`

 Lua is also a case-sensitive language. For example, using `else` is a reserved word, but *Else* and *ELSE* are two different, valid names.

Types of values

Lua is a dynamically typed language. There is no defined type in the language. Each value carries its own type.

As you have noticed, values can be stored in variables. They can be manipulated to give a value of any type. This also allows you to pass arguments to other functions and return as results.

The basic types of values that you'll deal with are the following:

- `nil`—It is the only type whose value is `nil`. Any uninitialized variable has `nil` as its value. Like global variables, it is `nil` by default and can be assigned `nil` to delete it.

- `Boolean`—The `Boolean` type has two values, `false` and `true`. You will notice that conditional expressions consider `false` and `nil` as false and anything else as true.

- `Numbers`—Represents real (double-precision floating-point) numbers.

- `String`—A `String` is a sequence of characters. 8-bit characters and embedded zeros are allowed.

- `Tables`—A data structure in Lua. It is implemented by an associative array, which is an array that can be indexed not only with numbers, but also with strings or any other value, except `nil`. (We will discuss more about this in the section *Tables* later in this chapter).

- `Functions`—Known as first-class values of Lua. Typically, functions can be stored in variables, passed as arguments to other functions and returned as results.

Time for action – printing values using blocks

Let's give it a shot and see how powerful a language Lua is. We're starting to get an idea of how variables work and what happens when you assign a value to it. What if you have a variable that has multiple values attached to it? How does Lua differentiate them? We'll be using the `Corona Terminal` so we can see the values outputted in the terminal box. Along the way, you'll pick up other programming techniques as you progress through this section. We will also be referring to chunks in this exercise. The unit of execution of Lua is called a **chunk**. A chunk is a sequence of statements, which are executed sequentially.

If you remember from the previous chapter, we learned how to create our own project folder and `main.lua` file for the Hello World application.

1. Create a new project folder on your desktop and name it `Variables`.

2. Open up your preferred text editor and save it as `main.lua` in your `Variables` project folder.

3. Create the following variables:

```lua
local x = 10 -- Local to the chunk
local i = 1  -- Local to the chunk
```

4. In the `while` loop, add the following code:

```lua
while i<=x do
  local x = i     -- Local to the "do" body
  print(x)        -- Will print out numbers 1 through 10
  i = i + 1
end
```

5. Create an `if` statement that will represent another local body:

```lua
if i < 20 then
  local x           -- Local to the "then" body
  x = 20
  print(x + 5)  -- 25
else
  print(x)          -- This line will never execute since the above
"then" body is already true
end
print(x)  -- 10
```

6. Save your script.

7. Launch the `Corona Terminal`. Make sure you see the **Corona SDK** screen and a terminal window pop up.

8. Navigate to your `Variables` project folder and open your `main.lua` file in the simulator. You will notice that the device in the simulator is blank, but if you look at your terminal window, there are some results from the code printed out as follows:

```
1
2
3
4
5
6
7
8
9
10
25
10
```

What just happened?

The first two variables that were created are local outside of each block of code. Notice in the beginning of the `while` loop, `i <= x` refers to the variables in lines 1 and 2. The statement `local x = i` inside the `while` loop is only local to the `do` body and is not the same as `local x = 10`. The `while` loop runs ten times and prints out a value that is incremented by 1 each time.

The `if` statement compares `i < 20`, where `i` equals 1 and uses another `local x` that is local to the `then` body. Since the statement is true, `x` equals 20 and prints out the value of `x + 5` which is 25.

The very last line, `print(x)` is not attached to any of the blocks of code in the `while` loop or the `if` statement. Therefore, it refers to `local x = 10` and prints out the value of `10` in the terminal window. This may seem confusing, but it's important to understand how local and global variables work in Lua.

Expressions

An **expression** is something that has a value. It can include numeric constants, quoted strings, variable names, unary and binary operations, and function calls.

Arithmetic operators

+, -, *, /, %, and ^ are called **arithmetic operators**.

The following is an example using *Binary arithmetic* operators:

```
t = 2*(2-5.5)/13+26
print(t)    -- 25.461538461538
```

The following is an example using the *Modulo* (division remainder) operator:

```
m = 18%4
print(m)     -- 2
```

The following is an example using the *Power of* operator:

```
n = 7^2
print(n)   --49
```

Relational operators

Relational operators always result in `false` or `true` and ask yes-or-no questions.

<, >, <=, >=, ==, and ~= are some of the relational operators.

The operator == tests for equality and the operator ~= is the negation of equality. If the value types are different, then the result is false. Otherwise, Lua compares the values to their types. Numbers and strings are compared in the usual way. Tables and functions are compared by reference, as long as two such values are considered equal only if they are the same object. When a new object is created, the new object is different from the previously existing one.

The following are the examples of relational operators. It will display a `Boolean` result and can't be concatenated with a string:

```
print(0 > 1)    --false
print(4 > 2)    --true
print(1 >= 1)   --true
print(1 >= 1.5)   --false
print(0 == 0)   --true
print(3 == 2)   --false
print(2 ~= 2)   --false
print(0 ~= 2)   --true
```

Logical operators

The **logical operators** in Lua are and, or, and not. All logical operators consider both false and nil as false and anything else as true.

The operator and returns its first argument if the value is false or nil; otherwise it returns its second argument. The operator or returns its first argument if the value is different from nil and false; otherwise, it returns its second argument. Both and and or use short-cut evaluation, which means, the second operand is evaluated only when necessary.

```
print(10 and 20)        -- 20
print(nil and 1)        -- nil
print(false and 1)      -- false
print(10 or 20)         -- 10
print(false or 1)       -- 1
```

The operator not always returns true or false:

```
print(not nil)        -- true
print(not true)       -- false
print(not 2)          -- false
```

Concatenation

The **string concatenation operator** in Lua is denoted by two dots . . . It takes two strings as operands and splices them together. If any of its operands are numbers, then they are also converted to a string.

```
print("Hello " .. "World")  -- Hello World

myString = "Hello"
print(myString .. " World")    -- Hello World
```

Length operator

The **length operator** #, measures the length of a string. The length of a string is simply the number of characters in it. A character is considered as 1 byte.

```
print(#"*") --1
print(#"\n") --1
print(#"hello") --5
myName = "Jane Doe"
print(#myName) --8
```

Precedence

Operator precedence in Lua is as follows, from higher to lower priority:

- ^
- not   #   - (unary)
- *   /
- +   -
- ..
- <   >   <=   >=   ~=   ==
- and
- or

All binary operators are left associative, except for ^ exponentiation and .. concatenation, which are right associative. You can use parentheses to change the precedence of an expression.

In cases where two operands of the same precedence compete for operands, the operand belongs to the operator on the left:

```
print(5 + 4 - 2) -- This returns the number 7
```

The preceding expression shows both the addition and subtraction operators, which have equal precedence. The second element (the number 4) belongs to the addition operator, so the expression is evaluated mathematically as follows:

```
print((5 + 4) - 2) -- This returns the number 7
```

Let's focus on the rules of precedence based on priority. For example:

```
print (7 + 3 * 9) -- This returns the number 34
```

An inexperienced programmer might think that the value of the preceding example is 90, if it were evaluated from left to right. The correct value is 34 because multiplication has a higher precedence over addition, so it is performed first. Adding parentheses to the same expression will make it easier to read:

```
print (7 + (3 * 9)) -- This returns the number 34
```

Strings

Earlier in this chapter, you saw some code examples using sequences of characters. Those sequences of characters are called **strings**. Strings may contain characters with any numeric value, including embedded zeros. This also means that binary data can be stored in a string.

Quoting strings

There are three ways to quote strings: with double quotes, with single quotes and with square brackets.

 When quoting strings, make sure that only straight up and down quotation characters are used in your code or else it will not compile.

Using double quote characters " mark the beginning and end of the string. For example:

```
print("This is my string.")   -- This is my string.
```

You can also quote strings by using the single quote character '. Single quotes work the same as double quotes except that single-quoted strings can contain a double quote.

```
print('This is another string.')   -- This is another string.

print('She said, "Hello!" ')   -- She said, "Hello!"
```

Lastly, using a pairs of square brackets will also quote strings. They are used mainly for strings when double or single quotes cannot be used. There are not many cases that this occurs, but they will do the job.

```
print([[Is it 'this' or "that?"]]) -- Is it 'this' or "that?"
```

Time for action – getting our hands full of strings

We're starting to familiarize ourselves with several blocks of code and how they interact with each other. Let's see what happens when we add in some expressions using strings and how different they are in comparison to just regular strings you print out in the terminal.

1. Create a new project folder on your desktop and name it `Working With Strings`.

2. Make a new `main.lua` file in your text editor and save it in your folder.

3. Type the following lines (Do not include the line numbers in the code, it is only used for line reference):

```
1 print("This is a string!") -- This is a string!
2 print("15" + 1) -- Returns the value 16
```

4. Add in the following variables. Notice that it uses the same variable name:

```
3 myVar = 28
4 print(myVar)   -- Returns 28

5 myVar = "twenty-eight"
6 print(myVar) -- Returns twenty-eight
```

5. Let's add in more variables with some string values and compare them using different operators.

```
7 Name1, Phone = "John Doe", "123-456-7890"
8 Name2 = "John Doe"

9 print(Name1, Phone) -- John Doe   123-456-7890
10 print(Name1 == Phone) -- false
11 print(Name1 <= Phone) -- false
12 print(Name1 == Name2) -- true
```

6. Save your script and launch your project in Corona. Observe the results in the terminal window.

```
This is a string!
16
28
twenty-eight
John Doe   123-456-7890
false
false
true
```

What just happened?

You can see that line 1 is just a plain string with characters printed out. In line 2, notice that the number 15 is inside the string and then added to the number 1 which is outside the string. Lua provides automatic conversions between number and strings at runtime. Numeric operations applied to a string will try to convert the string to a number.

When working with variables, you can use the same one and have them contain a string and a number at different times as in lines 3 and 5 (myVar = 28 and myVar = "twenty-eight").

In the last chunk of code (lines 7-12), we compared different variable names using relational operators. First, we printed the strings of Name1 and Phone. The next lines following the comparison between Name1, Name2, and Phone. When two strings have the same characters in the exact order, then they are considered as the same string and are equal to each other. When you look at print(Name1 == Phone) and print(Name1 <= Phone), the characters do not correlate with each other so they return false. In print(Name1 == Name2), both variables contain the same characters and therefore returns true.

Have a go hero – pulling some more strings

Strings are pretty simple to work with since they are just sequences of characters. Try making your own expressions similar to the preceding example with the following modifications:

♦ Create some variables with numerical values and another set of variables with numerical string values. Use relational operators to compare the values and then print out the results.

♦ Use the concatenation operator and combine several strings or numbers together and space them out equally. Print out the result in the terminal window.

Tables

Tables are the proprietary data structure in Lua. They represent arrays, lists, sets, records, graphs, an so on. A table in Lua is similar to an associative array. Associative arrays can be indexed with values of any type, not just numbers. Tables implement all these structures efficiently. For example, arrays can be implemented by indexing tables with integers. Arrays do not have a fixed size, but grow as needed. When initializing an array, its size is defined indirectly.

The following is an example of how tables can be constructed:

```
1 a = {}      -- create a table with reference to "a"
2 b = "y"
3 a[b] = 10      -- new entry, with key="b" and value=10
4 a[20] = "Monday"   -- new entry, with key=20 and value="Monday"
5 print(a["y"])      -- 10
6 b = 20
7 print(a[b])      -- "Monday"
8 c = "hello"      -- new value assigned to "hello" property
9 print( c )      -- "hello"
```

You will notice in line 5 that `a["y"]` is indexing the value from line 3. In line 7, `a[b]` uses a new value of variable `b` and indexes the value of 20 to the string, `"Monday"`. The last line, `c` is different from the previous variables and its only value is the string, `"hello"`.

Passing a table as an array

Keys of a table can be consecutive integers, starting at 1. They can be made into an array (or a list).

```
colors =  {
[1]  = "Green",
[2]  = "Blue",
[3]  = "Yellow",
[4]  ="Orange",
[5]  = "Red"
}
print(colors[4])  -- Orange
```

Another way of writing table constructors to build arrays in a faster and convenient way that doesn't require writing out each integer key is as follows:

```
colors = {"Green", "Blue", "Yellow", "Orange", "Red"}
print(colors[4])  -- Orange
```

Altering contents in a table

While working with tables, you can modify or remove the values already in it, and also add new values to it. This can be accomplished using the assignment statement. The following example creates a table with three people and their favorite type of drink. You can make an assignment to change one person's drink, add a new person-drink pair to the table, and remove an existing person-drink pair.

```
drinks = {Jim = "orange juice", Matt = "soda", Jackie = "milk"}
drinks.Jackie = "lemonade" -- A change.
drinks.Anne = "water" -- An addition.
drinks.Jim = nil -- A removal.
print(drinks.Jackie, drinks.Anne, drinks.Matt, drinks.Jim)
-- lemonade water soda nil
```

`drinks.Jackie = "lemonade"` overwrites the original value of `drinks.Jackie = "milk"`.

`drinks.Anne = "water"` adds a new key and value to the table. The value of `drinks.Anne` before this line would have been `nil`.

`drinks.Matt = "soda"` stays the same since there were no alterations to it.

`drinks.Jim = nil` overwrites the original value of `drinks.Jim = "orange juice"` with `nil`. It removes the key `Jim` from the table.

Populating a table

Ways to populate a table is to start with an empty table and add things to it one at a time. We'll be using constructors, which are expressions that create and initialize tables. The simplest constructor is the empty constructor, { }.

```
myNumbers = {} -- Empty table constructor

for i = 1, 5 do
  myNumbers[i] = i
end

for i = 1, 5 do
print("This is number " .. myNumbers[i])
end
```

The following is the result from the terminal:

```
--This is number 1
--This is number 2
--This is number 3
--This is number 4
--This is number 5
```

The preceding example shows that `myNumbers = {}` is an empty table constructor. A `for` loop is created and calls `myNumbers[i]` five times starting from the number 1. Each time it is called, it is incremented by 1 and then printed out.

Objects

Tables and functions are objects. Variables do not actually contain these values, only references to them. Tables are also used in what is known as **object-oriented programming**. Functions that deal with a particular type of value are part of that value. Such a value is called an **object** and its functions are called **methods**. In Corona, we'll be focusing more on display objects since they are essential for game development.

Display objects

Anything drawn to the screen is made by **display objects**. In Corona, the assets you see displayed in the simulator are instances of display objects. You have probably seen shapes, images, and text, which are all forms of display objects. When you create these objects, you'll be able to animate them, turn them into backgrounds, interact with them using touch events, and so on.

Display objects are created by calling a function known as a **factory function**. There is a specific kind of factory function for each type of display object. For example, `display.newCircle()` creates a vector object.

Instances of display objects behave similar to Lua tables. This enables you to add your own properties to an object as long as they do not conflict with the system assigned properties and method names.

Display properties

The dot operator is used to access properties. Display objects share the following properties:

- `object.alpha` is the object's opacity. A value of `0` is transparent and `1.0` is opaque. The default value is `1.0`.

- `object.height` is in local coordinates.

- `object.isVisible` controls whether the object is visible on the screen. `true` is visible and `false` is not. The default is `true`.

- `object.isHitTestable` allows an object to continue to receive hit events even if it is not visible. If `true`, objects will receive hit events regardless of visibility; if `false`, events are only sent to visible objects. Defaults to `false`.

- `object.parent` is a read-only property that returns the object's parent.

- `object.rotation` is the current rotation angle (in degrees). Can be a negative or positive number. Default is `0`.

- `object.contentBounds` is a table with properties xMin, xMax, yMin, and yMax in screen coordinates. Generally used to map the object in a group to the screen coordinates.

- `object.contentHeight` is the height in screen coordinates.

- `object.contentWidth` is the width in screen coordinates.

- `object.width` is in local coordinates.

- `object.x` specifies the x-position (in local coordinates) of the object relative to the parent—the parent's origin to be precise. It provides the x-position of the object's reference point relative to the parent. Changing the value will move the object in the x-direction.

- `object.xOrigin` specifies the x-position of the object's origin relative to the parent's origin. It is in the object's local coordinates. Changing the value of this property will move the object in the x-direction.

- `object.xReference` defines the x-position of the reference point relative to the object's local origin. For most display objects, the value defaults to 0, meaning the x-position of the origin and the reference point are the same.

- `object.xScale` gets or sets the X scaling factor. A value of 0.5 will scale the object to 50 percent in the X direction. The scaling occurs around the object's reference point. The default reference point for most display objects is center.

- `object.y` specifies the y-position (in local coordinates) of the object relative to the parent—the parent's origin to be precise.

- `object.yOrigin` specifies the y-position of the object's origin relative to the parent's origin. It is in the object's local coordinates. Changing the value of this property will move the object in the y-direction.

- `object.yReference` defines the y-position of the reference point relative to the object's local origin. For most display objects, the value defaults to 0, meaning the y-position of the origin and the reference point are the same.

- `object.yScale` gets or sets the Y scaling factor. A value of 0.5 will scale the object to 50 percent in the Y direction. The scaling occurs around the object's reference point. The default reference point for most display objects is center.

Object methods

Corona can create display objects to store object methods as properties. There are two ways this can be done, the dot operator (.) and the colon operator (:). Both are valid ways to create object methods.

The call to an object method using the dot operator is passed to the object if it's the first argument:

```
object = display.newRect(110, 100, 50, 50)
object:setFillColor(255, 255, 255)
object.translate( object, 10, 10 )
```

The colon operator method is merely a shortcut with less typing involved to create the function:

```
object = display.newRect(110, 100, 50, 50)
object:setFillColor(255, 255, 255)
object:translate( 10, 10 )
```

The display objects share the following methods:

◆ `object:rotate( deltaAngle )` or `object.rotate( object, deltaAngle )`—Effectively adds `deltaAngle` (in degrees) to the current rotation property.

◆ `object:scale( sx, sy )` or `object.scale(object, sx, sy )`—Effectively multiplies `xScale` and `yScale` properties by `sx` and `sy` respectively. If the current `xScale` and `yScale` values are 0.5 and `sx` and `sy` are also 0.5, the resulting scale will be 0.25 for `xScale` and `yScale`. This scales the object from 50 percent of its original size to 25 percent.

◆ `object:setReferencePoint( referencePoint )` or `object.setReferencePoint( object, referencePoint )`—Sets the reference point either to the center of the object (default) or to one of several convenient points along the bounding box of the object. The argument `referencePoint` should be one of the following:

  ❑ `display.CenterReferencePoint`

  ❑ `display.TopLeftReferencePoint`

  ❑ `display.TopCenterReferencePoint`

  ❑ `display.TopRightReferencePoint`

  ❑ `display.CenterRightReferencePoint`

  ❑ `display.BottomRightReferencePoint`

  ❑ `display.BottomCenterReferencePoint`

  ❑ `display.BottomLeftReferencePoint`

  ❑ `display.CenterLeftReferencePoint`

◆ `object:translate( deltaX, deltaY )` or `object.translate( object, deltaX, deltaY )`—Effectively adds `deltaX` and `deltaY` to the `x` and `y` properties respectively. This will move the object from its current position.

◆ `object:removeSelf( )` or `object.removeSelf( object )`—Removes the display object and frees its memory, assuming there are no other references to it. This is equivalent to calling `group:remove(IndexOrChild)` on the same display object, but is syntactically simpler. The `removeSelf()` syntax is also supported in other cases such as removing physics' joints in Physics.

Images

Many art assets used in Corona applications are sets of images. You will notice that bitmap image objects are types of display objects.

Loading an image

By using `display.newImage( filename [, baseDirectory] [, left, top] )`, an image object is returned. The image data is loaded from a filename you specified to your image and looks in the `system.ResourceDirectory` for that file. The acceptable types of image files that are supported are `.png` (PNG-24 or higher only) and `.jpg` files. Avoid high `.jpg` compression as it may take longer to load on a device. `.png` files have better quality over `.jpg` files and are used to display transparent images. `.jpg` files do not save transparent images.

Image autoscaling

The default behavior of `display.newImage()` is to autoscale large images. This is to conserve texture memory. However, there are times when you do not want to have images autoscaled and there is an optional Boolean flag in the parameter list to control this manually.

To override autoscaling and show the image at its full resolution, use the optional `isFullResolution` parameter. By default, it is `false`, but if you specify `true`, then the new image is loaded at its full resolution:

```
display.newImage( [parentGroup,] filename [, baseDirectory]
[, x, y] [,isFullResolution] )
```

The following are the limitations and known issues:

- Indexed PNG image files are not supported.

- Grayscale images are currently not supported; images must be RGB.

- Images will still be autoscaled if they are larger than the maximum possible texture dimensions of the device. This is usually 1024x1024 (iPhone 3G) or 2048x2048 (iPhone 3GS and iPad).

- If you reload the same image multiple times, the subsequent calls to `display.newImage` ignores the `isFullResolution` parameter and takes on the value passed the first time. In other words, the way you load an image file the first time affects the autoscaling setting the next time you load that same file. This is because Corona conserves texture memory by automatically re-using a texture that has already been loaded. As a result, you can use the same images as many times as you want without consuming additional texture memory.

More information on Corona SDK's documentation is located on Ansca's website: `http://www.anscamobile.com`.

Time for action – placing images on screen

We're finally getting into the visually appealing part of this chapter by starting to add in display objects using images. We don't have to refer to the terminal window for now. So let's focus on the simulator screen. We'll begin by creating a background image and some art assets.

1. First off, create a new project folder to your desktop and name it `Display Objects`.

2. In the `Chapter 2 Resources` folder, copy the `glassbg.png` and `moon.png` image files into your `Display Objects` project folder. You can download the project files accompanying this book from the Packt website.

3. Launch your text editor and create a new `main.lua` file for your current project.

4. Write out the following lines of code:

```
local background = display.newImage( "glassbg.png", true )
local image01 = display.newImage( "moon.png", 110, 30 )
local image02 = display.newImage( "moon.png" )
image02.x = 160; image02.y = 200
image03 = display.newImage( "moon.png" )
image03.x = 160; image03.y = 320
```

The display object for your background variable should contain the filename of the background image in your project folder. For example, if the background image filename is called `glassbg.png`, then you would display the image as follows:

```
local background = display.newImage( "glassbg.png", true )
```

Using `image02.x = 160; image02.y = 200` is the same as follows:

```
image02.x = 160
image02.y = 200
```

The semicolon (;) indicates the end of a statement and is optional. It makes it easier to separate two or more statements in one line and saves adding extra lines to your code.

5. Save your script and launch your project in the simulator.

 If you're using Corona SDK on a Mac OSX, the default device is the iPhone. If you're using Windows, the default device is the Droid.

6. You should see a background image and three other display objects that are the same as the image shown in as shown in the following screenshot. The display results will vary depending on which device you use to simulate.

The display objects for variables `image01`, `image02`, and `image03` should contain the `moon.png` filename. The filenames in your code are case-sensitive, so make sure that you write it exactly how it displays in your project folder.

What just happened?

Currently, `background` is set to full resolution because we specified `true` in the display object. We also have the image centered about its local origin since no `top` or `left` coordinates were applied.

When you observe the placement of `image01`, `image02`, and `image03` in the simulator, they're practically in line with each other vertically, though the script style for `image01` versus `image02`/`image03` are written differently. This is because the coordinates for `image01` are based on `(left, top)` of the display object. You can optionally specify that the image's top-left corner be located at the coordinate `(left, top)`; if you don't supply both coordinates, the image will be centered about its local origin.

Placement for `image02` and `image03` are specified from their local origin of the display object and positioned by local values of x and y properties of the device screen. The local origin is at the center of the image; the reference point is initialized at this point. Since we didn't apply (`left`, `top`) values to `image02` and `image03`, further access to x or y properties are referred to the center of the image.

Now, you've probably noticed that the output from the iPhone 3G looks fine and dandy, but the output from the Droid shows that the display objects are not centered and the background image doesn't even fill the entire screen. We see that all the objects we specified are there but the scaling is off. That is because each iOS and Android device has different screen resolutions. The iPhone 3G has a screen resolution of 320 x 480 pixels and the Droid has a screen resolution of 480 x 854 pixels. What may look fine on one type of device may not look exactly the same on a different one. Don't worry, there is a simple solution to fix all that by using a `config.lua` file that we will discuss in the next couple of sections.

Have a go hero – adjusting display object properties

Now that you know how to add images onto the device screen, try testing out the other display properties. Try doing any of the following:

- Change all the x and y coordinates of `image01`, `image02`, and `image03` display objects
- Choose any display object and change its rotation
- Change the visibility of a single display object

Refer to the display properties mentioned earlier in this chapter in case you're unsure how to do any of the preceding adjustments.

Runtime configuration

All project files not only contain a `main.lua` file but other `.lua` and related assets as needed for your project. Some Corona projects are configured using a `config.lua` file that is compiled into your project and accessed at runtime. This allows you to specify dynamic content scaling, dynamic content alignment, dynamic image resolution, frame rate control, and anti-aliasing all at the same time so that the output on every type of device is displayed similarly.

Dynamic content scaling

You can specify to Corona what the original screen size for your content is. Then allow it to scale your app to run on a device that has a different screen size to the original.

The following values should be used to scale content:

- `width` (number)—Screen resolution width of the original target device (in portrait orientation)

- `height` (number)—Screen resolution height of the original target device (in portrait orientation)

- `scale` (string)—Type of autoscaling from the following:

    - `none`—Dynamic content scaling turned off

    - `letterbox`—Uniformly scales up content as much as possible

    - `zoomEven`—Scales up content uniformly to fill the screen, while keeping the aspect ratio

    - `zoomStretch`—Scales up content non-uniformly to fill the screen and will stretch it vertically or horizontally

> `zoomStretch` works well with Android device scaling since many of them have different screen resolutions.

Dynamic content alignment

Content that is dynamically scaled is already centered by default. You may find cases where you don't want the content to be centered. Devices such as the iPhone 3G and the Droid have completely different screen resolutions. In order for the content displayed on the Droid to match the iPhone 3G, the alignment needs to be adjusted so the content fills the entire screen without leaving any empty black screen space.

`xAlign`: A string that specifies the alignment in the x-direction. The following values can be used:

- `left`
- `center` (Default)
- `right`

`yAlign`: A string that specifies the alignment in the y-direction. The following values can be used:

- `top`
- `center` (Default)
- `bottom`

Dynamic image resolution

Corona allows you to swap in higher-resolution versions of your images to higher-resolution devices, without having to change your layout code. This is a case to consider if building for multiple devices with different screen resolutions.

An example where you want to display high-resolution images is on an iPhone 4 where the resolution is 640 x 960 pixels. It is double the resolution of the earlier iOS devices such as the iPod Touch 2G or the iPhone 3GS which both are 320 x 480 pixels. Scaling up the content from the iPhone 3GS to fit the iPhone 4 screen works, but the images will not be as crisp and will look a little fuzzy on the device.

Images of higher resolution can be swapped in for the iPhone 4 by adding a `@2x` suffix to the end of filenames. For example, if your image filename is `myImage.png` then your higher resolution filename should be `myImage@2x.png`.

In your `config.lua` file, a table named `imageSuffix` needs to be added for the image naming convention and image resolutions to take effect. The `config.lua` file resides in your project folder where all your other `.lua` files and image files are stored. Look at the following example:

```
application =
{
    content =
    {
        width = 320,
        height = 480,
        scale = "letterbox",
        imageSuffix =
        {
            ["@2x"] = 2,
        },
    },
}
```

When calling your display objects, use `display.newImageRect( [parentGroup,] filename [, baseDirectory] w, h )` instead of `display.newImage()`. The target height and width need to be set to the dimensions of your base image.

Frame rate control and anti-aliasing

The frame rate is 30 fps (frames per second) by default. FPS refers to the speed at which the image is refreshed in games. 30 fps is the standard in mobile games, especially for older devices. You can set it to 60 fps when you add in the fps key. Using 60 fps makes your app run smoother. You can easily detect a life-like fluidity in the motion when it comes to running animations or collision detections.

Corona uses software anti-aliasing for vector objects. By default, it is turned off to improve the performance of the vector objects. You can turn it on by setting the `antialias` key to `true`.

See the following example:

```
application =
{
    content =
        {
            fps = 60,
        antialias = true,
        },
}
```

Time for action – scaling display objects on multiple devices

In our `Display Objects` project, we left off displaying a background image and three similar display objects in the simulator. When running the project on different devices, the coordinates and resolution size were most compatible with the iPhone only. When building applications for multiple devices across iOS and Android platforms, we can configure it using a `config.lua` file that is compiled into the project and accessed at runtime. So let's get to it!

1. In your text editor, create a new file and write out the following lines:

```
application =
{
        content =
        {
                width = 320,
                height = 480,
                scale = "letterbox",
                xAlign = "left",
                yAlign = "top"
        },
}
```

2. Save your script as `config.lua` in your `Display Objects` project folder.

3. Mac users, launch your application in Corona under the iPhone device. Once you have done so, under the **Corona Simulator** menu bar, select **Window | View As | iPhone 4**. You will notice that the display objects fit perfectly on the screen and that there are no empty black spaces showing either.

4. Windows users, launch your application in Corona under the Droid device. You will notice that all the content is scaled and aligned properly. Under the **Corona Simulator** menu bar, select **Window | View As | NexusOne**. Observe the similarities of content placement to that of the Droid. From left to right: iPhone 3G, iPhone 4, Droid, and NexusOne.

What just happened?

We have now learned a way to implement easy configuration to display our content across a variety of devices on iOS and Android. Content scaling features are useful for multiscreen development. If you look at the `config.lua` file we created, the content `width = 320` and `height = 480`. This is the resolution size that the content is originally authored for. In this case, it is the iPhone 3G. Since we used `scale = "letterbox"`, it enabled the content to uniformly scale up as much as possible, while still showing all content on the screen.

We also set `xAlign = "left"` and `yAlign = "top"`. This fills in the empty black screen space that shows on the Droid specifically. The content scaling is in the center by default so by aligning the content to the left and top of the screen the additional screen space will be taken away.

Dynamic resolution images

Earlier, we touched base with dynamic image resolution. iOS devices are a perfect example in this case. Corona has the capability to use base images (for devices on the 3GS and lower) and double-resolution images (for the iPhone 4 that has **retina display**) all within the same project file. Any of your double-resolution images can be swapped to your high-end iOS device without having to alter your code. This will allow your build to coincide with older devices and let you handle more complex multiscreen deployment cases. You will notice that dynamic image resolution works in conjunction with dynamic content scaling.

Using the line `display.newImageRect( [parentGroup,] filename [,` `baseDirectory] w, h )` will call out your dynamic resolution images.

`w` refers to the content *width* of the image and `h` refers to the content *height* of the image.

For example:

```
myImage = display.newImageRect( "image.png", 128, 128 )
```

Remember that the two values represent the base image size, *not* the onscreen position of the image. You must define the base size in your code so that Corona knows how to render the higher-resolution alternative images. The contents of your project folder will be set up similarly as follows:

```
My New Project/     name of your project folder
Icon.png            required for iPhone/iPod/iPad
Icon@2x.png         required for iPhone/iPod with Retina display
main.lua
config.lua
myImage.png         Base image (Ex. Resolution 128 x 128 pixels)
myImage@2x.png      Double resolution image (Ex. Resolution 256 x 256
pixels)
```

When creating your double resolution image, make sure that it is twice the size of the base image. It's best when creating your display assets that you start with the double resolution image. Corona lets you select your own image naming patterns. The @2x convention is one example that can be used but you have the option of naming suffixes to your personal preference. For now, we'll use the @2x suffix since it distinguishes the double resolution reference. When you create your double resolution image, name it with the @2x suffix included. Take the same image and resize it to 50 percent of the original size and then use the same filename without the @2x included.

Other examples on naming suffixes can be:

◆   @2

◆   -2

◆   -two

As mentioned earlier in the chapter, you have to define your image suffix for your double-resolution images in the `imageSuffix` table in your `config.lua` file. The content scale you set will allow Corona to determine the ratio between the current screen and base content dimensions. The following example uses the suffix @2x to define double-resolution images:

```
application =
{
    content =
```

```
{
    width = 320,
    height = 480,
    scale = "letterbox",
    imageSuffix =
        {
            ["@2x"] = 2,
        },
    },
}
```

Time for some shapes

Another way of creating display objects is using **vector objects**. You can use vector objects to create shapes, such as a rectangle, rounded rectangle, and circle by using the following:

- `display.newRect( [parentGroup,] left, top, width, height )` creates a rectangle using `width` by `height`. Location starts from the top-left corner of the device screen using `left` and `top` as your coordinates of placement.

- `display.newRoundedRect( [parentGroup,] left, top, width, height, cornerRadius )` creates a rounded rectangle using `width` by `height`. Location starts from the top-left corner of the device screen using `left` and `top` as your coordinates of placement. Rounding off the corners uses `cornerRadius`.

- `display.newCircle( [parentGroup,] xCenter, yCenter, radius )` creates a circle using `radius` centered at `xCenter, yCenter`.

Applying stroke width, fill color, and stroke color

All vector objects can be outlined using strokes. You can set the stroke width, fill color and stroke color.

- `object.strokeWidth`—Creates the stroke width in pixels.

- `object:setFillColor( r, g, b [, a] )`—Using the `r,g,b` codes between 0 and 255. `a` refers to the **alpha**, which is optional and defaulted at 255.

- `object:setStrokeColor( r, g, b [, a] )`—Using the `r,g,b` codes between 0 and 255. `a` refers to the alpha, which is optional and defaulted at 255.

The following is an example of displaying vector objects using strokes:

```
local rect = display.newRect(110, 100, 250, 250)
rect:setFillColor(255, 255, 255)
rect:setStrokeColor(45, 180, 100)
rect.strokeWidth = 10
```

Text, text, text

In *Chapter 1, Getting Started With Corona SDK*, we created the Hello World application using a text display object. Let's go in detail on how text is implemented onscreen.

`display.newText( [parentGroup,] string, x, y, font, size )` creates a text object using `x` and `y` values. There is no text color by default. In the `font` parameter, apply any of the font names in the library. The `size` parameter displays the size of the text. Some of the default constants can be used if you don't want to apply a font name:

- ◆ `native.systemFont`
- ◆ `native.systemFontBold`

Applying color and string value

The size, color, and text fields can be set or retrieved in text display objects.

- ◆ `object.size`—The size of the text
- ◆ `object:setTextColor( r, g, b [, a] )`—Using the `r,g,b` codes between 0 and 255. `a` refers to the alpha, which is optional and defaulted at 255
- ◆ `object.text`—Contains the text of the textfield. It allows you to update a string value for a test object

Functions

Functions can carry out a procedure or compute and return values. We can make a function call as a statement or we can use it as an expression. We have learned that functions can be variables. A table can use those variables to store them as properties.

Functions are the most important means of abstraction in Lua. One function that we have used many times is: print. In the following example, the print function is being told to execute one piece of data—the string, "My favorite number is 8":

```
print("My favorite number is 8") -- My favorite number is 8
```

Another way of saying this is that print is being called with one argument. print is only one of the many built-in functions that Lua has, but almost any program you write will involve you defining your own functions.

Defining a function

When trying to define a function, you have to give it a name that you can call out to when you want to return a value. You then have to create a statement of what the value will output and then apply end to your function after you have finished defining it. For example:

```
function myName()
  print("My name is Jane.")
end


myName()   -- My name is Jane.
```

Notice that the function name is myName and is used to call out what's inside the function definition print("My name is Jane.").

An alternative to defining a function is as follows:

```
function myName(Name)
  print("My name is " .. Name .. ".")
end

myName("Jane")   -- My name is Jane.
myName("Cory")   -- My name is Cory.
myName("Diane")   -- My name is Diane.
```

The new myName function has one argument using the variable Name. The string, "My name is " is concatenated with Name and then a period as the printed result. When the function is called, we used three different names as an argument and the result is printed with a new customized name for each line.

More display functions

In Corona, you can change the appearance of the status bar on your device. This is a one-line setting in your code that takes effect once you launch your application.

`display.setStatusBar( mode )`—Hides or changes the appearance of the status bar on iOS devices (iPad, iPhone, and iPod Touch) and Android 2.x devices. Android 3.x devices are not supported.

The argument mode should be one of the following:

- `display.HiddenStatusBar`: To hide the status bar, you can use the following line at the beginning of your code:

  `display.setStatusBar( display.HiddenStatusBar )`

- `display.DefaultStatusBar`: To show the default status bar, you can use the following line at the beginning of your code:

  `display.setStatusBar(display.DefaultStatusBar)`

- `display.TranslucentStatusBar`: To show the translucent status bar, you can use the following line at the beginning of your code:

```
display.setStatusBar(display.TranslucentStatusBar)
```

- `display.DarkStatusBar`: To show the dark status bar, you can use the following line at the beginning of your code:

```
display.setStatusBar(display.DarkStatusBar)
```

Content size properties

When you want to obtain display information on your device, you can use the content size properties to return the values.

- `display.contentWidth`—Returns the original width of the content in pixels. This will default to the screen width.

- `display.contentHeight`—Returns the original height of the content in pixels. This will default to the screen height.

- `display.viewableContentWidth`—A read-only property that contains the width of the viewable screen area in pixels, within the coordinate system of the original content. Accessing this property will display how the content is viewed, whether you're in portrait or landscape mode. For example:

```
print ( display.viewableContentWidth )
```

- `display.viewableContentHeight`—A read-only property that contains the height of the viewable screen area in pixels within the coordinate system of the original content. Accessing this property will display how the content is viewed, whether you're in portrait or landscape mode. For example:

```
print ( display.viewableContentHeight )
```

- `display.statusBarHeight`—A read-only property representing the height of the status bar in pixels (only valid on iOS devices). For example:

```
print (display.statusBarHeight)
```

Optimizing your workflow

So far, we have touched on the vital basics of programming in Lua and terminology used in Corona SDK. Once you start developing interactive applications to sell in the App Store or Google Play Store, you need to be aware of your design choices and how they affect the performance of your application. This means taking into consideration how much memory your mobile device is using to process the application. Here are some things to look for if you're just starting out on Corona SDK.

Using memory efficiently

In some of our earlier examples, we used global variables in our code. Cases like those are an exception since the examples did not contain a high volume of functions, loops to call out to or display objects. Once you start building a game that is heavily involved with function calls and numerous display objects, local variables will increase performance within your application and will be placed on the stack so Lua can interface with them faster.

The following code will cause memory leaks:

```
-- myImage is a global variable
    myImage = display.newImage( "image.png" )
myImage.x = 160;  myImage.y = 240

-- A touch listener to remove object
local removeBody = function( event )
  local t = event.target
  local phase = event.phase
```

```
    if "began" == phase then
      -- variable "myImage" still exists even if it's not displayed
      t:removeSelf() -- Destroy object
    end

    -- Stop further propagation of touch event
    return true
  end

myImage:addEventListener( "touch", removeBody )
```

The preceding code removes myImage from the display hierarchy once it is touched. The only problem is that the memory used by myImage leaks because the variable myImage still refers to it. Since myImage is a global variable, the display object it references will not be freed even though myImage does not display on the screen.

Unlike global variables, localizing variables help speed up the look-up process for your display object. Also, it only exists within the block or chunk of code that it's defined in. Using a local variable in the following code will remove the object completely and free up memory:

```
-- myImage is a local variable
   local myImage = display.newImage( "image.png" )
myImage.x = 160;  myImage.y = 240

-- A touch listener to remove object
local removeBody = function( event )
  local t = event.target
  local phase = event.phase

  if "began" == phase then
    t:removeSelf() -- Destroy object
  end

  -- Stop further propagation of touch event
  return true
end

myImage:addEventListener( "touch", removeBody )
```

Optimizing your display images

It's important to optimize your image file size as much as you can. Using full-screen images can impact the performance of your application. They require more time to load on a device and consume a lot of texture memory. When a lot of memory is consumed in an application, in most cases it'll be forced to quit.

iOS devices vary in available memory, depending which one you have:

◆ iPhone 3G, iTouch 2G—128 MB RAM

◆ iPhone 3GS, iPad, iTouch 3G/4G—256 MB RAM

◆ iPhone 4/4S, iPad 2—512 MB RAM

For example, texture memory on the iPhone 3GS should be kept under 25 MB before performance issues start occurring by slowing down your app or even forcing it to quit. An iPad 2 would have no problem going further down that boundary since it has more memory available.

Refer to the following link to apply memory warnings for iOS devices: `http://developer.anscamobile.com/reference/index/memorywarning-ios`.

For Android devices, there is around a 24 MB memory limit. So it's important to be aware of how many display objects you have in your scene and how to manage them when they are not needed anymore in your app.

In cases where you no longer need an image to be displayed on screen use the following code:

```
image.parent:remove( image ) -- remove image from hierarchy
-- or --
image:removeSelf( ) -- same as above
```

If you want to remove an image from the scene completely throughout the lifetime of your app, include the following line after your `image.parent:remove( image )` or `image:removeSelf()` code:

```
image = nil
```

Keeping memory usage low within your application will prevent crashes and improve performance. For more information on optimization, go to the following URL: `http://developer.anscamobile.com/content/performance-and-optimization`.

Pop quiz – basics of Lua

1. Which of the following are values?

   a. Numbers

   b. nil

   c. Strings

   d. All of the above

2. Which relational operator is false?

    a. `print(0 == 0)`

    b. `print(3 >= 2)`

    c. `print(2 ~= 2)`

    d. `print(0 ~= 2)`

3. What is the correct way to scale an object in the x direction?

    a. `object.scaleX`

    b. `object.xscale`

    c. `object.Xscale`

    d. `object.xScale`

Summary

This chapter discussed parts of Lua programming that will send you on your way to start creating your own apps in Corona. As you continue working with Lua, you'll start understanding the terminology better. Eventually you'll find new programming solutions that will benefit your development process.

The following are some skills you learned so far:

◆ Creating variables and assigning values to them

◆ Establishing expressions by using operators

◆ How to use the Corona Terminal to output or print results

◆ Use tables to structure lists, arrays, sets, and so on

◆ Adding display objects in the simulator

◆ Configuring your application build to work on different mobile devices

◆ Implementing dynamic resolution images

◆ Creating functions to run a block of code

There was definitely a lot to take in in this section. There is still a handful of information on Lua that we didn't get to touch base on but you have learned enough to get you started. For more information on programming in Lua, you can refer to `http://www.lua.org/pil/index.html` or the resources section on the Corona website at `http://www.anscamobile.com/resources/`.

In the next chapter, we'll start making our very first game called Breakout! You'll get some hands-on experience of creating a game framework in Corona and applying all the necessary assets to develop a mobile game. You'll be surprised at how fast and simple it is to create one.

3
Building our First Game: Breakout

Up until now, we have gone through some important basics of programming in Lua and applying some code to run in the Corona simulator. Knowing the terminology is a small part of learning how to make an application. We'll need to take a step further and get some hands on experience on what it's like to structure a project from beginning to finish. We're going to accomplish this by creating our first game from scratch. This will push you further into understanding larger chunks of code and applying some game logic to make a functional game.

By the end of this chapter, you will understand the following:

- Structuring game files in a Corona project
- Creating variables for the game
- Adding game objects to the screen
- Making an alert message
- Displaying score and level number

Let the fun begin!

Breakout—bringing back old-school gaming

You have probably seen many forms of the game Breakout in the past couple of decades, especially during the Atari days. To give you a good idea of what the game is about, here is a brief editorial by Big Fish Games about the history of Breakout: `http://www.bigfishgames.com/blog/the-history-of-breakout/`.

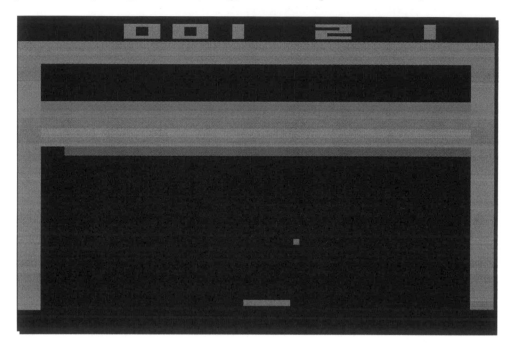

On the game screen, there are several columns and rows of bricks placed near the top of the screen. A ball travels across the screen, bouncing off the top and side walls of the screen. When a brick is hit, the ball bounces away and the brick is destroyed. The player loses the round when the ball touches the bottom of the screen. To prevent this from happening, the player has a movable paddle to bounce the ball upward, keeping it in play.

We're going to be creating a clone using touch events and the accelerometer for paddle movement that will be controlled by the player. We'll be adding some physics to the ball so it can bounce throughout the screen.

In the next chapter, we'll be adding the movement of the game objects, collision detection, score keeping, and win/lose conditions. Right now, we're going to focus on how to set up the game template of Breakout.

Understanding Corona physics API

Corona has made it convenient to add physics to your games, especially if you've never worked on one before. The engine uses **Box2D** and takes only a few lines to incorporate it into your application than what it normally takes to have it set up.

Working with the physics engine in Corona is fairly easy. You use display objects and set them as a physical body in your code. Images, sprites, and vector shapes can be turned into a physical object. This is substantial in visualizing how you want your objects to react in an environment you have created. You can see results right away rather than guessing how they might act in a physical world.

Setting up the physics world

Making the physics engine available in your app requires the following line:

```
local physics = require "physics"
```

Starting, pausing, and stopping physics

There are three main functions that affect the physics simulation:

- `physics.start()`: This will start or resume the physical environment. It is usually activated at the beginning of the application for physics bodies to take effect.
- `physics.pause()`: This stops the physics engine temporarily.
- `physics.stop()`: This basically destroys the physical world altogether.

physics.setGravity

This function returns the x and y parameters of the global gravity vector, in units of meter per second square (acceleration units). The default is (0, 9.8) to simulate standard Earth gravity, pointing downwards on the y-axis. For example,

Syntax: `physics.setGravity(gx, gy)`

```
physics.setGravity( 0, 9.8 ): Standard Earth gravity
```

physics.getGravity

This function returns the x and y parameters of the global gravity vector, in units of meter per second square (acceleration units).

Syntax: `gx, gy = physics.getGravity()`

Tilt-based gravity

When you have physics.setGravity(gx, gy) and accelerometer API applied, implementing tilt-based dynamic gravity is simple. The following is an example of creating the tilt-based function:

```
function movePaddle(event)

  paddle.x = display.contentCenterX - (display.contentCenterX *
(event.yGravity*3))

end

Runtime:addEventListener( "accelerometer", movePaddle )
```

The accelerometer is not present in the Corona Simulator; a device build must be created to see the effect.

physics.setScale

This function sets the internal pixels-per-meter ratio used in converting between the onscreen Corona coordinates and simulated physics coordinates. This should be done before any physical objects are instantiated.

The default scaling value is 30. For devices of higher resolution like iPad, Android, or iPhone 4, you may wish to increase this value to 60 or more.

Syntax: `physics.setScale( value )`

```
physics.setScale( 60 )
```

physics.setDrawMode

There are three rendering modes for the physics engine. This can be altered at any time.

Syntax: `physics.setDrawMode( mode )`

◆ `physics.setDrawMode( "debug" )`: This mode shows collision engine outlines only

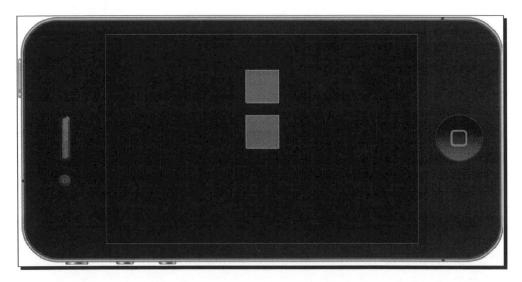

◆ `physics.setDrawMode( "hybrid" )`: This mode overlays collision outlines on normal Corona objects

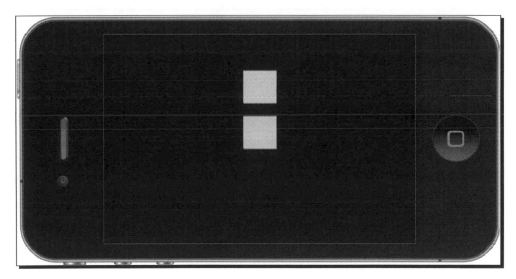

- ◆ `physics.setDrawMode( "normal" )`: This mode is the default Corona renderer, with no collision outlines

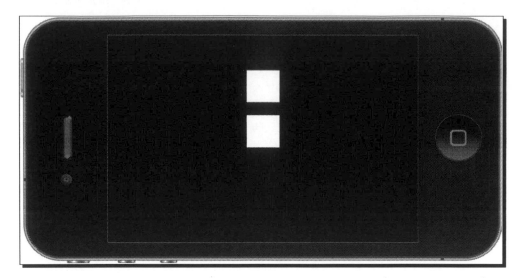

The physics data is displayed using color-coded vector graphics, which reflect different object types and attributes:

- ◆ **Orange**—dynamic physics bodies (the default body type)
- ◆ **Dark blue**—kinematic physics bodies
- ◆ **Green**—static physics bodies such as the ground or walls
- ◆ **Gray**—a body that is *sleeping* due to lack of activity
- ◆ **Light blue**—joints

physics.setPositionIterations

This function sets the accuracy of the engine's position calculations. The default value is 8, meaning that the engine will iterate through eight position approximations per frame for every object but will increase processor engagement, so it should be handled carefully because it might slow down the application.

Syntax: `physics.setPositionIterations( value )`

```
physics.setPositionIterations( 16 )
```

physics.setVelocityIterations

This function sets the accuracy of the engine's velocity calculations. The default value is 3, meaning that the engine will iterate through three velocity approximations per frame for every object but will increase processor engagement, so it should be handled carefully because it might slow down the application.

Syntax: `physics.setVelocityIterations( value )`

```
physics.setVelocityIterations( 6 )
```

Configuring the application

This tutorial is compatible for both iOS and Android devices. The graphics have been designed to accommodate the varying screen dimensions of both platforms.

Build configuration

By default, all items displayed on all device screens are shown in portrait mode. We'll be creating this game specifically in landscape mode, so we'll have to alter some build settings and configure how all the items on screen will be displayed. Playing the game in landscape mode will actually add more player interactivity since the paddle will have more screen space to move about and less airtime for the ball.

Time for action – adding build.settings file

Build-time properties can be provided in an optional `build.settings` file, which uses Lua syntax. The `build.settings` file is used to set application orientation and auto-rotation behavior, along with a variety of platform-specific build parameters.

1. Create a new project folder on your desktop called `Breakout`.

2. In your preferred text editor, make a new file called `build.settings` and save it to your project folder.

3. Type in the following lines:
   ```
   settings =
   {
     orientation =
       {
        default = "landscapeRight",
       }
   }
   ```

4. Save and close. The `build.settings` file is completed.

What just happened?

The default orientation setting determines the initial launch orientation on the device, and also the initial orientation of the Corona simulator.

The default orientation doesn't affect Android devices. The orientation is initialized to the actual orientation of the device (unless only one orientation is specified). Also, the only supported orientations are `landscapeRight` and portrait. On a device, you can flip to either `landscapeRight` or `landscapeLeft`, but the operating system only reports one flavor of landscape, and Corona's orientation event chooses `landscapeRight`.

We have created this application to work with landscape orientations, supporting `landscapeRight`. We have set this orientation as its default so it won't switch to `landscapeLeft` or even any portrait mode. While working on an iOS device, if the `build.settings` aren't set before launching the application, it will go to the default portrait mode.

Runtime configuration

Currently our project is not scaled to display evenly for cross-platform development. The contents will still display on the device, but most likely not in the correct aspect ratio.

For example, iPhone projects are designed for a 320 pixel wide screen and can be up scaled to the 480 pixel wide screen for Android devices. This makes porting easier, since the code and art assets do not need to be revised.

Corona can target builds made for iPhone 4 and other current iOS devices that display double resolution art assets while remaining iOS 3.0-compatible. This means that pre-iPhone 4 content will no longer upscale automatically to the larger iPhone 4 screen resolution. As iOS development progresses, content scaling will generally be required in new iPhone apps to be compatible with devices such as the iPhone 3GS and lower.

Time for action – adding config.lua file

If no content size is specified, the content width and height returned will be the same as the physical screen width and height of the device. If you specify a different content width and height in `config.lua`, the content width and height will take on those values.

1. In your text editor, create a new file called `config.lua` and save it to your project folder.

2. Type in the following lines:

```
application =
{
        content =
```

```
    {
        width = 320,
        height = 480,
        scale = "letterbox",
        fps = 60,
    },
}
```

3. Save and close your file.

What just happened?

The content width and height allow you to choose a virtual screen size that is independent of the physical device screen size. We have set the size to target the original iPhone since it displays the smallest dimensions across all the devices on both iOS and Android platforms. The original iPhone has dimensions of 320 x 480. With this configuration, it'll still scale evenly for the iPad, which has dimensions of 768 x 1024.

The scale used for this application is set to `letterbox`. It will uniformly scale up content as much as possible, while still showing all content on the screen. This will create a widescreen look, which will be compatible with the Droid, which has a longer screen than the iPhone 3GS.

We set `fps = 60`. By default, the frame rate is 30 fps. In this application, this will make the movement of the ball appear faster and allow us to increase the speed conveniently. We can stretch the frame rate to a maximum of 60 fps that Corona can allow.

Building the application

Now that we have configured our application to landscape mode and set the display contents to scale on multiple devices, we're ready to start designing the game. Before we start writing some code for the game, we need to add in some art assets that will be displayed on the screen. You can find them in the `Chapter 3 Resources` folder. You can download the project files accompanying this book from the Packt website. The following files that you'll need to add to your `Breakout` project folder are as follows:

- alertBox.png
- bg.png
- mmScreen.png
- ball.png
- paddle.png
- brick.png
- playbtn.png

Displaying groups

An important function we'll be introducing in this game is `display.newGroup()`. Groups allow you to add and remove child display objects. Initially, there are no children in a group. The local origin is at the parent object's origin; the reference point is initialised to this local origin. You can easily organize your display objects in separate groups and refer to them by their group name. For example, in Breakout, we'll combine menu items such as the **Title** screen and **Play** button in a group called `menuScreenGroup`. Every time we access `menuScreenGroup`, any display object defined by the group name will be called.

display.newGroup()

This function creates a group in which you can add and remove child display objects.

Syntax: `display.newGroup()`

Example:

```
local rect = display.newRect(0, 0, 150, 150)
rect:setFillColor(255, 255, 255)

local myGroup = display.newGroup()
myGroup:insert( rect )
```

Working with system functions

The system functions we're going to introduce in this chapter will return information about the system (get device information, current orientation) and control system functions (enabling Multi-touch, controlling the idle time, Accelerometer, GPS). We'll be using the following system functions to return environment information on which our application will be running and the response frequency for accelerometer events.

system.getInfo()

This function returns information about the system on which the application is running.

Syntax: `system.getInfo( param )`

```
print( system.getInfo( "name" ) ) -- display the deviceID
```

Valid values for parameters are as follows:

◆ `"name"`—returns the name. For example, on the iTouch, this would be the name of the phone as it appears in iTunes, *Pat's iTouch*.

- ◆ `"model"`—returns the device type. These include:
    - ❑ "iPhone"
    - ❑ "iPad"
    - ❑ "iPhone Simulator"
    - ❑ "Nexus One"
    - ❑ "Droid"
    - ❑ "myTouch"
    - ❑ "Galaxy Tab"

- ◆ `"deviceID"`—returns the unique id of the device.
- ◆ `"environment"`—returns the environment that the app is running in. These include:
    - ❑ `"simulator"`: The Corona Simulator
    - ❑ `"device"`: iOS, Android device, and the Xcode Simulator

- ◆ `"platformName"`—returns the platform name (the OS name), that is, one of the following:
    - ❑ Mac OS X (Corona Simulator on Mac)
    - ❑ Win (Corona Simulator on Windows))
    - ❑ iPhone OS (all iOS devices))
    - ❑ Android (all Android devices))

- ◆ `"platformVersion"`—returns a string representation of the platform version.
- ◆ `"version"`—returns the version of Corona used.
- ◆ `"build"`—returns the Corona build string.
- ◆ `"textureMemoryUsed"`—returns the texture memory usage in bytes.
- ◆ `"maxTextureSize"`—returns the maximum texture width or height supported by the device.
- ◆ `"architectureInfo"`—returns a string describing the underlying CPU architecture of the device you are running on.

system.setAccelerometerInterval()

This function sets the frequency of accelerometer events. The minimum frequency is 10 Hz and the maximum is 100 Hz on the iPhone. Accelerometer events are a significant drain on battery; so only increase the frequency when you need faster responses in games. Always try to lower the frequency whenever possible to conserve battery life.

Syntax: `system.setAccelerometerInterval( frequency )`

```
system.setAccelerometerInterval( 75 )
```

The function sets the sample interval in Hertz. Hertz is cycles per second, the number of measurements to take per second. If you set the frequency to 75, then the system will take 75 measurements per second.

After you have added the assets from the Chapter 3 Resources folder into your project folder, let's begin writing some code!

Time for action – creating variables for the game

For any application to start we'll need to make a `main.lua` file. This has been discussed in the previous chapter when we worked with some sample code and ran it with the simulator.

The code will be structured accordingly in your `main.lua` by the time the game is completed:

`Necessary Classes` (For example: physics or ui)

`Variables and Constants`

`Main Function`

  `Object Methods`

`Call Main Function` (This always has to be called or your application will not run)

Formatting your code to make it look like the preceding structure is good practice on keeping things organized and running your application efficiently.

In this section, we'll be introducing the display group that will show the **Main Menu** screen and a **Play** button that the user will be able to interact with to move on to the **Main Game** screen. All in-game elements such as the paddle, ball, brick objects, and heads-up display elements follow after the player interacts with the **Play** button. We'll also be introducing win and lose conditions that will be referred to as the `alertDisplayGroup`. All these game elements will be initialized in the beginning of our code.

1. Create a new `main.lua` file in your text editor and save it to your project folder.

2. We're going to hide the status bar (specifically for iOS devices) and load the physics engine. Corona uses the Box2D engine that is already built into the SDK.

   ```
   display.setStatusBar(display.HiddenStatusBar)

   local physics = require "physics"
   ```

```
physics.start()
physics.setGravity(0, 0)

system.setAccelerometerInterval( 100 )
```

> More information on the Corona Physics API can be found on the Corona website at: `http://developer.anscamobile.com/content/game-edition-box2d-physics-engine`.
>
> The Box2D physics engine used in Corona SDK was written by Erin Catto of Blizzard Entertainment. More information on Box2D can be found at: `http://box2d.org/manual.pdf`.

3. Add in the menu screen objects.

```
local menuScreenGroup   -- display.newGroup()
local mmScreen
local playBtn
```

4. Add in the in-game screen objects.

```
local background
local paddle
local brick
local ball
```

5. Add in HUD elements for the score and level.

```
local scoreText
local scoreNum
local levelText
local levelNum
```

> The HUD is also known as the heads-up display. It is a method of visually representing character information on the game screen.

6. Next, we'll add in the alert display group for the win/lose conditions.

```
local alertDisplayGroup    -- display.newGroup()
local alertBox
local conditionDisplay
local messageText
```

7. The following variables hold the values for the bricks display group, score, ball velocity, and in game events.

```
local _W = display.contentWidth / 2
local _H = display.contentHeight / 2
local bricks = display.newGroup()
local brickWidth = 35
local brickHeight = 15
local row
local column
local score = 0
local scoreIncrease = 100
local currentLevel
local vx = 3
local vy = -3
local gameEvent = ""
```

8. Accelerometer events can only be tested on a device, so we're going to add a variable for touch events on the paddle by calling the `"simulator"` environment. This is so we can test the paddle movement in the Corona simulator. If you were to test the application on a device, the event listeners for touch and accelerometer on the paddle won't conflict.

```
local isSimulator = "simulator" == system.getInfo("environment")
```

9. Lastly, add in the `main()` function. This will start our application.

```
function main()

end

--[[
This empty space will hold other functions and methods to run the
application
]]--

main()
```

What just happened?

The `display.setStatusBar(display.HiddenStatusBar)` is only applicable to iOS devices. It hides the appearance of the status bar.

A new Corona API we added to this game is the physics engine. We'll be adding physics parameters to the main game objects (paddle, ball, and bricks) for collision detection. Having `setGravity(0,0)` will allow the ball to bounce throughout the playing field freely.

`local menuScreenGroup`, `local alertDisplayGroup`, and `local bricks` are all forms of display groups we can separate and organize our display objects to. For example, `local menuScreenGroup` is designated for the objects that show up on the **Main Menu** screen; that way they can be removed as a group and not as individual objects.

Some of the variables added already have values that are applied to certain game objects. There is already a set velocity for the ball using `local vx = 3` and `local vy = -3`. The x and y velocity determines how the ball moves on the game screen. Depending on the position the ball collides with an object, the ball will follow a continuous path. The `brickWidth` and `brickHeight` have a value that will stay constant throughout the application so we can line the brick objects evenly onscreen.

`local gameEvent = " "` will store the game events such as `"win"`, `"lose"`, and `"finished"`. When a function checks the game status for any of these events, it will display the proper condition onscreen.

We have added some system functions as well. We created `local isSimulator = "simulator" == system.getInfo("environment")` so that it returns information about the system on which the application is running. This will be directed to the paddle touch events so that we can test the application in the simulator. If the build was to be ported on a device, you would only be able to use the accelerometer to move the paddle. The simulator can't test accelerometer events. The other system function is `system.setAccelerometerInterval( 100 )`. It sets the frequency of accelerometer events. The minimum frequency is 10 Hz and the maximum is 100 Hz on the iPhone.

The empty function `main()` set will start out the display hierarchy. Think of it as a storyboard. The first thing you see is an introduction and then some action happens in the middle that tells you about the main content. In this case, the main content is the gameplay. The last thing you see is some kind of ending or closure to tie the story altogether. The ending is the display of the win/lose conditions at the end of a level.

Understanding events and listeners

Events are sent to listeners. Functions or objects can be event listeners. When an event occurs, the listener is called by a table representing the event. All events will have a property name that identifies the kind of event.

Register events

Display objects and global Runtime objects can be event listeners. You can add and remove listeners for events using the following object methods:

- ◆ `object:addEventListener( )`: It adds a listener to the object's list of listeners. When the named event occurs, the listener will be invoked and be supplied with a table representing the event.
- ◆ `object:removeEventListener( )`: It removes the specified listener from the object's list of listeners so that it no longer is notified of events corresponding to the specified event.

In the following example, an image display object registers to receive a touch event. Touch events are not broadcast globally. Display objects that register for the event and lie underneath it will be candidates for receiving the touch.

```
local playBtn = display.newImage("playbtn.png")
playBtn.name = "playbutton"

local function listener(event)
  if event.target.name == "playbutton" then

print("The button was touched.")

  end
end

playBtn:addEventListener("touch", listener )
```

Runtime events are sent by the system. They broadcast to all listeners. The following is an example of registering for an `enterFrame` event:

```
local playBtn = display.newImage("playbtn.png")

local function listener(event)
  print("The button appeared.")
end

Runtime:addEventListener("enterFrame", listener )
```

Runtime events

The application we're creating uses runtime events. Runtime events have no specific target and are only sent to the global Runtime. They broadcast to all registered listeners. The following events all have string names and will be applied to the Breakout game:

enterFrame

`enterFrame` events occur at the frame interval of the application. They are only sent to the global Runtime object. For example, if the frame rate is 30fps, then it will occur approximately 30 times per second.

Properties are available in this event:

◆   `event.name` is the string `"enterFrame"`.

◆   `event.time` is the time in milliseconds since the start of the application.

accelerometer

Accelerometer events let you detect movements and determine the device's orientation in relation to gravity. These events are only sent to devices that support accelerometer. They are only sent to the global Runtime object.

The following properties are available for this event:

◆   `event.name` is the string `"accelerometer"`.

◆   `event.xGravity` is the acceleration due to gravity in the x-direction.

◆   `event.yGravity` is the acceleration due to gravity in the y-direction.

◆   `event.zGravity` is the acceleration due to gravity in the z-direction.

◆   `event.xInstant` is the instantaneous acceleration in the x-direction.

◆   `event.yInstant` is the instantaneous acceleration in the y-direction.

◆   `event.zInstant` is the instantaneous acceleration in the z-direction.

◆   `event.isShake` is true when the user shakes the device.

Touch events

When the user's finger touches the screen, a hit event is generated and dispatched to display objects in the display hierarchy. Only those objects that intersect with the location of the finger on the screen will receive the event.

touch (single touch)

Touch events are a special kind of hit event. When a user's finger touches the screen, they are starting a sequence of touch events, each with different phases.

◆   `event.name` is the string `"touch"`.

◆   `event.x` is the x-position in screen coordinates of the touch.

◆   `event.y` is the y-position in screen coordinates of the touch.

- ◆ `event.xStart` is the x-position of the touch from the `"began"` phase of the touch sequence.

- ◆ `event.yStart` is the y-position of the touch from the `"began"` phase of the touch sequence.

- ◆ `event.phase` is a string identifying where in the touch sequence the event occurred:

  - ❑ `"began"` a finger touched the screen.

  - ❑ `"moved"` a finger moved on the screen.

  - ❑ `"ended"` a finger was lifted from the screen.

  - ❑ `"cancelled"` the system cancelled tracking of the touch.

tap

tap generates a hit event when the user touches the screen. The event is dispatched to display objects in the display hierarchy. This is similar to the `touch` event except a hit count (number of taps) is available in the event callback.

- ◆ `event.name` is the string `"tap"`.

- ◆ `event.numTaps` returns the number of taps on the screen.

- ◆ `event.x` is the x-position in screen coordinates of the tap.

- ◆ `event.y` is the y-position in screen coordinates of the tap.

Transitions

In this chapter, we'll be touching base with `transition.to()` and `transition.from()`.

- ◆ `transition.to()`: It animates a display object's properties over time using the `easing` transitions.

  Syntax: `handle = transition.to( target, params )`

- ◆ `transition.from()`: It is similar to `transition.to()` except the starting property values are specified in the function's parameter table and the final values are the corresponding property values in the target prior to the call.

  Syntax: `handle = transition.from( target, params )`

  The parameters used are:

  `target` - A display object that will be the target of the transition.

  `params` - A table that specifies the properties of the display object, which will be animated, and one or more of the following optional non-animated properties:

- ❑ params.time: It specifies the duration of the transition in milliseconds. By default, the duration is 500 ms (0.5 seconds).

- ❑ params.transition: It is by default easing.linear.

- ❑ params.delay: It specifies the delay, in milliseconds, (none by default) before the tween begins.

- ❑ params.delta: It is a boolean specifying whether non-control parameters are interpreted as final ending values or as changes in value. The default is nil meaning false.

- ❑ params.onStart: It is a function or table listener called before the tween begins.

- ❑ params.onComplete: It is a function or table listener called after the tween completes.

For example:

```
_W = display.contentWidth
_H = display.contentHeight

local square = display.newRect( 0, 0, 100, 100 )
square:setFillColor( 255,255,255 )
square.x = _W/2; square.y = _H/2

local square2 = display.newRect( 0, 0, 50, 50 )
square2:setFillColor( 255,255,255 )
square2.x = _W/2; square2.y = _H/2

transition.to( square, { time=1500, x=250, y=400 } )
transition.from( square2, { time=1500, x=275, y=0 } )
```

The preceding example shows how two display objects transition throughout the space on a device screen. The square display object from it's current position will move to a new location of x = 250 and y = 400 in 1500 milliseconds. The square2 display object will transition from x = 275 and y = 0 to it's initial location in 1500 milliseconds.

Creating menu screens

Having menu screens allows the player to transition through different parts of your application. Typically a game will start out with some kind of screen displaying the game title with an interactive user interface button labeled **Play** or **Start** to give the player the option to play the game. It is standard in any mobile application to have a menu screen before transitioning to the main content.

Time for action – adding the main menu screen

The **Main Menu** screen will be the first thing in our menu system that the player interacts with after the application is launched. It's a great way to introduce the title of the game and also it gives the player an idea of what type of gaming environment they should expect. We wouldn't want the player to jump abruptly into the app without any proper notification. It's important to allow the player to prepare for what is to come when they launch the app.

1. We're going to create a function called `mainMenu()` to introduce the title screen. So after `function main()` ends, add in the following lines:

```
function mainMenu()

end
```

2. We'll be adding in a display group and two display objects to this function. One display object is the image that will represent the **Main Menu** screen and the other will be a UI button called **Play**. Add them inside of `function mainMenu()`.

```
menuScreenGroup = display.newGroup()

mmScreen = display.newImage("mmScreen.png", 0, 0, true)

  mmScreen.x = _W
  mmScreen.y = _H

  playBtn = display.newImage("playbtn.png")
  playBtn:setReferencePoint(display.CenterReferencePoint)
  playBtn.x = _W; playBtn.y = _H + 50
  playBtn.name = "playbutton"

menuScreenGroup:insert(mmScreen)

  menuScreenGroup:insert(playBtn)
```

3. Remember the empty `main()` function set? We need to call `mainMenu()` inside of it. The entire function should look like this:

```
function main()
  mainMenu()
end
```

4. After the `mainMenu()` function, we're going to create another function called `loadGame()`. It will initiate the event from `playbtn` to transition to the main game screen. The event will change the alpha of `menuScreenGroup` to 0, which makes it appear invisible on the screen. Complete the transition by calling the `addGameScreen()` function (`addGameScreen()` will be discussed later in the chapter in *Adding Game Objects* section).

```
function loadGame(event)
    if event.target.name == "playbutton" then

        transition.to(menuScreenGroup,{time = 0, alpha=0, onComplete =
addGameScreen})

        playBtn:removeEventListener("tap", loadGame)
    end
end
```

5. Next, we need to add in an event listener to `playBtn` so when it is tapped, it will call the `loadGame()` function. Add the following line in the `mainMenu()` function after the last method:

```
playBtn:addEventListener("tap", loadGame)
```

6. Run the project in the simulator. You should see the **Main Menu** screen display **Breakout** and the **Play** button.

What just happened?

Creating a **Main Menu** screen only requires a couple of blocks of code. For `loadGame(event)`, we set a parameter called `event`. When the `if` statement is called, it takes `playbutton`, which references the display object `playBtn` and checks to see if it is true. Since it is, the `menuScreenGroup` will be removed from the stage and wil call on the `addGameScreen()` function. At the same time the event listener for `playBtn` is removed from the scene.

Have a go hero – creating a help screen

Right now the design of the menu system is set up so that it goes from the **Main Menu** screen and then transitions to the **Gameplay** screen. You have the option to extend the menu screens without jumping into the game right away. After the **Main Menu** screen, we can add an additional **Help Menu** screen that will explain the player how to play the game.

Create a new image in your preferred image editing program and write out steps on how to play the game. You can then create a new button called **Next** and add both art assets to your project folder. In your code, you'll have to create a new function and event listener for your **Next** button that will transition to the gameplay screen.

Creating the gameplay scene

Now that we have a menu system in place, we can start on the gameplay elements of the application. We'll start adding all of the main game objects that the player will interact with. One thing to think about when adding in game objects is their placement on the screen. Given that this game will be played in landscape mode, we have to remember that there is plenty of space available in the x-direction and a smaller amount in the y-direction. Based on the original design of the game, the bottom wall of the screen causes the player to lose the level or turn if the ball lands in that area. So if you were to pinpoint an area to place the paddle object, we wouldn't set it near the top of the screen. It makes more sense for the paddle to be as close to the bottom of the screen to protect the ball better.

Time for action – adding game objects

Let's add in the display objects the player will see while in gameplay.

1. After the `loadGame()` function, we're going to create another function that will display all our game objects on screen. The following lines will display the art assets that were created for this tutorial:

    ```
    function addGameScreen()

      background = display.newImage("bg.png", 0, 0, true )
      background.x = _W
      background.y = _H

      paddle = display.newImage("paddle.png")
      paddle.x = 240; paddle.y = 300
      paddle.name = "paddle"

      ball = display.newImage("ball.png")
      ball.x = 240; ball.y = 290
      ball.name = "ball"
    ```

2. Next, we'll add in the text that will display the score and level number during the game.

    ```
    scoreText = display.newText("Score:", 5, 2, "Arial", 14)
    scoreText:setTextColor(255, 255, 255, 255)
    ```

```
scoreNum = display.newText("0", 54, 2, "Arial", 14)
scoreNum:setTextColor(255, 255, 255, 255)

levelText = display.newText("Level:", 420, 2, "Arial", 14)
levelText:setTextColor(255, 255, 255, 255)

levelNum = display.newText("1", 460, 2, "Arial", 14)
levelNum:setTextColor(255, 255, 255, 255)
```

3. To build the first game level we're going to call the `gameLevel1()` function, which will be explained later in this chapter. Don't forget to close the `addGameScreen()` function with `end`.

```
gameLevel1()

end
```

What just happened?

The `addGameScreen()` function displays all the game objects shown during gameplay. We have added the `background`, `paddle`, and `ball` from the art assets provided for this chapter.

We have added text for the score and level at the top of the game screen. `scoreNum` is initially set to `0`. We'll discuss in the next chapter how we will update the score number when a brick collision is made. `levelNum` starts at `1` and updates when the level is completed and moves on to the next one.

We ended the function by calling `gameLevel1()` which will be implemented in the next section to start the first level.

Time for action – building bricks

The bricks are the last of the game objects we need to add in for this application. We'll be creating two different levels for this game. Each one will have a different brick layout from the other.

1. We're going to create the function for the first level. Let's create a new function, `gameLevel1()`. We will also set the `currentLevel = 1` since the application begins at **Level 1**. Then we'll add in the `bricks` display group and set it `toFront()` so that it appears in front of the game background.

```
function gameLevel1()

currentLevel = 1

bricks:toFront()
```

The method, `object:toFront( )` moves the target object to the visual front of its parent group (object.parent). In this case, we are setting the `bricks` group to appear as the front most display group during gameplay so it appears in front of the background image.

2. Next, add some local variables that will show how many rows and columns of bricks will be displayed on screen and where in the playing field each brick will be placed.

```
local numOfRows = 4
local numOfColumns = 4
local brickPlacement = {x = (_W) - (brickWidth * numOfColumns )
/ 2  + 20, y = 50}
```

3. Create double `for` loops, one for `numOfRows` and the other for `numOfColumns`. Create a brick instance placed according to its width, height, and the number corresponding to `numOfRows` and `numOfColumns`. The art asset for the brick display object is provided with this chapter. Afterwards, close the function with `end`.

```
for row = 0, numOfRows - 1 do
  for column = 0, numOfColumns - 1 do

    local brick = display.newImage("brick.png")
    brick.name = "brick"
    brick.x = brickPlacement.x + (column * brickWidth)
    brick.y = brickPlacement.y + (row * brickHeight)
    physics.addBody(brick, "static", {density = 1, friction = 0,
bounce = 0})
    bricks.insert(bricks, brick)

  end
 end
end
```

4. The set up for **Level 2** is similar to how **Level 1** is arranged. The code is almost the same except our new function is called `gameLevel2()`, `currentLevel = 2`, and the values for `numOfRows` and `numOfColumns` have different values. Add this block after the `gameLevel1()` function.

```
function gameLevel2()

  currentLevel = 2
```

```
    bricks:toFront()

    local numOfRows = 5
    local numOfColumns = 8
    local brickPlacement = {x = (_W) - (brickWidth * numOfColumns )
/ 2  + 20, y = 50}

    for row = 0, numOfRows - 1 do
      for column = 0, numOfColumns - 1 do

        -- Create a brick
        local brick = display.newImage("brick.png")
        brick.name = "brick"
        brick.x = brickPlacement.x + (column * brickWidth)
        brick.y = brickPlacement.y + (row * brickHeight)
        physics.addBody(brick, "static", {density = 1, friction = 0,
bounce = 0})
        bricks.insert(bricks, brick)

      end
    end
end
```

5. Save your file and relaunch the simulator. You'll be able to interact with the **Play** button and see the transition from the **Main Menu** screen to the game screen. You will see the game layout for **Level 1** displayed on screen.

What just happened?

The `bricks` display group is set `bricks:toFront()`. This means that the group will always be put in front of the display hierarchy apart from the `background`, `paddle`, and `ball` display objects.

`gameLevel1()` has set values for the amount of brick objects displayed in the playing field. They will be centered based on the `contentWidth` of the device shell and set at 50 in the y-direction. The brick group is placed near the top left-hand corner by `brickPlacement` and takes the middle of the screen and subtracts it by half the width of all the brick objects put together. Then we add 20 more pixels in the x-direction to center it with the paddle.

We created double `for` loops for `numOfRows` and `numOfColumns`, which start the creation of the brick objects from the left-hand corner of the screen.

Notice that the `brick` display object is given the name `"brick"`. Just remember that `"brick"` cannot be used the same way as `brick` when calling the object. `"brick"` is an instance of `brick`. It is merely used as a string when event parameters are called on. For example:

```
if event.other.name == "brick" and ball.x + ball.width * 0.5  event.
other.x + event.other.width * 0.5 then
        vx = -vx
elseif event.other.name == "brick" and ball.x + ball.width * 0.5 >=
event.other.x + event.other.width * 0.5 then
        vx = vx
end
```

The physics body of `brick` is set to `"static"` so it is not affected by gravity pulling down. And then it is added to `bricks` group under `bricks.insert(bricks, brick)`.

Have a go hero – focused platform gaming

Upon completing this chapter and the following, feel free to redesign the display images to focus on a specific platform. For example, you can easily convert the code to be compatible with all iOS devices. This can be done by converting display objects to `display.newImageRect( [parentGroup,] filename [, baseDirectory] w, h )` so you can substitute higher resolution images on devices with retina display, (that is iPhone 4/iPod Touch 4G). Remember that you'll have to adjust your configuration settings to have the changes applied. This pertains to adding the `@2x` image suffix (or your preferred suffix naming convention) to your `config.lua` file.

Red alert!

In every game there is some kind of message that tells you the status of your progress when the main action has ended. For this application, we need a way to let the player know if they have won or lost a round, how they can play again or when the game is officially completed.

Time for action – displaying game messages

Let's set up some win/lose notifications so we can display these events occur in game:

  1. Create a new function called `alertScreen()` and pass two parameters called `title` and `message`. Add in a new display object called `alertbox` and have it transition from an `xScale` and `yScale` of 0.5 using `easing.outExpo`.

```
function alertScreen(title, message)

    alertBox = display.newImage("alertBox.png")
    alertBox.x = 240; alertBox.y = 160

    transition.from(alertBox, {time = 500, xScale = 0.5, yScale =
0.5, transition = easing.outExpo})
```

2. Store the `title` **parameter in the text object called** `conditionDisplay`.

```
    conditionDisplay = display.newText(title, 0, 0, "Arial", 38)
    conditionDisplay:setTextColor(255,255,255,255)
    conditionDisplay.xScale = 0.5
    conditionDisplay.yScale = 0.5
    conditionDisplay:setReferencePoint(display.CenterReferencePoint)
    conditionDisplay.x = display.contentCenterX
    conditionDisplay.y = display.contentCenterY - 15
```

3. Store the `message` **parameter in the text object called** `messageText`.

```
    messageText = display.newText(message, 0, 0, "Arial", 24)
    messageText:setTextColor(255,255,255,255)
    messageText.xScale = 0.5
    messageText.yScale = 0.5
    messageText:setReferencePoint(display.CenterReferencePoint)
    messageText.x = display.contentCenterX
    messageText.y = display.contentCenterY + 15
```

4. Create a new display group called `alertDisplayGroup` and insert all the objects into the group. Close the function.

```
    alertDisplayGroup = display.newGroup()
    alertDisplayGroup:insert(alertBox)
    alertDisplayGroup:insert(conditionDisplay)
    alertDisplayGroup:insert(messageText)
end
```

5. Save your file and run the project in the simulator. The functionality of the **Play** button still goes to the gameplay screen for **Level 1**. None of the objects have movement at the moment. We'll be adding touch events, ball movement, and collisions in the next chapter. All the game objects should be laid out like in the following screenshot:

What just happened?

We have set up the alert system for the game, but it is not operable at the moment until we add in more game functions to set the game objects in motion. The next chapter will demonstrate how the alertScreen() function passes two parameters, title and message. An alertBox display object is added as a background to the alert texts when they pop up after a condition occurs. When the alertBox pops up, it transitions from 0.5 of the xScale and yScale to full image scale in 500 milliseconds. That is basically the equivalent of half a second.

The conditionDisplay object passes the title parameter. This will be the text that displays, **You Win** or **You Lose**.

The messageText object passes the message parameter. The text with this parameter displays a message such as **Play Again** or **Continue** after a condition is reached.

All the objects in this function are then inserted into alertDisplayGroup = display.newGroup(). It will act as one group instead of individual objects when it will appear on and off the stage.

When running the code in the simulator; if errors pop up in your terminal window, be sure to check the line(s) causing the errors. Sometimes a simple capitalization error or even a comma or quotation mark that is missing can keep your app from running in the simulator. Make sure you're aware of those common mistakes. They can be easily overlooked.

You can refer to the `Breakout - Part 1` folder in the `Chapter 3` folder to see how the first half of the code for this tutorial is set up.

Pop quiz – building a game

1. When adding the physics engine in your code, which functions are valid to add to your application?

   a. `physics.start()`

   b. `physics.pause()`

   c. `physics.stop()`

   d. None of the above

2. Which is correct when adding an event listener?

   a. `button:addeventlistener("touch", listener )`

   b. `button:AddEventListener("touch", listener )`

   c. `button:addEventListener(touch, listener )`

   d. `button:addEventListener("touch", listener )`

3. What is the correct way to have the following display object transition to x = 300, y = 150, have the alpha changed to 0.5, in 2 seconds?

   ```
   local square = display.newRect( 0, 0, 50, 50 )
   square:setFillColor( 255,255,255 )
   square.x = 100 square2.y = 300
   ```

   a. `transition.to( square, { time=2000, x=300, y=150, alpha=0.5 } )`

   b. `transition.from( square, { time=2000, x=300, y=150, alpha=0.5 } )`

   c. `transition.to( square, { time=2, x=300, y=150, alpha=0.5 } )`

   d. None of the above

Summary

We have completed the first half of this game tutorial. Understanding how to structure a Corona project properly makes it easier to keep your code organized and tracks your assets better. We have gotten a taste of working with blocks of code that pertain to a small dose of the game logic needed to allow the application to run.

So far we have:

- Specified the build configuration on displaying the content for Android and iOS devices
- Introduced the main variables and constants that will run in the application
- Instantiated the physics engine and began to apply them to the game objects that require physical bodies
- Created transitions between menus to gameplay screens
- Added display objects and game messages to the screen

It's quite an accomplishment of how much we've done so far, including learning some new API in the process of coding the application. We still have a lot more to add before the game can be fully functional. We still have a lot more to add before the game can be fully functional.

In the next chapter, we'll be finishing the last half of this game tutorial. We'll be working with collision detection of the paddle, ball, brick, and wall objects. Also, we'll learn how to update the score when a brick is removed from the scene and get our win/lose conditions active as well. We're in the home stretch. Let's keep going!

4
Game Controls

So far we have completed the first half of our game in the previous chapter. We started on developing the initial structure for the project by introducing the game objects to the screen. Currently, the paddle and ball movement is inactive, but everything displayed in the simulator is scaled accordingly to the original game design. The last phase of completing this tutorial is to add in all the actions that will occur in the game, including object movement and updating the score.

In this chapter we will cover:

- Moving the paddle using touch events and accelerometer
- Collision detection between all game objects in the scene
- Removing objects upon collision detection
- Ball movement within screen boundaries
- Calculating the score
- Win and lose conditions

Home stretch! We can do it!

Moving in the up direction

If making objects appear on screen is exciting to you, wait until you see them move! The main object of Breakout is to keep the ball above the paddle position to stay in play and have it collide with all the bricks to complete the level. What keeps the suspense flowing is the anticipation of the ball movement throughout the game screen. This wouldn't be possible without adding physical boundaries on the game objects to react to collision detection.

Let's get even more physical

In the last chapter, we talked about how to integrate the physics engine into your code. We also started implementing physical bodies to the brick objects and now we'll need to do the same with other active game objects such as the paddle and the ball. Let's continue with this last half of the tutorial. We will continue using our `main.lua` file from the `Breakout` project folder.

physics.addBody()

Corona display objects can be turned into simulated physical objects using one line of code.

- ◆ If no shape information is specified, the display object takes on the form of the actual rectangular boundary of the original image to create the physics body. For example, if a display object is 100 x 100 pixels, then that would be the actual size of the physics body.

- ◆ If a shape is specified, then the body boundaries will follow the polygon provided by the shape. The shape coordinates must be defined in clockwise order, and the resulting shape must be convex-only.

- ◆ If a radius is specified, then the body boundaries will be circular and centered in the middle of the display object used to create the physics body.

A body shape is a table of local (x,y) coordinates, relative to the center of the display object.

Syntax:

- ◆ Circular shapes:

    ```
    physics.addBody(object, [bodyType,] {density=d, friction=f,
    bounce=b [,radius=r]})
    ```

- ◆ Polygon shapes:

    ```
    physics.addBody(object, [bodyType,] {density=d, friction=f,
    bounce=b [,shape=s]})
    ```

For example:

Circular bodies:

```
local ball = display.newImage("ball.png")

physics.addBody( ball, "dynamic" { density = 1.0, friction = 0.3,
bounce = 0.2, radius = 25 } )
```

Polygon bodies:

```
local rectangle = display.newImage("rectangle.png")

rectangleShape = { -6,-48, 6,-48, 6,48, -6,48 }

physics.addBody( rectangle, { density=2.0, friction=0.5, bounce=0.2,
shape=rectangleShape } )
```

Parameters:

- `Object` (Object): A display object.
- `bodyType` (String): Specifying the body type is optional. It uses a string parameter before the first body element. The possible types are `"static"`, `"dynamic"`, and `"kinematic"`. The default type is `"dynamic"` if no value is specified.
  - static bodies don't move, and don't interact with each other; examples of static objects would include the ground or the walls of a pinball machine.
  - dynamic bodies are affected by gravity and collisions with the other body types.
  - kinematic objects are affected by forces but not by gravity, so you should generally set draggable objects to `"kinematic"`, at least for the duration of the drag event.
- `Density` (Number): Multiplied by the area of the body's shape to determine mass. Based on a standard value of 1.0 for water. Lighter materials (such as wood) have a density below 1.0, and heavier materials (such as stone) have a density greater than 1.0. Default value is `1.0`.
- `Friction` (Number): May be any non-negative value; a value of 0 means no friction and 1.0 means fairly strong friction. The default value is `0.3`.
- `Bounce` (Number): Determines the amount of an object's velocity returned after a collision. The default value is `0.2`.
- `Radius` (Number): Radius of the bounding circle in pixels.
- `Shape` (Number): Shape value in the form of a table of the shape vertices, {x1,y1,x2,y2,...,xn,yn}. For example, `rectangleShape = { -6,-48, 6,-48, 6,48, -6,48 }`. The coordinates must be defined in clockwise order, and the resulting shape must be convex-only. (Physics assume the 0,0 point of an object, is the center of the object. A -x will be to the left of the object's center and -y will be at the top of object's center).

Time for action – starting physics for the paddle and ball

Right now, our display objects are rather stagnant. In order for gameplay to initiate, we have to activate physics for the paddle and ball in order for any kind of movement in the game to occur.

1. Above the `gameLevel1()` function, create a new function called `startGame()`.

```
function startGame()
```

2. Add in the following lines to instantiate the physics of the paddle and ball:

```
physics.addBody(paddle, "static", {density = 1, friction = 0,
bounce = 0})
physics.addBody(ball, "dynamic", {density = 1, friction = 0,
bounce = 0})
```

3. Create an event listener that uses the background display object to remove the `"tap"` event for `startGame()`. Close the function with `end`.

```
background:removeEventListener("tap", startGame)
end
```

4. In the `addGameScreen()` function that we created in the previous chapter, we have to add the following line after the call to the `gameLevel1()` function. This starts the actual game when the background is touched.

```
background:addEventListener("tap", startGame)
```

What just happened?

The paddle object has a `"static"` body type so it is not affected by any collision that occurs against it.

The ball object has a `"dynamic"` body type because we want it to be affected by the collisions on the screen due to directional changes by the wall borders, bricks and paddle.

The event listener on the background is removed from the `startGame()` function, that way it doesn't affect any of the other touch events that are applied in game.

Paddle movement

Getting the paddle to move side to side is one of the key actions that needs to be accomplished. Part of the game design is to protect the ball from reaching the bottom of the screen. We will be separating paddle movement in the simulator and the accelerometer. The movement in the simulator enables us to test with touch events since accelerometer actions cannot be tested in the simulator.

Time for action – dragging the paddle in the simulator

Right now, the paddle does not move at all. There are no coordinates set to translate on the screen, so let's create that.

1. Underneath the `addGameScreen()` function, create a new function called `dragPaddle(event)`.

```
function dragPaddle(event)
```

2. Next, we'll focus on moving the paddle side to side within the boundary of the game screen.

```
    if isSimulator then

      if event.phase == "began" then
        moveX = event.x - paddle.x
      elseif event.phase == "moved" then
        paddle.x = event.x - moveX
      end

      if((paddle.x - paddle.width * 0.5) < 0) then
        paddle.x = paddle.width * 0.5
      elseif((paddle.x + paddle.width * 0.5) > display.contentWidth)
then
        paddle.x = display.contentWidth - paddle.width * 0.5
      end

    end

    end
```

Add in the preceding block of code to enable paddle movement in the simulator and then close the function. The reason for adding this block is because the simulator does not support accelerometer events.

What just happened?

We have created a function where the drag event only works in the simulator. For `if event.phase == "began"`, a touch has been made to the paddle. On `elseif event.phase == "moved"`, a touch has been moved on the paddle.

In order to keep the paddle from moving past the wall boundaries, `paddle.x` does not go past `< 0` in the x-direction when it hits the coordinate. When the paddle slides to the right side of the screen, `paddle.x` does not go past `> display.contentWidth` in the x-direction.

There is no designated coordinate for the right side of the screen since the code is supposed to be universal for all screen sizes on iOS and Android devices. Both platforms have varying screen resolutions, so `display.contentWidth` takes them into account.

Time for action – moving the paddle with accelerometer

As mentioned earlier, accelerometer events cannot be tested in the simulator. They only work when a game build is uploaded to a device to see the results. The paddle movement will stay within the wall borders of the level across the x-axis.

1. Below the `dragPaddle()` function, create a new function called `movePaddle(event)`.

```
function movePaddle(event)
```

2. Add in the accelerometer movement using `yGravity`. It provides the acceleration due to gravity in the y-direction.

```
paddle.x = display.contentCenterX - (display.contentCenterX *
(event.yGravity*3))
```

3. Add in the wall borders for the level and close the function:

```
if((paddle.x - paddle.width * 0.5) < 0) then
  paddle.x = paddle.width * 0.5
  elseif((paddle.x + paddle.width * 0.5) > display.contentWidth)
then
    paddle.x = display.contentWidth - paddle.width * 0.5
  end
end
```

What just happened?

To make the accelerometer movement work with a device, we have to use `yGravity`.

 Accelerometer events are based on portrait scale when `xGravity` and `yGravity` are used accordingly. When display objects are designated for landscape mode, `xGravity` and `yGravity` values are switched to compensate for the events to work properly.

We have applied the same code for the paddle from `function dragPaddle()`:

```
if((paddle.x - paddle.width * 0.5) < 0) then
  paddle.x = paddle.width * 0.5
elseif((paddle.x + paddle.width * 0.5) > display.contentWidth) then
  paddle.x = display.contentWidth - paddle.width * 0.5
end
```

This still keeps the paddle from going past any wall border boundaries.

Ball collision with paddle

The motion of the ball has to flow in a fluid manner every time it collides with the paddle. This means proper directional changes on all sides of the game field.

Time for action – making the ball bounce against the paddle

We will check which side of the paddle the ball has hit to choose the side where it will move next. It's important to have the motion to follow through any directional hits as it would in a realistic environment. Through every paddle collision, we want to make sure the ball goes in the *up* direction.

1. Create a new function called `bounce()` for the ball after the `movePaddle()` function.

```
function bounce()
```

2. Add in a value of -3 for velocity in the y-direction. This will make the ball move in an upward motion:

```
vy = -3
```

3. Check when a collision is made with the `paddle` and `ball` and close the function:

```
if((ball.x + ball.width * 0.5) < paddle.x) then
  vx = -vx
elseif((ball.x + ball.width * 0.5) >= paddle.x) then
  vx = vx
end
end
```

What just happened?

When the ball collides with the paddle, the motion follows through depending on what side of the paddle is touched by the ball. In the first part of the `if` statement, the ball travels toward 0 in the x-direction. The last part of the `if` statement shows the ball travelling toward the opposite side of the screen in the x-direction.

Removing objects from the scene

There are limited resources on a device. As much as we wish they were as powerful as a desktop to hold so much memory, it's not at that point yet. This is why it is important to remove display objects from the display hierarchy when you no longer use them in your application. This helps the overall system performance by reducing memory consumption and eliminates unnecessary drawing.

When a display object is created, it is added by default to the root object of the display hierarchy. This object is a special kind of group object known as the **stage object**.

In order to keep an object from rendering on screen, it needs to be removed from the scene. The object needs to be removed explicitly from its parent. This removes the object from the display hierarchy. This can be done in either of the two following ways:

`myImage.parent:remove( myImage )` -- remove `myImage` from hierarchy

or

`myImage:removeSelf( )` -- same as above

This does not free all the memory from the display object. To make sure that the display object is removed properly, we need to eliminate all variable references to it.

Variable references

Even though a display object has been removed from the hierarchy, there are situations in which the object continues to exist. To do this, we set the property to `nil`.

```
local ball = display.newImage("ball.png")
local myTimer = 3

function time()
  myTimer = myTimer - 1
  print(myTimer)

  if myTimer == 0 then

    ball:removeSelf()
    ball = nil

  end
end

timer.performWithDelay( 1000, time, myTimer )
```

Brick by brick

The bricks in the game are the main obstacles since they have to be cleared in order to move onto the next round. In this version of Breakout, the player must destroy all the bricks in one turn. Failure to do so results in starting over from the beginning of the current level.

Time for action – removing the bricks

When the ball collides with a brick, we will use the same technique applied to the paddle to determine the side the ball will follow. When a brick is hit, we'll need to figure out which brick has been touched and then remove it from both the stage and the bricks group. Each brick removal will increment 100 points to the score. The score will be taken from the score constant and added to the current score as text.

1. Below the `gameLevel2()` function, create a function called `removeBrick(event)`:

```
function removeBrick(event)
```

2. Check which side of the brick the ball hits using the `if` statement. When checking for an event, we'll be referring the event to the object name, `"brick"`. This is the name we gave our `brick` display object:

```
if event.other.name == "brick" and ball.x + ball.width * 0.5 <
event.other.x + event.other.width * 0.5 then
     vx = -vx
  elseif event.other.name == "brick" and ball.x + ball.width *
0.5 >= event.other.x + event.other.width * 0.5 then
     vx = vx
  end
```

3. Add in the following `if` statement to remove the brick from the scene when the ball collides with one. After a collision has been made, increase the `score` by 1. Initiate the `scoreNum` to take the value of the `score` and multiply it by `scoreIncrease`:

```
if event.other.name == "brick" then
  vy = vy * -1
  event.other:removeSelf()
  event.other = nil
  bricks.numChildren = bricks.numChildren - 1

  score = score + 1
  scoreNum.text = score * scoreIncrease
  scoreNum:setReferencePoint(display.CenterLeftReferencePoint)
  scoreNum.x = 54
end
```

4. When all the bricks are destroyed from the level, create an `if` statement that pops up on the **Alert** screen for a win condition and set the `gameEvent` string to `"win"`.

```
if bricks.numChildren < 0 then
  alertScreen("YOU WIN!", "Continue")
  gameEvent = "win"
end
```

5. Close the function with `end`.

```
end
```

What just happened?

If you remember from the previous chapter, we gave the `brick` objects a name called `"brick"`.

When the ball hits the left side of any of the individual bricks, the ball travels towards the left. When the ball hits the right side of the bricks, it travels toward the right. The width of each object is taken as a whole to calculate the direction the ball travels.

When a brick is hit, the ball bounces upward (the y-direction). Upon every collision, the ball makes with a brick; the object is removed from the scene and destroyed from memory.

`bricks.numChildren - 1` subtracts the count from the total number of bricks it started out with originally. When a brick is removed, the score increments 100 points each time. The `scoreNum` text object updates the score every time a brick is hit.

When all bricks are gone, the **Alert** screen pops up with a notification that the player has won the level. We also set `gameEvent = "win"`, which will be used in another function that will transition the event to a new scene.

Directional changes

Aside from the ball motion against the paddle, other factors are the collision states against the wall borders. When a collision occurs, the ball diverts its direction the opposite way. For every action, there is a reaction, just like real world physics.

Time for action – updating the ball

The ball needs to move in a continuous motion without gravity affecting it. We'll have to take into account the side walls and top and bottom walls. The velocity in the x and y direction have to reflect the other way when a collision happens on any of the boundaries. We need to set coordinates that the ball is only allowed to move through and an alert when it passes through an area below the paddle region.

1. Create a new function called `function updateBall()` below the `removeBrick(event)` function.

   ```
   function updateBall()
   ```

2. Add in the ball movement:

   ```
   ball.x = ball.x + vx
   ball.y = ball.y + vy
   ```

3. Add in the ball movement for the x-direction:

   ```
   if ball.x < 0 or ball.x + ball.width > display.contentWidth then
     vx = -vx
   end
   ```

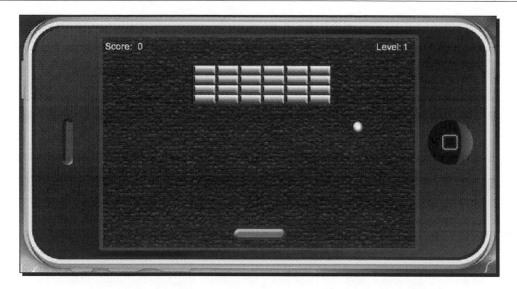

4. Add in the ball movement for the y-direction:

```
if ball.y < 0 then
    vy = -vy
end
```

5. Add in the ball movement when it collides with the bottom of the **Gameplay** screen. Create the lose **Alert** screen and a game event for `"lose"`. Close the function with `end`.

```
if ball.y + ball.height > paddle.y + paddle.height then
  alertScreen("YOU LOSE!", "Play Again") gameEvent = "lose"
end
end
```

What just happened?

Everywhere the ball travels, proper direction change is needed when it hits the wall. Any time the ball hits the side walls, we use `vx = -vx`. When the ball hits the top boundary, `vy = -vy` is used. The only time the ball doesn't reflect the opposite direction is when it hits the bottom of the screen.

The **Alert** screen displays the lose condition, which emphasizes to the player to **Play Again**. `gameEvent = "lose"` will be used in another `if` statement to reset the current level.

Transitioning levels

When a win or lose condition occurs, the game needs a way to transition to the next level or repeat the current one. The main game objects have to be reset to their starting position and the bricks redrawn. Pretty much the same idea when you start a game during first play.

Time for action – resetting and changing levels

We'll need to create functions that set up the first and second level in the game. If a level needs to be replayed, only the current level the user lost in can be accessed.

1. Create a new function called `changeLevel1()`. This will be placed below the `updateBall()` function:

```
function changeLevel1()
```

2. Clear the `bricks` group when the player loses the round and reset them:

```
bricks:removeSelf()

bricks.numChildren = 0
bricks = display.newGroup()
```

3. Remove the `alertDisplayGroup`:

```
alertBox:removeEventListener("tap", restart)
alertDisplayGroup:removeSelf()
alertDisplayGroup = nil
```

4. Reset the `ball` and `paddle` position:

```
ball.x = (display.contentWidth * 0.5) - (ball.width * 0.5)
ball.y = (paddle.y - paddle.height) - (ball.height * 0.5) -2

paddle.x = display.contentWidth * 0.5
```

5. Redraw the `bricks` for the current level:

```
gameLevel1()
```

6. Add an event listener to the `background` object for `startGame()`. Close the function.

```
    background:addEventListener("tap", startGame)
end
```

7. Next create a new function called `changeLevel2()`. Apply all the same code used for `changeLevel1()`, but make sure the `bricks` are redrawn for `gameLevel2()`.

```
function changeLevel2()

  bricks:removeSelf()

  bricks.numChildren = 0
```

```
bricks = display.newGroup()

alertBox:removeEventListener("tap", restart)
alertDisplayGroup:removeSelf()
alertDisplayGroup = nil

ball.x = (display.contentWidth * 0.5) - (ball.width * 0.5)
ball.y = (paddle.y - paddle.height) - (ball.height * 0.5) -2

paddle.x = display.contentWidth * 0.5


gameLevel2()  -- Redraw bricks for level 2

background:addEventListener("tap", startGame)
end
```

What just happened?

When a level needs to be reset or changed, the display objects have to be wiped from the board. In this case, we removed the `bricks` group using `bricks:removeSelf()`.

When any **Alert** screen pops up, whether win or lose, the entire `alertDisplayGroup` is removed during the reset as well. The `ball` and `paddle` are set back to their start game position.

`gameLevel1()` is called to redraw the bricks for level 1. The function holds the initial setup for the `brick` display objects and `bricks` group.

The `background` object is used again to call the `startGame()` function with an event listener. When level 2 needs to be set up, the same procedure is used like in function `changeLevel1()`, but called `changeLevel2()` and `gameLevel2()` is used to redraw the bricks.

Have a go hero – add more levels

Right now, the game only has two levels. What can be done to extend this game is add more levels. They can be created using the same logic made for `gameLevel1()` and `gameLevel2()` by adjusting the numbers used to create rows and columns for the bricks. You'll have to create a new function that resets the level. We can use the same method done on `changeLevel1()` and `changeLevel2()` to re-create a level and reset it.

You win some, you lose some

Nothing is more exhilarating than the anticipation of winning. That is until you make that one small mistake and it causes you to start over. Don't worry, it's not the end of the world, you can always try again and learn from your errors on beating the level.

Game events that occur within the program such as a win or lose condition has been made will alert the player of their progress. The game has to have some way of guiding the player to what action they need to make to replay the level or move on to the next one.

Time for action – making win and lose conditions

For any game alerts to even appear during gameplay, we need to create some `if` statements for every possible scenario available in each level. When this occurs, the score needs to be reset back to zero.

1. Below the `alertScreen()` function, create a new function called `restart()`:

    ```
    function restart()
    ```

2. Create an `if` statement for a `"win"` game event when the first level has been completed and transitions to **Level 2**.

    ```
    if gameEvent == "win" and currentLevel == 1 then
       currentLevel = currentLevel + 1
       changeLevel2()
       levelNum.text = tostring(currentLevel)
    ```

     `tostring()` converts any argument to a string. In the preceding example, the `currentLevel` value changes from 1 to 2 when a `"win"` game event occurs. The value will convert to a string format that the `levelNum` text object can display on screen for **Level 2**.

3. Add an `elseif` statement for a `"win"` game event when the second level has been completed and notifies the player that the game has been completed.

    ```
    elseif gameEvent == "win" and currentLevel == 2 then
       alertScreen("  Game Over", "  Congratulations!")
       gameEvent = "completed"
    ```

4. Add another `elseif` statement for `"lose"` game event on the first level. Reset the score to zero and replay level 1.

    ```
    elseif gameEvent == "lose" and currentLevel == 1 then
       score = 0
       scoreNum.text = "0"
       changeLevel1()
    ```

5. Add another `elseif` statement for a `"lose"` game event on the second level. Reset the score to zero and replay level 2.

```
elseif gameEvent == "lose" and currentLevel == 2 then
   score = 0
   scoreNum.text = "0"
   changeLevel2()
```

6. Lastly add another `elseif` statement for a `gameEvent = "completed"`. Close the function with `end`.

```
elseif gameEvent == "completed" then
   alertBox:removeEventListener("tap", restart)
end
end
```

7. Now we need to backtrack and add an event listener to the `alertScreen()` function using the `alertBox` object. We're going to add it to the bottom of the function. This will activate `function restart()`.

```
alertBox:addEventListener("tap", restart)
```

What just happened?

The `restart()` function checks all `gameEvent` and `currentLevel` variables happening during gameplay. When a game event checks for the string `"win"`, it also goes down the list of statements to see what comes out true. For example, if the player wins and is currently on level 1, then the player moves on to level 2.

During a case that the player loses, `gameEvent == "lose"` becomes true and the code checks what level the player lost in. For any level the player loses in, the score reverts back to 0 and the current level the player was on is set up again.

Activating event listeners

The event listeners in this game basically turn the movements of the objects on and off. We have already coded the functions that carry out the actions of our game objects to run the level. Now it's time to activate them using certain type of events. As you've noticed from the previous chapter, we can add event listeners to display objects or have them run globally.

Collision events

Collision events within the physics engine occur through Corona's event listener model. There are three new event types:

◆ `"collision"`: This event includes phases for `"began"` and `"ended"`, which signify the moments of initial contact and broken contact. These phases exist for both normal two-body collisions and body-sensor collisions. If you do not implement a `"collision"` listener, this event will not fire.

◆ `"preCollision"`: An event type that fires right before the objects start to interact. Depending on your game logic, you may wish to detect this event and conditionally override the collision. It may also result in multiply reports per contact and affect the application performance.

◆ `"postCollision"`: An event type that fires right after the objects have interacted. This is the only event in which the collision force is reported. If you do not implement a `"postCollision"` listener, this event will not fire.

 Collisions are reported between pairs of objects and can be detected either globally, using a runtime listener, or locally within an object, using a table listener.

Global collision listeners

When detected as a runtime event, each collision event includes `event.object1`, which contains the table ID of the Corona display object involved.

For example:

```
local physics = require "physics"
physics.start()

local box1 = display.newImage( "box.png" )
physics.addBody( box1, "dynamic", { density = 1.0, friction = 0.3,
bounce = 0.2 } )
box1.myName = "Box 1"

local box2 = display.newImage( "box.png", 0, 350)
physics.addBody( box2, "static", { density = 1.0, friction = 0.3,
bounce = 0.2 } )
box2.myName = "Box 2"

local function onCollision( event )
```

```
            if event.phase == "began" and event.object1.myName == "Box 1"
    then

                print( "Collision made." )

        end
end
```

```
    Runtime:addEventListener( "collision", onCollision )
```

Local collision listeners

When detected with a table listener within an object, each collision event includes `event.other`, which contains the table ID of the other display object involved in the collision.

For example:

```
local physics = require "physics"
physics.start()

local box1 = display.newImage( "box.png" )
physics.addBody( box1, "dynamic", { density = 1.0, friction = 0.3,
bounce = 0.2 } )
box1.myName = "Box 1"

local box2 = display.newImage( "box.png", 0, 350)
physics.addBody( box2, "static", { density = 1.0, friction = 0.3,
bounce = 0.2 } )
box2.myName = "Box 2"

local function onCollision( self, event )
        if event.phase == "began" and self.myName == "Box 1" then

                print( "Collision made." )

        end
end

box1.collision = onCollision
    box1:addEventListener( "collision", box1 )

box2.collision = onCollision
    box2:addEventListener( "collision", box2 )
```

Time for action – adding game listeners

For many of the functions we have created for our game objects we need to activate the event listeners so that they will run the code and disable them when gameplay has stopped.

1. The last function we need to create in order to complete this game is called `gameListeners()`, which will also have a parameter called `event`. This should be added right after the `gameLevel2()` function.

```
function gameListeners(event)
```

2. Add in the following event listeners that will start several events in the application using an `if` statement:

```
if event == "add" then
   Runtime:addEventListener("accelerometer", movePaddle)
   Runtime:addEventListener("enterFrame", updateBall)
   paddle:addEventListener("collision", bounce)
   ball:addEventListener("collision", removeBrick)
   paddle:addEventListener("touch", dragPaddle)
```

3. Next we'll add in an `elseif` statement for the event listeners that will remove the events and then close the function.

```
elseif event == "remove" then
   Runtime:removeEventListener("accelerometer", movePaddle)
   Runtime:removeEventListener("enterFrame", updateBall)
   paddle:removeEventListener("collision", bounce)
   ball:removeEventListener("collision", removeBrick)
   paddle:removeEventListener("touch", dragPaddle)

   end
end
```

4. In order for `function gameListeners()` to work properly, we need to instantiate it in the `startGame()` function using the `"add"` string in the parameter. Place it before the end of the function.

```
gameListeners("add")
```

5. In the `alertScreen()` function, add the `"remove"` string in the parameter and place it at the start of the function.

```
gameListeners("remove")
```

6. All the code has been written! Go ahead and run the game in the simulator. The application is also device ready. Make a simple icon image that fits the required dimensions for the device you're developing on. Compile a build and run it on your device.

What just happened?

There are two sets of `if` statements for the `event` parameter, `"add"` and `"remove"`.

All the event listeners in this function play an important role in making the game run. `"accelerometer"` and `"enterframe"` are used as runtime events since they have no specific target.

Both the `paddle` and `ball` have `"collision"` events that will carry out their purpose in any object contact made.

The `"touch"` event allows the user to touch and drag the paddle so it can move back and forth in the simulator.

Notice `event == "remove"` removes all event listeners that were active in the game. When the game starts, `gameListeners("add")` is activated. When a win or lose condition is achieved, `gameListeners("remove")` is activated.

Have a go hero – let's turn everything upside down

What if we decided to flip the game upside down? In other words, place the paddle near the top of the screen, the ball below the paddle, and the group of bricks closer to the bottom of the screen.

Things you'll have to consider:

- The top wall is now an area you have to keep the ball from entering
- The y-direction the ball travels when it collides with the bricks
- The ball has to reflect off the bottom wall when it collides with it

As you can see, there are a couple things to consider before switching values from negative to positive and vice versa. Be sure to verify your logic and that it makes sense when creating this new variation.

The results are in!

Let's reiterate block by block to make sure that we have everything added into our game. You can also refer to the Breakout Final folder in the Chapter 4 folder to see the final code. We made sure that we introduced our variables used in the game. We also initialized the main() function that starts the gameplay. A **Main Menu** screen was implemented with the game title and a **Play** button.

```
-- Hide Status Bar
display.setStatusBar(display.HiddenStatusBar)

-- Physics Engine
local physics = require "physics"
physics.start()
physics.setGravity(0, 0)

-- Accelerometer
system.setAccelerometerInterval( 100 )

-- Menu Screen
local menuScreenGroup   -- display.newGroup()
local mmScreen
local playBtn

-- Game Screen
local background
local paddle
local brick
local ball

-- Score/Level Text
local scoreText
local scoreNum
local levelText
local levelNum

-- alertDisplayGroup
local alertDisplayGroup   -- display.newGroup()
local alertBox
local conditionDisplay
local messageText

-- Variables
local _W = display.contentWidth / 2
local _H = display.contentHeight / 2
```

```
local bricks = display.newGroup()
local brickWidth = 35
local brickHeight = 15
local row
local column
local score = 0
local scoreIncrease = 100
local currentLevel
local vx = 3
local vy = -3
local gameEvent = ""

local isSimulator = "simulator" == system.getInfo("environment")

-- Main Function

function main()
  mainMenu()
end

function mainMenu()
  menuScreenGroup = display.newGroup()

  mmScreen = display.newImage("mmScreen.png", 0, 0, true)
  mmScreen.x = _W
  mmScreen.y = _H

  playBtn = display.newImage("playbtn.png")
  playBtn:setReferencePoint(display.CenterReferencePoint)
  playBtn.x = _W; playBtn.y = _H + 50
  playBtn.name = "playbutton"

  menuScreenGroup:insert(mmScreen)
  menuScreenGroup:insert(playBtn)

  -- Button Listeners
  playBtn:addEventListener("tap", loadGame)
end
```

Next we transitioned the menuScreenGroup away from the stage to load the main playing field. The main display objects of the game, such as the paddle, ball, and bricks were added. The score and the level number were displayed as the UI elements and updated throughout gameplay. Paddle movement in both the simulator and accelerometer were added as well as the collision detection with the paddle and the ball.

```
function loadGame(event)
  if event.target.name == "playbutton" then
    -- Start Game
    transition.to(menuScreenGroup,{time = 0, alpha=0, onComplete =
addGameScreen})
    playBtn:removeEventListener("tap", loadGame)
  end
end

function addGameScreen()

  background = display.newImage("bg.png", 0, 0, true )
  background.x = _W
  background.y = _H

  paddle = display.newImage("paddle.png")
  paddle.x = 240; paddle.y = 300
  paddle.name = "paddle"

  ball = display.newImage("ball.png")
  ball.x = 240; ball.y = 290
  ball.name = "ball"

  -- Text

  scoreText = display.newText("Score:", 5, 2, "Arial", 14)
  scoreText:setTextColor(255, 255, 255, 255)

  scoreNum = display.newText("0", 54, 2, "Arial", 14)
  scoreNum:setTextColor(255, 255, 255, 255)

  levelText = display.newText("Level:", 420, 2, "Arial", 14)
  levelText:setTextColor(255, 255, 255, 255)

  levelNum = display.newText("1", 460, 2, "Arial", 14)
  levelNum:setTextColor(255, 255, 255, 255)

  -- Build Level Bricks

  gameLevel1()

  -- Start Listener
```

```
      background:addEventListener("tap", startGame)
end

-- Used to drag the paddle on the simulator

function dragPaddle(event)

  if isSimulator then

    if event.phase == "began" then
      moveX = event.x - paddle.x
    elseif event.phase == "moved" then
      paddle.x = event.x - moveX
    end

    if((paddle.x - paddle.width * 0.5) < 0) then
      paddle.x = paddle.width * 0.5
    elseif((paddle.x + paddle.width * 0.5) > display.contentWidth)
then
      paddle.x = display.contentWidth - paddle.width * 0.5
    end

  end

end

function movePaddle(event)

  -- Accelerometer Movement

  --must be yGravity since it's landscape
  paddle.x = display.contentCenterX - (display.contentCenterX *
(event.yGravity*3))


  -- Wall Borders

  if((paddle.x - paddle.width * 0.5) < 0) then
    paddle.x = paddle.width * 0.5
  elseif((paddle.x + paddle.width * 0.5) > display.contentWidth) then
    paddle.x = display.contentWidth - paddle.width * 0.5
  end
end
```

```
function bounce()
  vy = -3

  -- Paddle Collision, check the which side of the paddle the ball
hits, left, right

  if((ball.x + ball.width * 0.5) < paddle.x) then
    vx = -vx
  elseif((ball.x + ball.width * 0.5) >= paddle.x) then
    vx = vx
  end
end
```

The physical properties of the paddle and ball were added to the start of the game. The brick layouts for each of the two levels were created. We have added event listeners to all our game objects from the point when they need to be activated during the game and removed when gameplay is over.

```
function startGame()
  -- Physics
  physics.addBody(paddle, "static", {density = 1, friction = 0, bounce
= 0})
  physics.addBody(ball, "dynamic", {density = 1, friction = 0, bounce
= 0})

  background:removeEventListener("tap", startGame)
  gameListeners("add")
end

-- HOW TO BUILD BLOCKS

function gameLevel1()

  currentLevel = 1

  bricks:toFront()

  local numOfRows = 4
  local numOfColumns = 4
  local brickPlacement = {x = (_W) - (brickWidth * numOfColumns ) / 2
+ 20, y = 50}

  for row = 0, numOfRows - 1 do
    for column = 0, numOfColumns - 1 do
```

```
        -- Create a brick
        local brick = display.newImage("brick.png")
        brick.name = "brick"
        brick.x = brickPlacement.x + (column * brickWidth)
        brick.y = brickPlacement.y + (row * brickHeight)
        physics.addBody(brick, "static", {density = 1, friction = 0,
bounce = 0})
        bricks.insert(bricks, brick)

    end
  end
end

function gameLevel2()

  currentLevel = 2

  bricks:toFront()

  local numOfRows = 5
  local numOfColumns = 8
  local brickPlacement = {x = (_W) - (brickWidth * numOfColumns ) / 2
+ 20, y = 50}

  for row = 0, numOfRows - 1 do
    for column = 0, numOfColumns - 1 do

      -- Create a brick
      local brick = display.newImage("brick.png")
      brick.name = "brick"
      brick.x = brickPlacement.x + (column * brickWidth)
      brick.y = brickPlacement.y + (row * brickHeight)
      physics.addBody(brick, "static", {density = 1, friction = 0,
bounce = 0})
      bricks.insert(bricks, brick)

    end
  end
end


function gameListeners(event)
  if event == "add" then
    Runtime:addEventListener("accelerometer", movePaddle)
    Runtime:addEventListener("enterFrame", updateBall)
```

```
        paddle:addEventListener("collision", bounce)
        ball:addEventListener("collision", removeBrick)
        -- Used to drag the paddle on the simulator
        paddle:addEventListener("touch", dragPaddle)

    elseif event == "remove" then
        Runtime:removeEventListener("accelerometer", movePaddle)
        Runtime:removeEventListener("enterFrame", updateBall)
        paddle:removeEventListener("collision", bounce)
        ball:removeEventListener("collision", removeBrick)
        -- Used to drag the paddle on the simulator
        paddle:removeEventListener("touch", dragPaddle)

    end
end
```

Every time the ball collides with a brick, the brick is removed from the scene. The directional changes are updated to the ball for every wall, paddle, or brick collision made. Every time a win or lose condition occurred, all game objects are reset to begin at the start of the current or new level.

```
--BRICK REMOVAL

function removeBrick(event)

    -- Check the which side of the brick the ball hits, left, right

    if event.other.name == "brick" and ball.x + ball.width * 0.5 <
event.other.x + event.other.width * 0.5 then
        vx = -vx
    elseif event.other.name == "brick" and ball.x + ball.width * 0.5
>= event.other.x + event.other.width * 0.5 then
        vx = vx
    end

    -- Bounce, Remove
    if event.other.name == "brick" then
        vy = vy * -1
        event.other:removeSelf()
        event.other = nil
        bricks.numChildren = bricks.numChildren - 1
        -- Score
        score = score + 1
        scoreNum.text = score * scoreIncrease
```

```
      scoreNum:setReferencePoint(display.CenterLeftReferencePoint)
      scoreNum.x = 54
    end

    -- Check if all bricks are destroyed

    if bricks.numChildren < 0 then
      alertScreen("YOU WIN!", "Continue")
      gameEvent = "win"
    end
end

-- BALL FUNCTION

function updateBall()

    -- Ball Movement

  ball.x = ball.x + vx
  ball.y = ball.y + vy

    -- Wall Collision

  if ball.x < 0 or ball.x + ball.width > display.contentWidth then
    vx = -vx
  end--Left

  if ball.y < 0   then
    vy = -vy
  end--Up

  if ball.y + ball.height > paddle.y + paddle.height then
    alertScreen("YOU LOSE!", "Play Again") gameEvent = "lose"
  end--down/lose
end


-- RESET LEVEL

function changeLevel1()

    -- Clear Level Bricks
```

```
    bricks:removeSelf()

    bricks.numChildren = 0
    bricks = display.newGroup()

    -- Remove Alert

    alertBox:removeEventListener("tap", restart)
    alertDisplayGroup:removeSelf()
    alertDisplayGroup = nil

    -- Reset Ball and Paddle position

    ball.x = (display.contentWidth * 0.5) - (ball.width * 0.5)
    ball.y = (paddle.y - paddle.height) - (ball.height * 0.5) -2

    paddle.x = display.contentWidth * 0.5

    -- Redraw Bricks

    gameLevel1()

    -- Start

    background:addEventListener("tap", startGame)
end

function changeLevel2()

    -- Clear Level Bricks

    bricks:removeSelf()

    bricks.numChildren = 0
    bricks = display.newGroup()

    -- Remove Alert

    alertBox:removeEventListener("tap", restart)
    alertDisplayGroup:removeSelf()
    alertDisplayGroup = nil

    -- Reset Ball and Paddle position
```

```
    ball.x = (display.contentWidth * 0.5) - (ball.width * 0.5)
    ball.y = (paddle.y - paddle.height) - (ball.height * 0.5) -2

    paddle.x = display.contentWidth * 0.5

    -- Redraw Bricks

    gameLevel2()

    -- Start

    background:addEventListener("tap", startGame)
end
```

When a condition occurs, an **Alert** screen pops out, notifying the player what has happened. The display objects that initiate the alerts are created into a function. Lastly, the win and lose arguments are created to determine if the current level has to be replayed, goes to the next level, or if the game has been completed.

```
function alertScreen(title, message)
  gameListeners("remove")

  alertBox = display.newImage("alertBox.png")
  alertBox.x = 240; alertBox.y = 160

  transition.from(alertBox, {time = 300, xScale = 0.5, yScale = 0.5,
transition = easing.outExpo})

  conditionDisplay = display.newText(title, 0, 0, "Arial", 38)
  conditionDisplay:setTextColor(255,255,255,255)
  conditionDisplay.xScale = 0.5
  conditionDisplay.yScale = 0.5
  conditionDisplay:setReferencePoint(display.CenterReferencePoint)
  conditionDisplay.x = display.contentCenterX
  conditionDisplay.y = display.contentCenterY - 15

  messageText = display.newText(message, 0, 0, "Arial", 24)
  messageText:setTextColor(255,255,255,255)
  messageText.xScale = 0.5
  messageText.yScale = 0.5
  messageText:setReferencePoint(display.CenterReferencePoint)
  messageText.x = display.contentCenterX
  messageText.y = display.contentCenterY + 15
```

```
    alertDisplayGroup = display.newGroup()
    alertDisplayGroup:insert(alertBox)
    alertDisplayGroup:insert(conditionDisplay)
    alertDisplayGroup:insert(messageText)

    alertBox:addEventListener("tap", restart)
end

-- WIN/LOSE ARGUMENT

function restart()
    if gameEvent == "win" and currentLevel == 1 then
        currentLevel = currentLevel + 1
        changeLevel2()--next level
        levelNum.text = tostring(currentLevel)
    elseif gameEvent == "win" and currentLevel == 2 then
        alertScreen(" Game Over", " Congratulations!")
        gameEvent = "completed"
    elseif gameEvent == "lose" and currentLevel == 1 then
        score = 0
        scoreNum.text = "0"
        changeLevel1()--same level
    elseif gameEvent == "lose" and currentLevel == 2 then
        score = 0
        scoreNum.text = "0"
        changeLevel2()--same level
    elseif gameEvent == "completed" then
        alertBox:removeEventListener("tap", restart)
    end
end

main()
```

Beware of case-sensitive variables and functions in case you run into errors. Also be sure to check if you're missing any punctuation required in your code. These can be easily overlooked. Refer to your **Terminal** window in the simulator for any error references.

Pop quiz – working with game controls

1. How do you properly remove a display object from the stage?

    a. `remove()`

    b. `object: remove()`

    c. `object:removeSelf(); object = nil`

    d. None of the above

2. What is the correct way to make the following display object into a physical object?

   ```
   local ball = display.newImage("ball.png")
   ```

    a. `physics.addBody( circle, { density=2.0, friction=0.5, bounce=0.2, radius = 25 } )`

    b. `physics.addBody( circle, "dynamic", { density=2.0, friction=0.5, bounce=0.2, radius = 15 } )`

    c. a and b

    d. None of the above

3. What best represents what `"began"` means in the following function?

   ```
   local function onCollision( event )
           if event.phase == "began" and event.object1.myName ==
   "Box 1" then

                   print( "Collision made." )

           end
   end
   ```

    a. A finger moved on the screen

    b. A finger was lifted from the screen

    c. The system cancelled tracking the start touch

    d. A finger touched the screen

Summary

Congratulations! You have completed making your very first game! You should be very proud of yourself. Now you have experienced how simple it is to make an application with Corona. It can take merely a few hundred lines of code to make an application.

In this chapter, we covered the following:

- Added movement to the paddle with touch events
- Introduced the accelerometer features
- Implemented collision event listeners for all game objects affected
- Removed objects from memory when they weren't needed on the game screen
- Implemented movement of the ball as a physical object
- Updated a scoreboard for every brick collision
- Learned how to handle win and lose conditions

The past two chapters weren't so bad now were they? We're getting familiar with the workflow as we continue programming in Lua. It will definitely get easier to understand as long as you keep working with different game frameworks.

What the next chapter holds will be another game that will surely catch your attention. We'll be creating animated sprite sheets for our display objects. How's that for eye candy?

5
Animating our Game

We're off to a great start in our mobile game development journey. We have already gone through a great deal of programming, from displaying objects on screen to writing game logic that is displayed to the user. One of the most powerful things about the Corona SDK is that any display object can be animated. This is a testament to the flexible graphics model that Corona offers.

Animation adds a lot of character to the user experience in a game. This is accomplished by generating a sequence of frames that evolve smoothly from frame to frame. We'll be learning this first hand and applying it to the new game that we're going to create.

In this chapter we will:

◆ Work with motion and transitions

◆ Animate with movieclips

◆ Animate with sprite sheets

◆ Create a game loop for display objects

◆ Build our next game framework

Let's animate!

Panda star catcher

This section involves creating our second game called Panda Star Catcher. The main premise is a panda named Ling Ling who needs to launch toward the skies and catch as many stars as possible before the timer runs out. The panda will be animated and have separate movements for every course of action that is applied such as the set up before launch and while it's in the air. The slingshot mechanics will also be applied to launch Ling Ling into the air. You may have seen similar features in games such as Angry Birds and Crush the Castle.

Let's get everything moving

We have introduced transitions in *Chapter 3, Building our First Game: Breakout* and briefly touched base with it. Let's go into more detail with them.

Transitions

The transition library allows you to create animations with only a single line of code by allowing you to tween one or more properties of a display object. We discussed the basics of transitions back in *Chapter 3, Building our First Game: Breakout*.

This can be done through the `transition.to` method, which takes a display object and a table containing the control parameters. The control parameters specify the duration of the animation and the final values of properties for the display object. The intermediate values for a property are determined by an easing function that is also specified as a control parameter.

`transition.to()`: Animates a display object's properties over time using the `easing` transitions.

Syntax: `handle = transition.to( target, params )`

Parameters used are as follows:

- `target`: A display object that will be the target of the transition.
- `params`: A table that specifies the properties of the display object, which will be animated, and one or more of the following optional non-animated properties:
    - `params.time`: It specifies the duration of the transition in milliseconds. By default, the duration is 500 ms (0.5 seconds).
    - `params.transition`: It is by default `easing.linear`.

❑ `params.delay`: Specifies the delay, in milliseconds, (none by default) before the tween begins.

❑ `params.delta`: It is a boolean specifying whether non-control parameters are interpreted as final ending values or as changes in values. The default is `nil` meaning false.

❑ `params.onStart`: It is a function or table listener called before the tween begins.

❑ `params.onComplete`: It is a function or table listener called after the tween completes.

Easing

The `easing` library is a collection of interpolation functions used by the transition library:

◆ `easing.linear( t, tMax, start, delta )`: This function defines a constant motion with no acceleration.

◆ `easing.inQuad( t, tMax, start, delta )`: This function performs a quadratic interpolation of animated property values in a transition.

◆ `easing.outQuad( t, tMax, start, delta )`: This function starts motion fast and then decelerates motion to a zero velocity as it executes.

◆ `easing.inOutQuad( t, tMax, start, delta )`: This function starts animation from a zero velocity, accelerates, then decelerate to a zero velocity.

◆ `easing.inExpo( t, tMax, start, delta )`: This function starts motion from a zero velocity and then accelerates motion as it executes.

◆ `easing.outExpo( t, tMax, start, delta )`: This function starts motion fast and then decelerates motion to a zero velocity as it executes.

◆ `easing.inOutExpo( t, tMax, start, delta )`: This function starts motion from a zero velocity, accelerates, then decelerates to a zero velocity using an exponential easing equation.

You can create your own easing function to interpolate between a start and a final value. The arguments of the function are defined as:

◆ `t`: Is the time in milliseconds since the transition started

◆ `tMax`: Is the duration of the transition

◆ `start`: Is the starting value

◆ `delta`: Is the change in value (final value = start + delta)

For example:

```
local square = display.newRect( 0, 0, 50, 50 )
square:setFillColor( 255,255,255 )
square.x = 50; square.y = 100

local square2 = display.newRect( 0, 0, 50, 50 )
square2:setFillColor( 255,255,255 )
square2.x = 50; square2.y = 300

transition.to( square, { time=1500, x=250, y=0 } )
transition.from( square2, { time=1500, x=250, y=0, transition =
easing.outExpo } )
```

The value of timed functions

Using a function that can be called at a later time can be helpful when organizing the timing of the appearance of your game objects in an application. The timer library will allow us to handle our functions in a timely manner.

Timers

The `timer` function enables you to trigger events at a specific delay (in milliseconds) of your choosing.

◆ `timer.performWithDelay( delay, listener [, iterations] )`

Invokes the listener after a delay in milliseconds and returns a handle you can pass to `timer.cancel()` to cancel the timer before it invokes the listener.

Example:

```
local function myEvent()
     print( "myEvent called" )
end
timer.performWithDelay( 1000, myEvent )
```

◆ `timer.cancel( timerId )`

Cancels a timer operation initiated with `timer.performWithDelay()`.

Parameters:

❑ `timerId`: Handle returned by the call to `timer.performWithDelay()`.

Example:

```
local count = 0

local function myEvent()
    count = count + 1
    print( count )

    if count >= 3 then
        timer.cancel( myTimerID ) -- Cancels myTimerID
    end
 end

myTimerID = timer.performWithDelay( 1000, myEvent, 0 )
```

◆ `timer.pause( timerId )`

Pauses a timer started with `timer.performWithDelay()`.

Parameters:

❑ `timerId`: **The Timer ID from** `timer.performWithDelay()`.

Example:

```
local count = 0

local function myEvent()
    count = count + 1
    print( count )

    if count >= 5 then
        timer.pause( myTimerID ) -- Pauses myTimerID
    end
 end

myTimerID = timer.performWithDelay( 1000, myEvent, 0 )
```

◆ `timer.resume( timerId )`

Resumes a timer that was paused with `timer.pause( timerId )`.

Parameters:

❑ `timerID`: **The Timer ID from** `timer.performWithDelay()`.

Example:

```
local function myEvent()
    print( "myEvent called" )
end

myTimerID = timer.performWithDelay( 3000, myEvent )  -- wait 3
seconds

result = timer.pause( myTimerID ) -- Pauses myTimerID
print( "Time paused at " .. result )

result = timer.resume( myTimerID ) -- Resumes myTimerID
print( "Time resumed at " .. result )
```

Movieclips or sprite sheets. What's the difference?

Corona SDK includes a *sprite sheet* feature for constructing animated sprites. Refer to the following link for more information on sprite sheets at: `http://developer.anscamobile.com/reference/sprite-sheets`.

Sprite sheets are an efficient way to save texture memory. They are recommended for complex character animation or when numerous types of animations are involved.

Sprite sheets will require more coding and have more of an advanced setup. They require the construction of a large sheet of animation frames. The movieclip library is easier to get started with, and can be more rapidly used to port Flash content, since movieclip frames can be exported from Flash as PNG sequences.

Movieclips

The external movieclip library allows you to create animated sprites from sequences of images, which can be moved around the screen using the same techniques as any other Corona display object.

The movieclip library is an external module, `movieclip.lua`, that can be included with your projects and loaded using the `require` command.

The movieclip library can be found in the `Movieclip` sample project in the `SampleCode/Graphics` folder inside of the Corona SDK.

Movieclip functions

An animation object is returned using a list of images. You can use methods of the returned animation object to control its playback such as `play()`, `stop()`, and `reverse()`.

◆ `movieclip.newAnim( frames )`: Creates an animated sprite using an array of image filenames provided in the frames table:

```
myAnimation = movieclip.newAnim{ "1.png", "2.png", "3.png",
"4.png", "5.png"}
```

◆ `object:play()`: Starts the animated sprite playing in the forward direction. When the end of the sequence is reached, it repeats from the beginning.

◆ `object:play{ startFrame=a, endFrame=b, loop=c, remove=shouldRemove }`: Starts the animated sprite in forward motion. When the frame number given by `endFrame` is reached, it will cycle back to the frame number given by `startFrame` and continue playing:

```
myAnimation:play{ startFrame=1, endFrame=4, loop=5, remove=true }
```

An animation can loop as many times based on the number you indicate. Using `0` will loop the animation forever.

The remove parameter is a boolean flag, and if set to true, the movieclip will automatically delete itself when the given sequence is completed. The default value is `false`.

◆ `object:reverse()`: Plays the animated sprite in reverse direction. When the beginning of the image set is reached, it will cycle back to the last image and continue playing backwards.

◆ `object:reverse{ startFrame=a, endFrame=b, loop=c, remove=shouldRemove }`: Starts the animated sprite in reverse order. When the frame number given by `endFrame` is reached, it will cycle back to the frame number given by `startFrame` and continue playing.

An animation can loop as many times based on the number you indicate. Using `0` will loop the animation forever.

The remove parameter is a boolean flag, and if set to true, the movieclip will automatically delete itself when the given sequence is completed. The default value is `false`.

◆ `object:nextFrame()`: Resets any animation sequence in progress, moves the animation to the next image in the total sequence, and stops.

◆ `object:previousFrame()`: Resets any animation sequence in progress, moves the animation to the previous image in the total sequence, and stops.

- ◆ `object:setLabels( labels )`: Adds optional labels to an object previously created, using a table to assign label names to selected frame numbers:

  Syntax: `object:setLabels{ frameLabel1=num1, frameLabel2=num2, ..., frameLabelN = numN }`

  Example:

  ```
  myAnimation:setLabels{ main=1, end=30 }
  ```

- ◆ `object:stop()`: Stops the animation of the sprite at its current frame.

- ◆ `object:stopAtFrame( frame )`: Jumps the animation to the specified frame, given either as a frame number or by an optional frame label.

  ```
  myAnimation:stopAtFrame(2)
  myAnimation:play()

  myAnimation:stopAtFrame("label")
  myAnimation:reverse()
  ```

- ◆ `object:setDrag`: Turns any movieclip into a draggable object when drag is set as true. `limitX` and `limitY` parameters limit the dragging to either the x or y axis, and the bounds parameter can be used to specify drag boundaries for the object as `{left, top, width, height}`.

  The `onPress`, `onDrag`, and `onRelease` parameters take the names of functions to be called when those events occur. All parameters are optional.

  ```
  myAnimation:setDrag{ drag=true, limitX=false, limitY=false,
  onPress=myPressFunction, onDrag=myDragFunction,
  onRelease=myReleaseFunction, bounds={ 20, 20, 100, 25 }}
  ```

  To turn off the draggable property again, set drag to `false`:

  ```
  myAnimation:setDrag{ drag=false }
  ```

It's sprite mania!

Sprite sheets are 2D animations compiled to multiple frames into a single texture image. This is an efficient way to save on texture memory. It is beneficial for mobile devices and minimizes loading time.

Sprite API

The following line makes the sprite features available under the sprite namespace:

```
require "sprite"
```

◆ `sprite.newSpriteSheet`: **The function creates a new sprite sheet.**

   `spriteSheet = sprite.newSpriteSheet("myImage.png", frameWidth, frameHeight) -- the width/height of each animation in the sprite sheet`

   For example, the number of frames in the sprite sheet is assumed to be `floor(imageWidth/frameWidth) * floor(imageHeight/frameHeight)`. The first frame is placed at the top-left position and reads left to right and follows the next row if applicable. The following sprite sheet has 5 frames that are 128 x 128 pixels each. The sprite sheet image altogether is 384 x 256 pixels. If it were to be integrated in Corona, a sample method would be displayed as follows:

   `spriteSheet = sprite.newSpriteSheet("pandaSheet.png", 128, 128)`

◆ `spriteSet = sprite.newSpriteSet(spriteSheet, startFrame, frameCount)`: **Creates a new sprite set from a sprite sheet. A sprite set defines the collection of frames that belong to the same character or another moving asset, which may then be subdivided into different animation sequences for playback. A sprite set is a Lua table containing keys to one or more animation sequences for a given character.**

◆ `sprite.add( spriteSet, "sequenceName", startFrame, frameCount, time, [loopCount])`: **Adds a sequence named** `"sequenceName"` **to the sprite set with the specified frames. The sequence has** `frameCount` **frames, and it will play for the time specified in milliseconds. The frame rate of each sequence can be controlled individually by altering the** `time` **parameter.**

- `spriteSheet:dispose()`: Disposes of a sprite sheet and releases its texture memory. It also calls `removeSelf()` on all sprite instances using the sheet, removing them from the stage. All sprites, sequences, and sets that belong to the removed sprite sheet are no longer accessible.

```
local sprite = require("sprite")
local spriteSheet = sprite.newSpriteSheet("mySprite.png")

spriteSheet:dispose()
```

- `si = sprite.newSprite( spriteSet )`: Creates a new instance of a sprite.

- `si:prepare([sequence])`: Stops playing the current animation sequence, sets the new current sequence, and also moves to the first frame of that sequence.

- `si:play()`: Plays animation sequence, starting at the current frame.

- `si:pause()`: Stops the animation, but the frame remains on the last displayed frame. Playback can resume later with `play()`.

- `si:addEventListener("sprite", listener)`: notifies the listener as to when the sprite instance animation has an event. The event, passed to the listener, has the following fields:

  `event.sprite`: The sprite that fired the event; its current properties may also be accessed via the event.

  `event.phase`: The phase is one of:

    - `"end"`: the sprite stops playing

    - `"loop"`: the sprite loops (from last to first, or reverses direction)

    - `"next"`: the sprite's next frame is played

Game time!

Now that we have learned how to set up object movement, movieclips, and sprite sheets, let's try to incorporate them into Panda Star Catcher! You can download the project files accompanying this book from the Packt website. There is a project folder called `Panda Star Catcher` in the `Chapter 5` file folder. It already has the `config.lua` and `build.settings` files set up for you. The art assets are included in the folder as well. You will notice that the build and runtime configuration has a similar setup from *Chapter 3, Building our First Game: Breakout* and *Chapter 4, Game Controls*. This tutorial is compatible with both iOS and Android devices.

The graphics included in the project folder have been designed to display properly on both platforms.

Time for action – setting up the variables

Let's start off with introducing all the variables needed to run the game.

1. Create a brand new main.lua file and add it in the Panda Star Catcher project folder.

2. Let's hide the status bar from the devices and set all the variables needed in game:

```
display.setStatusBar( display.HiddenStatusBar ) -- Hides the
status bar

-- Display groups
local hudGroup = display.newGroup() -- Displays the HUD
local gameGroup = display.newGroup()
local levelGroup = display.newGroup()
local stars = display.newGroup() -- Displays the stars

-- Modules
local sprite = require("sprite")
local physics = require ("physics")

local mCeil = math.ceil
local mAtan2 = math.atan2
```

```
local mPi = math.pi
local mSqrt = math.sqrt

-- Game Objects
local background
local ground
local powerShot
local arrow
local panda
local poof
local starGone
local scoreText
local gameOverDisplay

-- Variables
local gameIsActive = false
local waitingForNewRound
local restartTimer
local counter
local timerInfo
local numSeconds = 30 -- Time the round starts at
local counterSize = 50
local gameScore = 0 -- Round starts at a score of 0
local starWidth = 30
local starHeight = 30
```

What just happened?

We hid the status bar at the start of the application. This is only applicable for iOS devices. There are four different groups set up and they all play an important role in the game.

You will notice `gameIsActive` = `false`. This enables us to activate properties of the application to affect the round when the display objects need to stop animating, appear on screen, and become affected by touch events.

Elements for the timer have been set in the beginning of the code as well. `numSeconds` = 30. This is how long the round will count down from in seconds. `starWidth` and `starHeight` depicts the dimensions of the object altogether.

Let's start the round

We'll need to load the panda to the game screen before it can launch. The panda will transition from the bottom of the screen and move upward on the screen before any touch event can occur.

Time for action – starting the game

Right now we need to set the off screen position for the panda and have it transition to its starting launch location so the user can interact with it.

1. After adding the variables, create a new local function called `startNewRound()` and add an `if` statement to initiate the `panda` object into the scene.

```
local startNewRound = function()

  if panda then
```

2. Add a new local function called `activateRound()` within `startNewRound()`. Set the starting position of the `panda` display object on screen and add `ground:toFront()` so that ground appears in front of the panda character.

```
    local activateRound = function()

      waitingForNewRound = false

      if restartTimer then
        timer.cancel( restartTimer )
      end

      ground:toFront()
      panda.x = 240;
      panda.y = 300;
      panda.rotation = 0
      panda.isVisible = true
      panda.isBodyActive = true
```

3. Create another local function called `pandaLoaded()`. Set `gameIsActive = true` and set the `panda` object's air and hit properties to `false`. Add `panda:toFront()` so that it appears in front of all the other game objects on screen and set the body type to `"static"`.

```
    local pandaLoaded = function()

      gameIsActive = true
      panda.inAir = false
      panda.isHit = false
      panda:toFront()

      panda.bodyType = "static"

    end
```

4. Transition the panda to `y=225` in 1000 milliseconds. When the tween is completed, call the `pandaLoaded()` function using the `onComplete` command. Close the `activateRound()` function with `end` and call out to it. Close the `if` statement for panda and the `startNewRound()` function with `end`.

```
        transition.to( panda, { time=1000, y=225,
onComplete=pandaLoaded } )
      end

      activateRound()

    end
  end
```

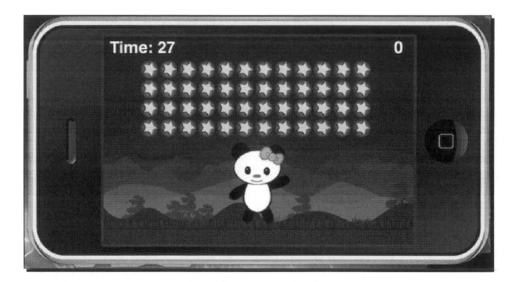

What just happened?

When the level is activated, the panda is placed below the ground before it is visible to the player. For `pandaLoaded()`, the game is activated by `gameIsActive = true` and the panda is ready for launch by the player. The panda transitions from the ground level to an area on the screen where it can be accessed.

Poof begone!

The panda needs to disappear from the stage after a turn has been made. Instead of having it disappear into thin air, we'll be adding a poof effect when it collides with any object on screen.

Time for action – reloading the panda on the stage

When the panda has been in the air for a certain amount of time or has hit any out of bounds area off the screen, it will turn into a cloud of smoke. The panda will be replaced with a *poof* image when a collision event occurs with the edge of the screen or the ground. The visible properties of the panda have to be turned off for the *poof* effect to work. When the collision has been made, the panda needs to be reloaded back on to the screen while the game is still activated.

1. Create a local function called `callNewRound()`. Include a local variable called `isGameOver` and set it to `false`.

```
local callNewRound = function()
   local isGameOver = false
```

2. Within the current function, create a new local function called `pandaGone()`. Add in new properties for the panda so it no longer displays on the game stage.

```
local pandaGone = function()

   panda:setLinearVelocity( 0, 0 )
   panda.bodyType = "static"
   panda.isVisible = false
   panda.isBodyActive = false
   panda.rotation = 0

   poof.x = panda.x; poof.y = panda.y
   poof.alpha = 0
   poof.isVisible = true
```

3. Add in a new function for the `poof` object called `fadePoof()`. With the `onComplete` command, transition with `time=50` and `alpha=1`. Have the `poof` object fade out with `time=100` and `alpha=0`. Close the `pandaGone()` function and call out to it using `timer.peformWithDelay`.

```
local fadePoof = function()
   transition.to( poof, { time=100, alpha=0 } )
end
transition.to( poof, { time=50, alpha=1.0, onComplete=fadePoof
} )

restartTimer = timer.performWithDelay( 300, function()
   waitingForNewRound = true;
   end, 1)

end

local poofTimer = timer.performWithDelay( 500, pandaGone, 1 )
```

4. When `isGameOver` is still `false`, add in a `timer.peformWithDelay` for `startNewRound()`. Close the `callNewRound()` function.

```
if isGameOver == false then
    restartTimer = timer.performWithDelay( 1500, startNewRound, 1
)
    end
end
```

What just happened?

A new round is called when the panda is no longer displayed on screen and the clock is still counting down. When `isGameOver` is still `false`, then the panda reloads by calling `startNewRound()`.

The panda collision occurs through `pandaGone()`. All physical properties become inactive by applying `panda.isVisible = false` and `pandaisBodyActive = false`.

The exact placement the panda disappears, the smoke will appear. This happens when `poof.x = panda.x; poof.y = panda.y`. `poof` will become visible for a short while through `fadePoof()`. Once it has faded, a new round awaits, which makes `waitingForNewRound = true`.

Earn some points

Points are earned when the panda catches any stars in the sky. The game is run on a timer, so it is the player's job to catch as many stars as he/she can before the time runs out. Let's rack up some points!

Time for action – tracking the score

The score updates through a parameter called `scoreNum` and displays it during gameplay. The score number is received through `gameScore`.

1. The next function that will be created is called `setScore()` with a parameter called `scoreNum`.

```
local setScore = function( scoreNum )
```

2. Use a local variable called `newScore` and set it equal to `scoreNum`. Set the `gameScore = newScore`. Provide an `if` statement for `gameScore` so that the score during gameplay is set at `0`.

```
local newScore = scoreNum
gameScore = newScore

if gameScore < 0 then gameScore = 0; end
```

3. Add in the `scoreText` display object and have it equal to `gameScore`. Close the function.

```
scoreText.text = gameScore
scoreText.xScale = 0.5; scoreText.yScale = 0.5
scoreText.x = (480 - (scoreText.contentWidth * 0.5)) - 15
scoreText.y = 20
end
```

What just happened?

For `setScore = function(scoreNum)`, we set a parameter called `scoreNum`. `scoreNum` will update the game score continuously through `local newScore`. `newScore` will update through `gameScore`, which provides the base of the score keeping. At the same time, `scoreText` will display the value of `gameScore` during the game.

When the game ends

There are no losers in this game. Everyone wins! You'll still keep your adrenaline pumping by trying to catch as many stars as you can before the timer runs out. When it's all over we still need to be notified when the time is up.

Time for action – displaying the game over screen

We need to set up the game over screen and have it display the final score the player has achieved at the end of the round.

1. Create a new local function called `callGameOver()`.

```
local callGameOver = function()
```

2. Set `gameIsActive = false` and pause the physics engine. Remove the `panda` and `stars` objects from the stage.

```
gameIsActive = false
physics.pause()

panda:removeSelf()
panda = nil
stars:removeSelf()
stars = nil
```

3. Display the game over objects and insert them into the `hudGroup` group. Use the `transition.to` method to display the game over objects on screen.

```
local shade = display.newRect( 0, 0, 480, 320 )
shade:setFillColor( 0, 0, 0, 255 )
shade.alpha = 0

gameOverDisplay = display.newImage( "gameOverScreen.png")
gameOverDisplay.x = 240; gameOverDisplay.y = 160
gameOverDisplay.alpha = 0

hudGroup:insert( shade )
hudGroup:insert( gameOverDisplay )

transition.to( shade, { time=200, alpha=0.65 } )
transition.to( gameOverDisplay, { time=500, alpha=1 } )
```

4. Update the final score with a local variable called `newScore`. Set `isVisible = false` for the `counter` and `scoreText`. Introduce the `scoreText` again to display the final score in a different location on the device screen. Close the function.

```
local newScore = gameScore
setScore( newScore )

counter.isVisible = false

scoreText.isVisible = false
scoreText.text = "Score: " .. gameScore
scoreText.xScale = 0.5; scoreText.yScale = 0.5
scoreText.x = 280
scoreText.y = 160
scoreText:toFront()
timer.performWithDelay( 1000, function() scoreText.isVisible =
true; end, 1 )

end
```

What just happened?

`callGameOver()` displays the game over screen when time runs out or if all the stars are collected. We set `gameIsActive = false` and paused all the physics so the panda cannot be moved with any other screen touches. The panda and stars are then removed from the scene.

`shade` and `gameOverDisplay` are visible through `transition.to` so it notifies the player that the round is over. The final score will display at the end of the round in front of the `gameOverDisplay` object.

Background display

The panda needs a general setting of where it's located in the game. Let's set the background and ground objects.

Time for action – adding the background elements

1. Add in the `background` and `ground` display objects to the `drawBackground()` function. Insert the objects in the group called `gameGroup`.

```
local drawBackground = function()

  background = display.newImage( "background.png" )
  background.x = 240; background.y = 160
```

```
gameGroup:insert( background )

ground = display.newImage( "ground.png" )
ground.x = 240; ground.y = 300

local groundShape = { -240,-18, 240,-18, 240,18, -240,18 }
physics.addBody( ground, "static", { density=1.0, bounce=0,
friction=0.5, shape=groundShape } )

gameGroup:insert( ground )

end
```

What just happened?

The background and ground display objects are placed in the function called drawBackground(). ground has a customized physical shape that is not the same size as the original display object. If the panda happens to hit the ground, it will be able to collide with it and not fall through.

Heads up!

Before the game can be played, we need a general idea of how to operate the controls of the game. Luckily, we'll only be adding a help screen that explains how to play. The **HUD (Heads Up Display)** needs to be displayed as well so the player can be updated on the time left on the clock and how many points have been accumulated.

Time for action – displaying the timer and score

Let's set up the help screen and HUD elements that need to be displayed during the game.

1. Create a new local function called hud().

```
local hud = function()
```

2. Display helpText at the start of the game for 10 seconds. Have it transition by sliding it to the left and turning visibility to false. Add the helpText to the hudGroup group.

```
local helpText = display.newImage("help.png")
helpText.x = 240; helpText.y = 160
helpText.isVisible = true
```

```
      hudGroup:insert( helpText )

      timer.performWithDelay( 10000, function() helpText.isVisible =
   false; end, 1 )

      transition.to( helpText, { delay=9000, time=1000, x=-320,
   transition=easing.inOutExpo })
```

3. Display `counter` and `scoreText` near the top of the screen. Add `scoreText` to the `hudGroup` group as well. Close the function with `end`.

```
      counter = display.newText( "Time: " .. tostring( numSeconds ),
   0, 0, "Helvetica-Bold", counterSize )
      counter:setTextColor( 255, 255, 255, 255 )
      counter.xScale = 0.5; counter.yScale = 0.5
      counter.x = 60; counter.y = 15
      counter.alpha = 0

      transition.to( counter, { delay=9000, time=1000, alpha=1,
   transition=easing.inOutExpo })

      hudGroup:insert( counter )

      scoreText = display.newText( "0", 470, 22, "Helvetica-Bold", 52
   )
      scoreText:setTextColor( 255, 255, 255, 255 )   --> white
      scoreText.text = gameScore
      scoreText.xScale = 0.5; scoreText.yScale = 0.5
      scoreText.x = (480 - (scoreText.contentWidth * 0.5)) - 15
      scoreText.y = 15
      scoreText.alpha = 0

      transition.to( scoreText, { delay=9000, time=1000, alpha=1,
   transition=easing.inOutExpo })

      hudGroup:insert( scoreText )

   end
```

What just happened?

`helpText` appears before the game starts and stays on the main device display for 9 seconds and transitions to -320 in the x-direction in 1 second. This happens through `transition.to( helpText, { delay=9000, time=1000, x=-320, transition=easing.inOutExpo })`.

counter **displays** "Time: " .. tostring(numSeconds).numSeconds **being the seconds that are counted down, starting from 30. It is located near the top-left corner of the screen.**

scoreText **displays** gameScore **and is updated for every star collision made. This will be placed on the top right corner of the screen. All the objects in** local hud = function() **are inserted in** hudGroup.

Time after time

This game has a timer that the player has to work against in order to catch as many stars as possible before it runs out. We're going to start the countdown as soon as the help text leaves the stage.

Time for action – setting up the timer

We'll need to create a couple of functions that activate the countdown and also stops the countdown at 0 seconds when the game is over.

1. Set up the timer countdown for the game with a local function called myTimer().

```
local myTimer = function()
```

2. Have the seconds for the timer countdown by an increment of 1. With the counter text object, display the time using numSeconds. Print out numSeconds to see the countdown in the **Terminal** window.

```
numSeconds = numSeconds - 1
counter.text = "Time: " .. tostring( numSeconds )
print(numSeconds)
```

3. Create an if statement for when the timer runs out or if all the stars are gone. Within the block, cancel the timer and call callGameOver() to end the round. Close the myTimer() function with end.

```
if numSeconds < 1 or stars.numChildren <= 0 then
    timer.cancel(timerInfo)
    panda:pause()
    restartTimer = timer.performWithDelay( 300, function()
callGameOver(); end, 1 )
    end

end
```

4. Initiate the `myTimer()` function with a new local function called `startTimer()`. This will start the countdown at the beginning of gameplay.

```
local startTimer = function()
      print("Start Timer")
      timerInfo = timer.performWithDelay( 1000, myTimer, 0 )
end
```

What just happened?

The main timer function is within `myTimer()`. We countdown the seconds using `numSeconds = numSeconds - 1`. The seconds will update in the `counter` display object. `print(numSeconds)` will be updated in the terminal window to see how fast the countdown runs inside the code.

When time runs out or all stars have been collected, an `if` statement is created to check if any of the arguments are `true`. When any statement evaluates to `true`, the timer stops counting down, the panda animation pauses, and the `callGameOver()` function is called. This will call the function to display the game over screen.

The timer initiates the countdown through `local startTimer = function()` at a rate of 1000 milliseconds, which is equivalent to 1 second.

It's so glowy

The panda needs another element that will display how much force is added before it launches into the sky. We're going to add a subtle glow-like display object that will represent that.

Time for action – making the power shot

We need to create a separate function for the `powerShot` so it can be called when the panda is set for launch.

1. Display the `powerShot` object through a new local function called `createPowerShot()`. Insert it into the `gameGroup` group.

```
local createPowerShot = function()
  powerShot = display.newImage( "glow.png" )
  powerShot.xScale = 1.0; powerShot.yScale = 1.0
  powerShot.isVisible = false

  gameGroup:insert( powerShot )
end
```

What just happened?

The powerShot object is created through the createPowerShot() function and is called when the panda is setting up for launch.

Pandas!

It will be exciting to see something animated on screen for once. Our main character will have designated animations for every action applied during gameplay.

Time for action – creating the panda character

We need to set up the panda collision event and animate it with the sprite sheet accordingly.

1. We need to create a local function that will introduce the collision and touch events for the panda. We shall call it createPanda().

    ```
    local createPanda = function()
    ```

2. When the panda collides with the stars, use onPandaCollision() with the parameters self and event. Reload panda every time a collision occurs with the stars or the edge of the screen by using callNewRound().

    ```
    local onPandaCollision = function( self, event )
      if event.phase == "began" then

        if panda.isHit == false then

          panda.isHit = true

          if event.other.myName == "star" then
            callNewRound( true, "yes" )
          else
            callNewRound( true, "no" )
          end

          if event.other.myName == "wall" then
            callNewRound( true, "yes" )
          else
    ```

```
              callNewRound( true, "no" )
          end

      elseif panda.isHit then
          return true
      end
  end
end
```

3. Create a directional arrow to allow the user to aim for an area to launch the panda. Insert it into the gameGroup **group.**

```
arrow = display.newImage( "arrow.png" )
arrow.x = 240; arrow.y = 225
arrow.isVisible = false

gameGroup:insert( arrow )
```

4. Create the sprite sheet for the panda display object that has three different animation sequences called "set", "crouch", and "air".

```
local pandaSheet = sprite.newSpriteSheet( "pandaSprite.png",
128, 128 )

local spriteSet = sprite.newSpriteSet(pandaSheet, 1, 5)
sprite.add( spriteSet, "set", 1, 2, 200, 0 )
sprite.add( spriteSet, "crouch", 3, 1, 1, 0 )
sprite.add( spriteSet, "air", 4, 2, 100, 0 )

panda = sprite.newSprite( spriteSet )

panda:prepare("set")
panda:play()
```

5. Add properties to panda **before it launches into the air.**

```
panda.x = 240; panda.y = 225
panda.isVisible = false

panda.isReady = false
panda.inAir = false
panda.isHit = false
panda.isBullet = true
```

```
panda.trailNum = 0

panda.radius = 12
physics.addBody( panda, "static", { density=1.0, bounce=0.4,
friction=0.15, radius=panda.radius } )
panda.rotation = 0
```

6. Set up collisions for `panda` using `"collision"` and apply an event listener.

```
panda.collision = onPandaCollision
panda:addEventListener( "collision", panda )
```

7. Create the `poof` object.

```
poof = display.newImage( "poof.png" )
poof.alpha = 1.0
poof.isVisible = false
```

8. Insert the `panda` and `poof` into the `gameGroup` group. Close the function.

```
gameGroup:insert( panda )
gameGroup:insert( poof )
end
```

9. We'll need to scroll up to the `activateRound()` function and add the `"set"` animation sequence for the panda.

```
panda:prepare("set")
panda:play()
```

What just happened?

The collision events that occur for the panda start with `if event.phase == "began"`. The panda reloads on screen through several cases of `if` statements. `event.other.myName == "star"` will call a new round as well as when the panda launches off screen towards the right, left, or top sides of the stage.

The sprite sheet for the panda has three sets of animations. They are called `"set"`, `"air"`, and `"crouch"`. There are a total of five frames in the sprite sheet.

The physical properties of the panda are set before launch. The body type is set to `"static"` and will change when it's in the air.

The collision event for the panda is called by `panda:addEventListener( "collision", panda )`.

Now that the sprite sheet is set up, the `"set"` animation needs to be added in the `activateRound()` function to initiate movement.

Starry skies

The stars play a big part in the game. It is the main obstacle that the panda has to get past to achieve points before the clock runs out.

Time for action – creating star collisions

Star collisions need to be made and removed from the stage so points can be accumulated for the player.

1. Create a function for the star collision called `onStarCollision()` and have a `self` and `event` parameter.

    ```
    local onStarCollision = function( self, event )
    ```

2. Add in `if` statements that removes the `stars` children from the game screen when a collision is made. Increment the score by 500 for each star removed on screen. Close the function with `end`.

    ```
    if event.phase == "began" and self.isHit == false then

      self.isHit = true
      print( "star destroyed!")
      self.isVisible = false
      self.isBodyActive = false

      stars.numChildren = stars.numChildren - 1

      if stars.numChildren < 0 then
        stars.numChildren = 0
      end

      self.parent:remove( self )
    ```

```
        self = nil

        local newScore = gameScore + 500
        setScore( newScore )
    end
end
```

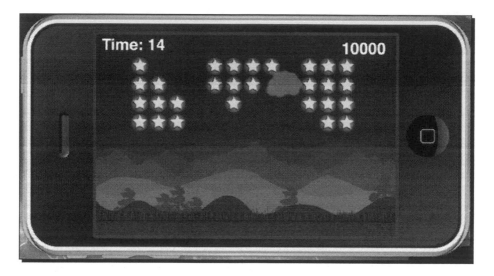

What just happened?

The star collision occurs on first contact with `if event.phase == "began"` and `self.isHit == false` assuming the star has not been touched by the panda. The stars are removed from the screen by `self.parent:remove( self )` and `self = nil`. The score is incremented by 500 through `gameScore` and updated to `setScore = (scoreNum)`.

Have a go hero – tracking the star count

Try tracking how many stars the panda has caught during gameplay. The logic is similar to how the game score was created. Each star caught will have to increment by 1 as the count for every collision made. The star count is placed within the `onStarCollision()` function. A new function and method will have to be created to display the text of the star count and will have to be updated every time the count changes.

Screen touches

The way the panda will get across the playing field to reach the stars is by creating a launch mechanic similar to a slingshot. Force will play a big role to push the panda in an upward motion.

Time for action – launching the panda

Let's add a touch event for the panda so that it flings towards the stars. The `powerShot` object will play a role by helping the player visualize how much power is applied to the panda before it launches into the air.

1. Implement touch events for the panda. Create a local function called `onScreenTouch()` with an event parameter.

```
local onScreenTouch = function( event )
```

2. With `gameIsActive` initiated, add in an `if` statement for when the touch event starts by using `event.phase == "began"`. During this event, use the `"crouch"` animation set to prepare panda for launch.

```
if gameIsActive then
   if event.phase == "began" and panda.inAir == false then

      panda.y = 225
      panda.isReady = true
      powerShot.isVisible = true
      powerShot.alpha = 0.75
      powerShot.x = panda.x; powerShot.y = panda.y
      powerShot.xScale = 0.1; powerShot.yScale = 0.1

      arrow.isVisible = true

      panda:prepare("crouch")
      panda:play()
```

3. Add an `elseif` statement for when the touch event ends by using `event.phase == "ended"`. Create a new local function called `fling()` that will hold the properties of `panda` when it is launched toward the `star` objects. Apply a force opposite of where the touch event is dragged. Scale the `powerShot` display object outward when the touch event is pulled farther from the character.

```
   elseif event.phase == "ended" and panda.isReady then

      local fling = function()
         powerShot.isVisible = false
         arrow.isVisible = false

         local x = event.x
         local y = event.y
```

```
                        local xForce = (panda.x-x) * 4
                        local yForce = (panda.y-y) * 4

                        panda:prepare("air")
                        panda:play()

                        panda.bodyType = "dynamic"
                        panda:applyForce( xForce, yForce, panda.x, panda.y )
                        panda.isReady = false
                        panda.inAir = true

                    end

                transition.to( powerShot, { time=175, xScale=0.1,
            yScale=0.1, onComplete=fling} )

                end

            if powerShot.isVisible == true then

                local xOffset = panda.x
                local yOffset = panda.y

                local distanceBetween = mCeil(mSqrt( ((event.y - yOffset) ^
            2) + ((event.x - xOffset) ^ 2) ))

                powerShot.xScale = -distanceBetween * 0.02
                powerShot.yScale = -distanceBetween * 0.02

                local angleBetween = mCeil(mAtan2( (event.y - yOffset),
            (event.x - xOffset) ) * 180 / mPi) + 90

                panda.rotation = angleBetween + 180
                arrow.rotation = panda.rotation
            end

        end
    end
```

What just happened?

Once the game is active and the panda has been loaded on the screen, a touch event to launch the panda can begin. The panda will go from a `"static"` physics state to a `"dynamic"` physics state. The `powerShot` display object size increases, the farther back the panda is pulled by an event touch.

The force from the panda launch is applied by `local fling = function()`. Force launch is created by `xForce` and `yForce`. The panda object is propelled by `panda:applyForce( xForce, yForce, panda.x, panda.y )`. Notice that the body type changes to `"dynamic"` so gravity can affect the object.

Organizing display objects

When the round has been set, the display hierarchy of the game objects needs to be rearranged. The objects of most importance are displayed towards the front of the screen.

Time for action – reordering layers

1. A new local function, `reorderLayers()` needs to be created to organize the display hierarchy of objects on screen during gameplay.

```
local reorderLayers = function()

    gameGroup:insert( levelGroup )
    ground:toFront()
    panda:toFront()
    poof:toFront()
    hudGroup:toFront()

end
```

What just happened?

The `gameGroup`, `hudGroup`, and other display objects are reorganized in the display hierarchy of the game screen. The most significant object is set to the front, while the least important one is towards the back.

Create stars

The stars will fill the game so that the panda can catch as many as possible. The skies will surely be full of them.

Time for action – creating stars in the level

We need to add the layout of the stars in the game and have them moving to add a little effect that they're active. A collision event will need to be applied so they are removed when the panda collides with them.

1. Create a new function called `createStars()` and lay out the `star` objects in a `for` loop. Add in the `"collision"` event that will be called by `onStarCollision()` to remove the stars when they are hit by the panda. Rotate the stars forwards and backwards at 10 seconds and 1080 and -1080 degrees each. This will allow the stars to rotate three full intervals backwards and forwards. Create the walls for the left and right side of the screen.

```
local createStars = function()

    local numOfRows = 4
```

```
    local numOfColumns = 12
    local starPlacement = {x = (display.contentWidth  * 0.5) -
(starWidth * numOfColumns ) / 2  + 10, y = 50}
for row = 0, numOfRows - 1 do
for column = 0, numOfColumns - 1 do

        -- Create a star
        local star = display.newImage("star.png")
        star.name = "star"
        star.isHit = false
        star.x = starPlacement.x + (column * starWidth)
        star.y = starPlacement.y + (row * starHeight)
        physics.addBody(star, "static", {density = 1, friction = 0,
bounce = 0})
        stars.insert(stars, star)

        star.collision = onStarCollision
        star:addEventListener( "collision", star )

        local function starAnimation()
          local starRotation = function()
            transition.to( star, { time=10000, rotation = 1080,
onComplete=starAnimation })
          end

            transition.to( star, { time=10000, rotation = -1080,
onComplete=starRotation })
        end

        starAnimation()

    end
  end

  local leftWall  = display.newRect (0, 0, 0, display.
contentHeight)
  leftWall.name = "wall"

   local rightWall = display.newRect (display.contentWidth, 0, 0,
display.contentHeight)
    rightWall.name = "wall"
```

```
        physics.addBody (leftWall, "static", {bounce = 0.0, friction =
    10})
        physics.addBody (rightWall, "static", {bounce = 0.0, friction
    = 10})

        reorderLayers ()
    end
```

What just happened?

The amount of stars displayed on screen is set by numOfRows and numOfColumns. A for loop is made to display each individual star object and placed in the stars group. The collision for star is detected by an event listener through onStarCollision().

leftWall and rightWall have physical properties as well and will take into account the collision detection with the panda.

The stars are animated by starAnimation() and starRotation(). Each function rotates each star object for 10 seconds (10000 milliseconds), and alternates between 1080 and -1080 degrees.

Have a go hero – creating a movieclip

Right now the stars have some movement by rotating simultaneously. Try adding some more characteristics to the image by having them change in a variety of sizes. This can be done by making a series of the same image and changing the size of the asset itself, not the image size. An image manipulation software program will be needed to accomplish this. Create as many images you see fit, and set them into a movieclip function. Let it run during gameplay.

Starting the game

The game starts when the clock starts counting down and the panda is loaded on the screen. Once the panda is set on screen, the player needs to aim and launch it quickly so reloading of the panda can occur immediately.

Time for action – initializing the game

The physics and remaining game functions need to be initialized to run the game. All game actions need to be delayed until the **Help** screen has left the stage.

1. Start the game by creating a new function called `gameInit()` that will hold the `physics` properties and activate the display objects on the stage.

```
local gameInit = function()
  physics.start( true )
  physics.setGravity( 0, 9.8 )

  drawBackground()
  createPowerShot()
  createPanda()
  createStars()
  hud()
```

2. Add in a `Runtime` event listener using `"touch"` for `onScreenTouch()`.

```
Runtime:addEventListener( "touch", onScreenTouch )
```

3. Have the level and timer start 10 seconds later so the user has time to read through the help text. Close the function and start the game with `gameInit()`.

```
local gameTimer = timer.performWithDelay( 10000, function()
startNewRound(); end, 1 )
  local gameTimer = timer.performWithDelay( 10000, function()
startTimer(); end, 1 )
end

gameInit()
```

All the code is complete! Run the game in the simulator and see for yourself how it works.

What just happened?

The round is initialized through `gameInit()`. The physics engine and remaining functions are run at this time. The event listener for `onScreenTouch()` is added as well. The `startNewRound()` and `startTimer()` functions initiate 10 seconds after launching the application through `timer.performWithDelay`.

Pop quiz – animating graphics

1. What is the proper way to stop the animation of a sprite sheet?

   a. `sprite:stop()`

   b. `sprite:pause()`

   c. `sprite:dispose()`

   d. **None of the above**

2. How do you make a movieclip animation loop forever?

   a. `myAnimation:play{ startFrame=1, endFrame=4, loop=1, remove=true }`

   b. `myAnimation:play{ startFrame=1, endFrame=4, loop=-1, remove=true }`

   c. `myAnimation:play{ startFrame=1, endFrame=4, loop=0, remove=true }`

   d. `myAnimation:play{ startFrame=1, endFrame=4, loop=100, remove=true }`

3. How do you create a new sprite sheet?

   a. `spriteSheet = sprite.newSpriteSheetFromData( "myImage.png", spriteData )`

   b. `spriteSheet = sprite.newSpriteSheetFromData( "myImage.png", spriteSet )`

   c. `spriteSheet = sprite.newSpriteSheet("myImage.png", frameWidth, frameHeight)`

   d. **None of the above**

Summary

Our second game, Panda Star Catcher is finally completed! We're now getting a great grasp on writing more functions and different types of game logic. Now we have animation under our belt! Way to go!

We looked at:

◆ Transitions and applying easing techniques in more depth

◆ Understanding the difference between movieclips and sprite sheets

- Creating a game loop for display objects that have to be reloaded continuously on screen
- Applying force to a display object that propels it towards a designated direction
- Adding a collision event that switches from one display object to another

We have pushed through making another game in one whole chapter! Working in Corona SDK is so simple and fast to learn. It doesn't even require thousands of lines of code to create a simple game.

In the next chapter, we'll be learning another vital element in creating games, sound effects, and music! You're in for a treat.

6
Playing Sounds and Music

We hear sound effects and music in almost every type of media we encounter daily. Many notable games such as PAC-MAN, Angry Birds, and Fruit Ninja can be recognized just by their theme music or sound effects alone. Aside from the visual imagery we see in games, sounds help impact the mood conveyed in the storyline and/or during game play. Quality sound effects and music that pertain to the theme of your game helps to give your audience a realistic feel to the experience.

In this chapter, you will learn how to apply sound effects and music that can be added to your applications. We have the visual appeal down from creating Breakout and Panda Star Catcher in the previous chapters. Now let's enhance the sensory experience with our ears!

The main points we'll be going over are:

- Loading, playing, and looping audio
- Understanding how to play, pause, resume, rewind, and stop
- Memory management (disposing audio)
- Volume control
- Performance and encoding tips

Let's create some more magic!

Corona Audio System

The Corona Audio System has advanced **OpenAL (Open Audio Library)** features. OpenAL is designed for efficient rendering of multichannel three-dimensional positional audio. The general functionality of OpenAL is encoded in source objects, audio buffers, and a single listener. A source object contains a pointer to a buffer, the velocity, position and direction of the sound, and the intensity of the sound. Buffers contain audio data in PCM format, either 8 or 16-bit, in either mono or stereo format. The listener object contains the velocity, position and direction of the listener, and the general gain applied to all sound.

 For more information on the Corona Audio System you can go to: `http://developer.anscamobile.com/partner/audionotes`. General information on OpenAL can be found at: `http://www.openal.com.`.

Sound formats

The following are sound formats that are compatible with iOS and Android platforms:

- All platforms support 16-bit, little endian, linear, `.wav` files
- The iOS and Mac simulator support `.mp3`, `.caf`, and `.aac`
- The Windows simulator supports `.mp3` and `.wav`
- Android supports `.mp3` and `.ogg` formats

Sound filename limitations on Android

File extensions are ignored when building in Android, so files are considered the same regardless of extension. The workaround for the mean time is to change the filenames to differentiate file extensions. See the following examples:

- `tap_aac.aac`
- `tap_aif.aif`
- `tap_caf.caf`
- `tap_mp3.mp3`
- `tap_ogg.ogg`

Mono sounds at their best

Using mono sounds take half the amount of memory than stereo sounds. Since the Corona Audio System uses OpenAL, it will only apply spatialized/3D effects to mono sounds. OpenAL does not apply 3D effects to stereo samples.

Maximum number of simultaneous channels

The maximum number of channels that can be run is 32. This allows up to 32 distinct sounds to be played simultaneously. The API to see the resulting number of channels in your code is:

```
audio.totalChannels
```

Time to play

Audio can be loaded in two different ways as follows:

- ◆ `loadSound()` preloads an entire sound into memory
- ◆ `loadStream()` prepares the sound to be played by reading small chunks at a time to save memory

audio.loadSound()

Loads an entire file completely into memory and returns a reference to the audio data. Files that are loaded completely into memory can be reused, played, and shared simultaneously on multiple channels so you only need to load one instance of the file. Sounds that you would use as sound effects in your game would fit in this category.

Syntax:

```
audio.loadSound(audiofileName [, baseDir ])
```

Parameters:

- ◆ `audiofileName` - Specifies the name of the audio file you want to load. Supported file formats are determined by the platform you are running the audio file on.
- ◆ `baseDir` - By default, sound files are expected to be in the application resources directory. If the sound file is in the application documents directory, use `system.DocumentsDirectory`.

Example:

- ◆ `tapSound = audio.loadSound("tap.wav")`
- ◆ `smokeSound = audio.loadSound("smoke.mp3")`

audio.loadStream()

This loads a file to be read as a stream. Streamed files are read in small chunks at a time to minimize memory use. Files that are large in size and have a long duration are intended for this. These files cannot be shared simultaneously across multiple channels. If need be, you must load multiple instances of the file.

Syntax:

```
audio.loadStream(audioFileName [, baseDir ])
```

Parameters:

◆ `audiofileName` - Specifies the name of the audio file you want to load. Supported file formats are determined by the platform you are running the audio file on.

◆ `baseDir` - By default, sound files are expected to be in the application resources directory. If the sound file is in the application documents directory, use `system. DocumentsDirectory`.

Example:

◆ `music1 = audio.loadStream("song1.mp3")`

◆ `music2 = audio.loadStream("song2.wav")`

audio.play()

Plays the audio specified by the audio handle on a channel. If a channel is not specified, an available channel will be automatically chosen for you.

Syntax:

```
audio.play(audioHandle [, {[channel=c] [, loops=1] [, duration=d] [,
fadein=f] [, onComplete=o] }])
```

Parameters:

◆ `audioHandle` - This is the audio data you want to play.

◆ `channel` - The channel number you want to play on. Channel number 1 to the maximun number of channels, which is 32, are valid channels. Specify 0 or omit this parameter to have a channel automatically picked for you.

◆ `loops` - The number of times you want the audio to loop. 0 means the audio will loop 0 times which means that the sound will play once and not loop. Passing -1 will tell the system to infinitely loop the sample.

◆ `duration` - In milliseconds, this will cause the system to play the audio for the specified amount of time.

◆ `fadein` - In milliseconds, this will start playing a sound at the minimum channel volume and transition to the normal channel volume over the specified number of milliseconds.

◆ `onComplete` - A callback function you want to be called when playback ends. The `onComplete` callback function passes back an event parameter.

Example:

```
backgroundMusic = audio.loadStream("backgroundMusic.mp3")
backgroundMusicChannel = audio.play( backgroundMusic, { channel=1,
loops=-1, fadein=5000 })
-- play the background music on channel 1, loop infinitely, and fadein
over 5 seconds
```

Looping

Highly compressed formats like mp3, aac, ogg vorbis, can remove samples at the end of an audio sample and possibly break a clip that is looped correctly. If you experience gaps in looping playback, try using WAV (compatible with iOS and Android) and make sure your lead-in and ending points are clean.

Simultaneous playback

Sounds loaded via `loadSound()` can be played back simultaneously on multiple channels. For example, you can load a sound effect like so:

```
bellSound = audio.loadSound("bell.wav")
```

If you want to make a variety of bell sounds occur for multiple objects, you can. The audio engine is highly optimized to handle this case. Call `audio.play()` using that same handle as many times as you need it (up to the maximum number of channels).

```
audio.play(bellSound)
audio.play(bellSound)
audio.play(bellSound)
```

Time for action – playing audio

We're going to listen to how sound effects and music are implemented in Corona to get an idea of how it really works:

1. Create a new project folder on your desktop called `Playing Audio`.

2. In the `Chapter 6 Resources` folder, copy the `ring.wav` and `song1.mp3` sound files into your project folder and create a new `main.lua` file. You can download the project files accompanying this book from the Packt website.

3. Preload the following audio with `loadSound()` and `loadStream()`:

```
ringSound = audio.loadSound("ring.wav")
backgroundSound = audio.loadStream("song1.mp3")
```

4. Play `backgroundSound` by setting it to channel 1, loop it infinitely, and fade in after for 3 seconds:

```
mySong = audio.play(backgroundSound, {channel=1, loops=-1,
fadein=3000})
```

5. Add in `ringSound` and have it played once:

```
myRingSound = audio.play(ringSound)
```

6. Save and run the project in the Corona simulator to hear the results.

What Just Happened?

For audio that is merely a short sound effect, we used `audio.loadSound()` to prepare the sound. For audio that is large in size or long in duration, `audio.loadStream()` is used.

The `backgroundSound` file is set to channel 1 and fades in at 3 seconds when it starts playing. `loops = -1` means that the file loops infinitely from beginning to end.

Have a go hero – repeating audio with delay

As you can see, loading and playing audio is really simple. It only takes 2 lines of code to play a simple sound. Let's see if you can take it up a notch.

Use the `ring.wav` file and load it through `loadSound()`. Create a function that plays the audio. Play the sound five times at an interval of 2 seconds.

Time to take control

We have the ability to control our sounds now that we can have them play in the simulator. If you think back to the days of cassette tape players, they had the ability to use functions such as pause, stop, and rewind. Corona's audio API library can do just that.

audio.stop()

Stops playback on a channel and clears the channel so it can be played again.

Syntax:

```
audio.stop([channel])
```

or:

```
audio.stop([{channel = c}])
```

Parameters:

- ◆ Having no parameters stops all active channels.
- ◆ `channel` - The channel to stop. Specifying 0 stops all channels.

audio.pause()

This pauses playback on a channel and has no effect on channels that aren't playing.

Syntax:

```
audio.pause([channel])
```

or:

```
audio.pause([{channel = c}])
```

Parameters:

- ◆ Having no parameters pauses all active channels.
- ◆ `channel` - The channel to pause. Specifying 0 pauses all channels.

audio.resume()

This resumes playback on a channel that is paused. It has no effect on channels that aren't paused.

Syntax:

```
audio.pause([channel])
```

or:

```
audio.pause([{channel = c}])
```

Parameters:

- ◆ Having no parameters resumes all paused channels.
- ◆ `channel` - The channel to resume. Specifying 0 resumes all channels.

audio.rewind()

This rewinds audio to the beginning position on either an active channel or directly on the audio handle.

Syntax:

```
audio.rewind([, audioHandle ] [, {channel=c} ])
```

Parameters:

◆ `audioHandle` - The audio handle of the data you want to rewind. Best for audio loaded with `audio.loadStream()`. Don't try using this with the channel parameter in the same call.

◆ `channel` - The channel you want the rewind operation to apply to. Best for audio loaded with `audio.loadSound()`. Don't try using this with the `audioHandle` parameter in the same call.

Time for action – controlling audio

Let's simulate our own little music player by creating user interface buttons that will control the audio calls:

1. In the `Chapter 6` folder, copy the `Controlling Audio` project folder to your desktop. You will notice several art assets, a `ui.lua` library and a `song2.mp3` file inside. You can download the project files accompanying this book from the Packt website:

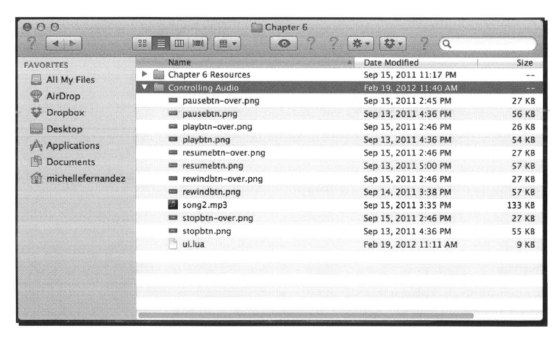

2. In the same project folder, create a brand new `main.lua` file.

3. Load the audio file via `loadStream()`, name it `backgroundSound`, and call the UI library. Also add in a local variable called `myMusic`:

```
local ui = require("ui")

local backgroundSound = audio.loadStream("song2.mp3")

local myMusic
```

4. Create a local function called `onPlayTouch()` with an event parameter to play the audio file. Add an `if` statement that contains `event.phase == "release"`, so that the music starts playing upon button release. Apply the `playBtn` display object as a new UI button:

```
local onPlayTouch = function( event )
        if event.phase == "release" then
                myMusic = audio.play(backgroundSound, {channel=1,
loops=-1})
        end
end

playBtn = ui.newButton{
        defaultSrc = "playbtn.png",
        defaultX = 100,
        defaultY = 50,
        overSrc = "playbtn-over.png",
        overX = 100,
        overY = 50,
        onEvent = onPlayTouch,
        id = "PlayButton",
        text = "",
        font = "Helvetica",
        textColor = {255, 255, 255, 255},
        size = 16,
        emboss = false
}

playBtn.x = 160; playBtn.y = 100
```

5. Create a local function called onPauseTouch() with an event parameter to pause the audio file. Add an if statement when event.phase == "release", so that the music pauses. Apply the pauseBtn display object as a new UI button:

```
local onPauseTouch = function(event)
        if event.phase == "release" then
                myMusic = audio.pause(backgroundSound)
                print("pause")
        end
end

pauseBtn = ui.newButton{
        defaultSrc = "pausebtn.png",
        defaultX = 100,
        defaultY = 50,
        overSrc = "pausebtn-over.png",
        overX = 100,
        overY = 50,
        onEvent = onPauseTouch,
        id = "PauseButton",
        text = "",
        font = "Helvetica",
        textColor = {255, 255, 255, 255},
        size = 16,
        emboss = false
}

pauseBtn.x = 160; pauseBtn.y = 160
```

6. Add a local function called onResumeTouch() with an event parameter to resume the audio file. Add an if statement when event.phase == "release", so that the music resumes. Apply the resumeBtn display object as a new UI button:

```
local onResumeTouch = function(event)
        if event.phase == "release" then
                myMusic = audio.resume(backgroundSound)
                print("resume")
        end
end

resumeBtn = ui.newButton{
        defaultSrc = "resumebtn.png",
        defaultX = 100,
```

```
        defaultY = 50,
        overSrc = "resumebtn-over.png",
        overX = 100,
        overY = 50,
        onEvent = onResumeTouch,
        id = "ResumeButton",
        text = "",
        font = "Helvetica",
        textColor = {255, 255, 255, 255},
        size = 16,
        emboss = false
}

resumeBtn.x = 160; resumeBtn.y = 220
```

7. Add a local function called `onStopTouch()` with an event parameter to stop the audio file. Create an `if` statement when `event.phase == "release"`, so that the music stops. Apply the `stopBtn` display object as a new UI button:

```
local onStopTouch = function(event)
        if event.phase == "release" then
                myMusic = audio.stop(backgroundSound)
                print("stop")

        end
end

stopBtn = ui.newButton{
        defaultSrc = "stopbtn.png",
        defaultX = 100,
        defaultY = 50,
        overSrc = "stopbtn-over.png",
        overX = 100,
        overY = 50,
        onEvent = onStopTouch,
        id = "StopButton",
        text = "",
        font = "Helvetica",
        textColor = { 255, 255, 255, 255 },
        size = 16,
        emboss = false
}

stopBtn.x = 160; stopBtn.y = 280
```

8. Add a local function called `onRewindTouch()` with an `event` parameter to rewind the audio file. Create an `if` statement when `event.phase == "release"`, that the music rewinds to the beginning of the track. Apply the `rewindBtn` display object as a new UI button:

```
local onRewindTouch = function(event)
      if event.phase == "release" then
            myMusic = audio.rewind(backgroundSound)
            print("rewind")
      end
end

rewindBtn = ui.newButton{
      defaultSrc = "rewindbtn.png",
      defaultX = 100,
      defaultY = 50,
      overSrc = "rewindbtn-over.png",
      overX = 100,
      overY = 50,
      onEvent = onRewindTouch,
      id = "RewindButton",
      text = "",
      font = "Helvetica",
      textColor = { 255, 255, 255, 255 },
      size = 16,
      emboss = false
}

rewindBtn.x = 160; rewindBtn.y = 340
```

9. Save your project and run it in the simulator. You now have created a functional media player!

What Just Happened?

We added a UI library for our user interface buttons by calling `require("ui")`. This produces the "on press" look when a button has been pushed down on.

A variety of functions were created to run each button:

◆ `onPlayTouch()` **calls out** `myMusic = audio.play(backgroundSound, {channel=1, loops=-1})` **when the event is triggered by the user pressing the button**

◆ `onPauseTouch()` **calls out** `myMusic = audio.pause(backgroundSound)` **to pause the song when the button is pressed**

- ◆ `onResumeTouch()` **calls out** `myMusic = audio.resume(backgroundSound)` to resume the song if it has been paused

- ◆ `onStopTouch()` **calls out** `myMusic = audio.stop(backgroundSound)` **if the** song is currently playing and will stop the audio

- ◆ `onRewindTouch()` **calls out** `myMusic = audio.rewind(backgroundSound)` to rewind the song to the beginning of the track

 When a song is paused, it resumes only by pressing the **Resume** button. The **Play** button will have no effect when the **Pause** button is pressed.

Memory management

It is important to call `audio.dispose()` on your loaded audio when you are completely done with the audio file. Doing so allows you to recover the memory.

audio.dispose()

Releases audio memory associated with the handle.

Syntax:

```
audio.dispose(audioHandle)
```

Parameters:

`audioHandle` - **The handle returned by the** `audio.loadSound()` **or** `audio.loadStream()` **functions that you want to free.**

 You must not use the handle once the memory is freed. The audio should not be playing or paused on any channel when you try to free it.

Example:

```
mySound = audio.loadSound("sound1.wav")
myMusic = audio.loadStream("music.mp3")

audio.dispose(mySound)
audio.dispose(myMusic)

mySound = nil
myMusic = nil
```

Have a go hero – disposing audio

You have just learned how to dispose audio files properly to recover memory in your application. Try the following:

1. Load your audio file and have it played over a set duration. Create a function that will dispose of the file when calling an `onComplete` command.

2. In the `Controlling Audio` project file, dispose of the audio in the `onStopTouch()` function.

Alterations to audio

The audio system also has the ability to alter the minimum and maximum states of audio volume as well as audio fades when needed in your application.

Volume control

The volume of audio can be set with values ranging from 0 to 1.0. This setting can be adjusted at any time before or during the extended sound playback.

audio.setVolume()

Syntax:

```
audio.setVolume( volume [, {[channel=c]} ] )
```

Parameters:

- `volume` - The new volume level you want to apply. Valid numbers range from 0.0 to 1.0, where 1.0 is the maximum volume value. Default volume is based on your device ringer volume and will vary.

- `channel` - The channel number you want to set the volume on. Channel number 1 to the maximum number of channels. Specify 0 to apply the volume to all the channels. Omitting this parameter entirely sets the master volume, which is different than the channel volume.

Example:

- `audio.setVolume(0.75) -- set master volume`
- `audio.setVolume(0.5, {channel=2}) -- set volume on channel 2`

audio.setMinVolume()

Clamps the minimum volume to the set value. Any volumes that go below the minimum volume will be played at the minimum volume level.

Syntax:

```
audio.setMinVolume(volume, {channel=c})
```

Parameters:

- `volume` - The new minimum volume level you want to apply. Valid numbers range from 0.0 to 1.0, where 1.0 is the maximum volume value.

- `channel` - The channel number you want to set the minimum volume on. Channel number 1 to the minimum number of channels are valid channels. Specify 0 to apply the minimum volume to all the channels.

Example:

```
audio.setMinVolume(0.10, {channel=1}) -- set the min volume on
channel 1
```

audio.setMaxVolume()

Clamps the maximum volume to the set value. Any volumes that exceed the maximum volume will be played at the maximum volume level.

Syntax:

```
audio.setMaxVolume(volume, {channel=c})
```

Parameters:

- `volume` - The new maximum volume level you want to apply. Valid numbers range from 0.0 to 1.0, where 1.0 is the maximum value.

- `channel` - The channel number you want to set the maximum volume on. 1 to the maximum number of channels are valid channels. Specify 0 to apply the maximum volume to all the channels.

Example:

```
audio.setMaxVolume(0.90, {channel=1}) -- set the max volume on
channel 1
```

audio.getVolume()

This gets the volume either for a specific channel or gets the master volume.

Syntax:

```
audio.getVolume([{[channel=c]}])
```

Parameters:

`channel` - The channel number you want to get the volume on. There can be a maximum number of 32 channels that are valid. Specifying 0 will return the average volume across all channels. Omitting this parameter entirely gets the master volume, which is different than the channel volume.

Example:

- ◆ `masterVolume = audio.getVolume() -- get the master volume`
- ◆ `channel1Volume = audio.getVolume({channel=1}) -- get the volume on channel 1`

audio.getMinVolume()

This gets the minimum volume for a specific channel.

Syntax:

```
audio.getMinVolume({channel=c})
```

Parameters:

`channel` - The channel number you want to get the minimum volume on. There can be a maximum number of 32 channels that are valid. Specifying 0 will return the average minimum volume across all channels.

Example:

```
channel1MinVolume = audio.getMinVolume({channel=1}) -- get the min
volume on channel 1
```

audio.getMaxVolume()

This gets the maximum volume for a specific channel.

Syntax:

```
audio.getMaxVolume({channel=c})
```

Parameters:

`channel` - The channel number you want to get the maximum volume on. There can be a maximum number of 32 channels that are valid. Specifying 0 will return the average volume across all channels.

Example:

```
channel1MaxVolume = audio.getMaxVolume({channel=1}) -- get the max
volume on channel 1
```

Fading audio

You can fade in volume at the time any audio starts playing, but there are other ways to control it as well.

audio.fade()

This fades a playing sound in a specified amount to a specified volume. The audio will continue playing after the fade completes.

Syntax:

```
audio.fade([{ [channel=c] [, time=t] [, volume=v] }])
```

Parameters:

♦   `channel` - The channel number you want to fade on. 1 to the maximum number of channels are valid channels. Specify 0 to apply fade to all the channels.

♦   `time` - The amount of time from now that you want the audio to fade over and stop. Omitting this parameter invokes a default fade time, which is 1000 milliseconds.

♦   `volume` - The target volume you want to change the fade to. Valid numbers are 0.0 to 1.0 where 1.0 is the maximum volume. If this parameter is omitted, the default value is 0.0.

Example:

```
audio.fade({channel=1, time=3000, volume=0.5})
```

audio.fadeOut()

This stops playing sound in a specified amount of time and fades to the minimum volume. The audio will stop at the end of the time and the channel will be freed.

Syntax:

```
audio.fadeOut([{ [channel=c] [, time=t] }])
```

Parameters:

- ◆ `channel` - The channel number you want to fade out on. 1 to the maximum number of channels are valid channels. Specify 0 to apply `fadeOut` to all the channels.

- ◆ `time` - The amount of time from now that you want the audio to fade out over and stop. Omitting this parameter invokes a default fade out time, which is 1000 milliseconds.

Example:

```
audio.fadeOut({ channel=1, time=5000 })
```

Performance tips

The following are some helpful notes when creating good quality audio for your games.

Pre-loading phase

It is best to pre-load all your files at the startup of your application. While `loadStream()` is generally fast, `loadSound()` may take awhile since it must load and decode the entire file the instant it needs to be used. Generally, you don't want to be calling `loadSound()` in the parts of your app where users expect it to be running smoothly when events occur, such as during gameplay.

audioPlayFrequency

In your `config.lua` file, you may specify a field called `audioPlayFrequency`.

```
application =
{
  content =
  {
    width = 320,
    height = 480,
    scale = "letterbox",
    audioPlayFrequency = 22050
  },
}
```

This tells the OpenAL system what sample rate to mix and playback at. For best results, set this no higher than you actually need. So if you never need better than 22050 Hz playback, set this to 22050. It produces quality speech recordings or middle-quality recordings of music. If you really do need high quality, then set this to 44100 to produce audio CD quality at playback.

It is best to have all your audio files encoded at the same frequency when you have this set. Supported values are 11025, 22050, and 44100.

Patents and royalties

For highly compressed formats, such as MP3 and AAC, AAC is the better option. AAC is the official successor to MP3 by the MPEG group. MP3 has patent and royalty issues you may need to concern yourself with if you distribute anything yourself. You may need to consult your lawyers for guidance. When AAC was ratified, it was agreed there would be no royalties required for distribution. If you prefer to use AAC over MP3, here's a tutorial on how to convert MP3s to AAC or any file format of your preference on the Apple website: `http://support.apple.com/kb/ht1550`.

Ogg Vorbis is a royalty free and patent free format. However, this is not supported on iOS devices.

More information on audio formats can be found at: `http://www.nch.com.au/acm/formats.html`. Ray Wenderlich, a mobile developer also has a tutorial available based on file and data formats for audio at: `http://www.raywenderlich.com/204/audio-101-for-iphone-developers-file-and-data-formats`.

Pop quiz – all about audio

1. What is the proper way to clear audio files from memory?

    a. `audio.pause()`

    b. `audio.stop()`

    c. `audio.dispose()`

    d. `audio.fadeOut()`

2. How many channels of audio can be played simultaneously in an application?

    a. 10

    b. 18

    c. 25

    d. 32

3. How do you make your audio file loop infinitely?

    a. loops = -1

    b. loops = 0

    c. loops = 1

    d. None of the above

Summary

We're now caught up on understanding the important aspects of using audio files in the Corona SDK. Now you can go off and add your own sound effects and music to your games or even add them to any of the samples we have made in the previous chapters. In doing so, you add another layer to the user experience that will draw players into the environment you created.

Up until now, you have learned how to:

- Pre-load and play sound effects and music using `loadSound()` and `loadStream()`
- Control audio functions that pause, resume, stop, and rewind a music track under the Audio System API
- Dispose audio from memory when it is no longer in use
- Adjust the volume in your audio files

In the next chapter, we will be combining everything we have learned thus far into creating our final game in this book. We'll also be going over other ways to implement physical objects and collision mechanics that are popular in mobile games in the market to date. More exciting information to learn awaits us. Let's power through!

Physics: Falling Objects

There are many variations on how to incorporate the physics engine using display objects. So far we have worked with removing objects with collisions, moving objects through the stage area, and launching objects by applying force against gravity, just to name a few. Now we're going to explore another mechanism that allows gravity to control the environment. The next game we'll be creating deals with falling physical objects.

Points that will be discussed in this chapter are:

- ◆ Working with more physics bodies
- ◆ Customizing the body construction
- ◆ Tracking the objects caught
- ◆ Working with post-collisions
- ◆ Creating falling objects

Here's to creating another fun simple game in this segment. Let's get cracking!

Creating our new game: Egg Drop

Every step taken so far has taught us more about game development on the iOS/Android devices. In this new segment, our game will include sound effects, which will enhance the sensory experience in our games.

 Be sure that you are using the latest stable build of Corona SDK Version 2011.704.

The new game we will be creating is called **Egg Drop**. The player controls the main character, which is a lumberjack with a frying pan. During gameplay, eggs start falling from the sky and it is the lumberjack's job to catch the eggs in his frying pan and not let them hit the ground. Every egg caught earns 500 points. The player starts with 3 lives. When an egg fails to hit the frying pan and hits the ground, a life is lost. When all 3 lives are gone, the game is over.

When starting the new game project, be sure to grab the `Egg Drop` file from the `Chapter 7` folder. You can download the project files accompanying this book from the Packt website `www.packt.com`. It contains all the necessary files that are built-out for you, such as the `build.settings`, `config.lua`, `ui.lua`, audio files, and art assets needed for the game. You'll then have to create a brand new `main.lua` file in the project folder before you start coding.

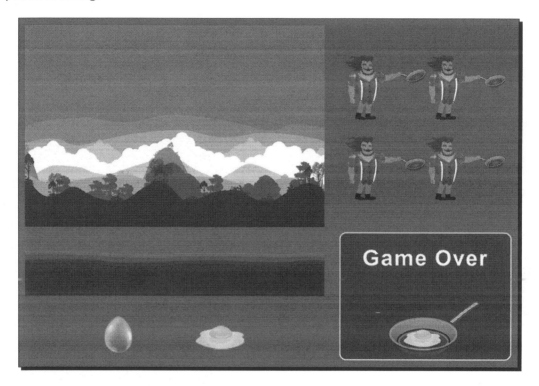

Starting variables

This will be our first full game setup filled with notable Corona SDK features. We'll be combining our base knowledge of what we learned so far with variables, display objects, the physics engine, touch/accelerometer events, and audio. Many of Corona's APIs are easy to use and understand. This shows the fast learning curve with Corona just by having basic to no knowledge of programming.

Time for action – setting up the variables

Let's get started with introducing the variables we'll be using to create our game. There will be a combination of display objects, integers to keep count, and pre-loading the main sound effects during gameplay.

1. Hide the status bar and add in `display.newGroup()` **called** `gameGroup`.

```
display.setStatusBar( display.HiddenStatusBar )
local gameGroup = display.newGroup()
```

2. Include the external modules in the game.

```
local sprite = require "sprite"
local physics = require "physics"
local ui = require "ui"
```

3. Add in the display objects.

```
local background
local ground
local charObject
local friedEgg
local scoreText
local eggText
local livesText
local shade
local gameOverScreen
```

4. Add in the variables.

```
local gameIsActive = false
local startDrop
local gameLives = 3
local gameScore = 0
local eggCount = 0
local mRand = math.random
```

5. Create the egg boundaries and density.

```
local eggDensity = 1.0
local eggShape = { -12,-13, 12,-13, 12,13, -12,13 }
local panShape = { 15,-13, 65,-13, 65,13, 15,13 }
```

6. Set up the accelerometer and audio.

```
system.setAccelerometerInterval( 100 )
local eggCaughtSound = audio.loadSound( "friedEgg.wav" )
local gameOverSound = audio.loadSound( "gameover.wav" )
```

What just happened?

We have continued creating a similar setup of our variables like in the Panda Star Catcher game. It's more efficient to organize them by separating groups, display objects, audio, and so on.

Many of the variables displayed have designated integers that fulfill the goals of gameplay. This includes values such as gameLives = 3 and eggCount = 0.

Controlling the main character

Accelerometer events work best with the main scope of the game. It enables you to view the full real estate of the game environment without having to interact with touches on the screen. Necessary touch events would make sense for user interface buttons such as pause, menu, play, and so on.

Time for action – moving the character

Eggs will be falling in all different areas of the screen from the sky. Let's prepare our main character to move through all potential areas on the screen.

1. Set up a new local function called moveChar() with an event parameter.

    ```
    local moveChar = function(event)
    ```

2. Add in the accelerometer movement for the character.

    ```
    charObject.x = display.contentCenterX -
        (display.contentCenterX * (event.yGravity * 3))
    ```

3. Create character boundaries where they moves on the screen. This enables the character to stay within the game screen and not go past the offscreen boundaries.

    ```
    if((charObject.x - charObject.width * 0.5) < 0) then
      charObject.x = charObject.width * 0.5
    elseif((charObject.x + charObject.width * 0.5) >
          display.contentWidth) then
      charObject.x = display.contentWidth - charObject.width *
        0.5
    end
    end
    ```

What just happened?

To make the accelerometer movement work with a device, we have to use yGravity.

 Accelerometer events are based on portrait scale when xGravity and yGravity are used accordingly. When display objects are designated for landscape mode, xGravity and yGravity values are switched to compensate for the events to work properly.

You will notice that the code in step 3 keeps the charObject from going past any wall border boundaries.

Have a go hero – adding touch events

The character is currently controlled by the accelerometer. Another option to control the character is through a touch event. Try replacing the event listener with "touch" and using event parameters so the touch event works properly.

If you remember how we incorporated the paddle movement with Breakout in *Chapter 3, Building our First Game: Breakout* and *Chapter 4, Game Controls* for the simulator, it should be very similar.

Updating the score

When the score is updated, it refers to our text display objects and translates the value from the number into a string.

For example:

```
gameScore = 100
scoreText = display.newText( "Score: " .. gameScore, 0, 0, "Arial",
           45 )
scoreText:setTextColor( 255, 255, 255, 255 )
scoreText.x = 160; scoreText.y = 100
```

In the previous example, you will notice that we have set a values of 100 to gameScore. In the following lines for scoreText, the gameScore is used to concatenate the string, "Score: " and the value of gameScore. Doing so displays the value of gameScore in a string format by scoreText.

Time for action – setting the score

Who doesn't like some friendly competition? We're familiar with scoreboards from the games we've made in the previous chapters. So we are no strangers on how to track the score.

1. Create a local function called `setScore()` with a parameter called `scoreNum`.

```
local setScore = function( scoreNum )
```

2. Set variables to count the score.

```
local newScore = scoreNum
gameScore = newScore
if gameScore < 0 then gameScore = 0; end
```

3. Have the score updated when points are earned in gameplay and close the function.

```
scoreText.text = "Score: " .. gameScore
scoreText.xScale = 0.5; scoreText.yScale = 0.5
scoreText.x = (scoreText.contentWidth * 0.5) + 15
scoreText.y = 15
end
```

What just happened?

When `setScore(scoreNum)` is called within any function, it will refer to all methods using the variable `gameScore`. Assuming that the `gameScore = 0` at the start of the application, the value increments to what the `gameScore` is set to.

In `scoreText.text = "Score: " .. gameScore`, `"Score: "` is the string that displays on the device during gameplay. `gameScore` takes the current value given to the variable and displays it as a string.

Displaying the environment

A logical setting for your display objects helps the player envision the relationship between the main character and the environment. Since our main character is a lumberjack, it would make sense to have him set in a forest or an area focused entirely on nature.

Time for action – drawing the background

In this section, we'll be filling the screen with our environment display objects. This includes our background and ground objects respectively and adding physical elements to our ground so that we can designate collision events for it.

1. Create a local function called `drawBackground()`.

```
local drawBackground = function()
```

2. Add in the background image.

```
background = display.newImageRect( "bg.png", 480, 320 )
background.x = 240; background.y = 160
gameGroup:insert( background )
```

3. Add in the ground elements and create the ground physical boundary. Close the function.

```
ground = display.newImageRect( "grass.png", 480, 75 )
ground.x = 240; ground.y = 325
ground.myName = "ground"
local groundShape = { -285,-18, 285,-18, 285,18, -285,18 }
physics.addBody( ground, "static", { density=1.0, bounce=0,
   friction=0.5, shape=groundShape } )
gameGroup:insert( ground )
end
```

What just happened?

The `background` and `ground` display objects are placed in the function called `drawBackground()`. The function `display.newImageRect()` is used since we are incorporating **Dynamic Scaling** on some of our images. The `ground` display object has a customized physical shape that is not of the same size as the original display object.

Our `background` object is centered to the dimensions of the device screen area and inserted into `gameGroup`.

The `ground` display object is placed near the bottom of the display area. It is assigned a name through `ground.myName = "ground"`. We'll be using the name `"ground"` later on for determining collision events. A customized physical boundary is made for ground through `groundShape`. This allows the body of the ground to affect the assigned dimensions of the display object. When `physics.addBody()` is initialized, we use `groundShape` as the shape parameter. Next, `ground` is set to `gameGroup` as well.

Displaying the heads-up display

In gaming, the **heads-up display (HUD)** is the method used to relay information visually to the player. In many games, the common features displayed are health/lives, time, weapons, menus, maps, and so on. This keeps your player on alert to what is currently happening during gameplay. When it comes to tracking your lives, you want to be informed how many are left before your character runs out of chances to continue playing and the game ends.

Time for action – designing the HUD

While trying to make the player's gaming experience an enjoyable one, it's important that the information displayed is relevant to the game and placed strategically so it doesn't interfere with the main gaming area.

1. Create a new local function called `hud()`.

```
local hud = function()
```

2. Display the text for the eggs that are caught during gameplay.

```
eggText = display.newText( "Caught: " .. eggCount, 0, 0,
   "Arial", 45 )
eggText:setTextColor( 255, 255, 255, 255 )
eggText.xScale = 0.5; eggText.yScale = 0.5
eggText.x = (480 - (eggText.contentWidth * 0.5)) - 15
eggText.y = 305
gameGroup:insert( eggText )
```

3. Add in the text to track the lives.

```
livesText = display.newText( "Lives: " .. gameLives, 0, 0,
   "Arial", 45 )
livesText:setTextColor( 255, 255, 255, 255 )  --> white
livesText.xScale = 0.5; livesText.yScale = 0.5  --> for
   clear retina display text
livesText.x = (480 - (livesText.contentWidth * 0.5)) - 15
livesText.y = 15
gameGroup:insert( livesText )
```

4. Add in text for the score and close the function.

```
scoreText = display.newText( "Score: " .. gameScore, 0, 0,
   "Arial", 45 )
scoreText:setTextColor( 255, 255, 255, 255 )  --> white
scoreText.xScale = 0.5; scoreText.yScale = 0.5  --> for
   clear retina display text
scoreText.x = (scoreText.contentWidth * 0.5) + 15
scoreText.y = 15
gameGroup:insert( scoreText )
end
```

What just happened?

The `eggText` display object will be found near the bottom-right corner of the screen. It's still in view to the user while in gameplay and stays out of the main focus point at the same time. Notice that `eggText = display.newText( "Caught: " .. eggCount, 0, 0, "Arial", 45 )` will refer to `eggCount` when the value is updated.

The `livesText` display object setup is similar to `eggText`. It is placed in the top right-hand corner of the screen. The placement for this object is rather prominent because of its importance in the game. It's in an area that is noticeable from the background and allows the player to refer to during the game. `livesText` decrements the number when `gameLives` is updated.

The initial setup for `scoreText` starts in the `hud()` function. It is placed on the top left-hand corner of the screen, opposite from `livesText`.

Creating the game lives

If there are no consequences in a game, then there is no sense of urgency to complete the main objectives. To keep a player engaged during gameplay, introducing elements that add some challenging aspects will keep the competitiveness and excitement going. Adding consequences in a game creates tension for the player and gives them more motivation to stay alive.

Time for action – counting the lives

Tracking the lives left in the game keeps the player updated on how much sooner it will be until the game is over.

1. Set up the function called `livesCount()`.

```
local livesCount = function()
```

2. Display the text for lives every time the number is decremented.

```
gameLives = gameLives - 1
livesText.text = "Lives: " .. gameLives
livesText.xScale = 0.5; livesText.yScale = 0.5  --> for
  clear retina display text
livesText.x = (480 - (livesText.contentWidth * 0.5)) - 15
livesText.y = 15
print(gameLives .. " eggs left")
if gameLives < 1 then
  callGameOver()
end
end
```

What just happened?

`livesCount()` is a separate function that updates `gameLives`. It makes sure that you're aware that `gameLives = gameLives - 1`. This decreases the set value instantiated at the beginning of the code. When `gameLives` changes values, it displays the update through `livesText`. The `print` statement is used towards the end of the function to track the count in the terminal window.

When `gameLives < 1`, the `callGameOver()` function will be called, which will show the game over elements of the game.

Have a go hero – adding images for the game lives

Currently, the game uses display text on screen to show the count of how many lives are left during gameplay. A way to make the HUD display more appealing is by creating/adding small icons that correlate with the game such as eggs or a frying pan.

Three separate display objects need to be created and placed in an orderly fashion so that when a life is taken away, the alpha of the object is reduced to `0.5`.

A method needs to be created so that all the three display objects are affected when the game lives are reduced to `0`.

Introducing the main character

Our main character will be animated for every action applied during gameplay. We will also create a **complex body construction** since the focus on its collision points will be towards the object he is holding and not his entire body.

Complex body construction

It is also possible to construct a body from multiple elements. Each body element is specified as a separate polygon shape with its own physical properties.

Since collision polygons in **Box2D** must be convex, any game object with a concave shape must be constructed by appending multiple body elements.

The constructor for a complex body is the same as the simple polygon body constructor, except with more than one body element listed:

```
physics.addBody( displayObject, [bodyType,] bodyElement1,
    [bodyElement2, ...] )
```

Each body element may have its own physical properties, along with a shape definition for its collision boundaries. For example:

```
local hexagon = display.newImage("hexagon.png")
hexagon.x = hexagon.contentWidth
hexagon.y = hexagon.contentHeight
hexagonShape = { -20,-40, 20, -40, 40, 0, 20,40, -20,40, -40,0 }
physics.addBody( hexagon, "static", { density = 1.0, friction = 0.8,
    bounce = 0.3, shape=hexagonShape } )
```

As in simpler cases, the `bodyType` attribute is optional and will default to `"dynamic"` if not specified.

Time for action – creating the character

The main character was created with a sprite sheet and needs to be set up to view the animation it provides. Other display images that will make an appearance include a cracked egg when a collision to a physical object has been made.

1. Create a new local function called `createChar()`.

    ```
    local createChar = function()
    ```

2. Create the sprite sheet for the main character.

```
local characterSheet = sprite.newSpriteSheet
  ( "charSprite.png",128, 128 )
local spriteSet = sprite.newSpriteSet(characterSheet, 1, 4)
sprite.add( spriteSet, "move", 1, 4, 400, 0 )
charObject = sprite.newSprite( spriteSet )
charObject:prepare("move")
charObject:play()
```

3. Set the starting position and physical properties for the main character.

```
charObject.x = 240; charObject.y = 250
physics.addBody( charObject, "static", { density=1.0,
  bounce=0.4, friction=0.15, shape=panShape } )
charObject.rotation = 0
charObject.isHit = false
charObject.myName = "character"
```

4. Add in the transition image after the egg has made a collision.

```
friedEgg = display.newImageRect( "friedEgg.png", 40, 23 )
friedEgg.alpha = 1.0
friedEgg.isVisible = false
gameGroup:insert( charObject )
gameGroup:insert( friedEgg )
end
```

What just happened?

The sprite sheet being referred to is called `spriteSet` and takes the first 4 frames of animation from `"charSprite.png"`. We created an animation set through `sprite.add( spriteSet, "move", 1, 4, 400, 0 )`. Every time `"move"` is called, it starts the animation from frame 1 and plays 4 frames from the start at 400 milliseconds.

The main display object is called `charObject` that takes on the characteristics of `spriteSet`. When it calls `prepare("move")`, that animation sequence plays when the `play()` command is executed.

An important change to the physical body of the character is that its main collision point will be directed towards the frying pan used in the animation. Any collision detection on the character's body will not be read. The `charObject` is given a name called `"character"`, which will be used to detect the collision even with the falling egg.

We have also placed the fried egg in this function for preparation on the collision.

Adding post-collisions

We want to make sure that an event type occurs right after an object has interacted with another object. At the instance of a post-collision, we can confirm the collision force between two objects. This helps us determine that the object that is destroyed was completed with a set amount of force.

Collision handling

Be careful on how you handle the Box2D physics engine. It will crash during a collision if Corona code attempts to modify objects still involved in the collision, since Box2D is still working out iterated mathematics on them.

For crash-proof collision detection, do not have collisions occur immediately.

Do not modify/create/destroy physics objects during a collision in order to prevent crashing.

If you need to modify/create/destroy an object as a result of a collision, your collision handler should set a flag or add a time delay so the change can occur later with `timer.performWithDelay()`.

Body properties

Many of the native Box2D methods have been made into simpler dot properties for display objects. The following examples show that a body, `newBody`, has been created using one of the constructor methods.

body.isAwake

This is a Boolean for the current awake state. By default, all bodies automatically *go to sleep* when there is no interaction with them for a couple of seconds. Bodies stop simulating until some kind of collision or other interaction wakes them up.

```
newBody.isAwake = true
local object = newBody.isAwake
```

body.isBodyActive

This is a Boolean for the active state of a body. Inactive bodies are not destroyed, but they are removed from the simulation and cease to interact with other bodies.

```
newBody.isBodyActive = true
local object = newBody.isBodyActive
```

body.isBullet

This is a Boolean for a body that is treated like a *bullet*. Bullets are subject to continuous collision detection. The default is `false`.

```
newBody.isBullet = true
local object = newBody.isBullet
```

body.isSensor

This is a Boolean property that sets the `isSensor` property across all elements in the body. A sensor passes through other objects instead of bouncing off them, but detects some collision. This property acts across all body elements and will override any `isSensor` settings on the elements themselves.

```
newBody.isSensor = true
```

body.isSleepingAllowed

This is a Boolean for a body that is allowed to go to sleep. A body that is awake is useful in cases such as tilt-gravity since sleeping bodies do not respond to changes in global gravity. The default is `true`.

```
newBody.isSleepingAllowed = true
local object = newBody.isSleepingAllowed
```

body.isFixedRotation

This is a Boolean for a body whose rotation should be locked, even if the body is about to load or subjected to off-center forces. The default is `false`.

```
newBody.isFixedRotation = true
local object = newBody.isFixedRotation
```

body.angularVelocity

This is the value of the current rotational velocity in degrees per second.

```
newBody.angularVelocity = 50
local myVelocity = newBody.angularVelocity
```

body.linearDamping

This is the value for how much the linear motion of a body is damped. This is the rate of decrease of angular velocity over time. The default is `0`

```
newBody.linearDamping = 5
local object = newBody.linearDamping
```

body.angularDamping

The value for how much the rotation of a body should be damped. The default is `0`.

```
newBody.angularDamping = 5
local object = newBody.angularDamping
```

body.bodyType

This is a string value for the type of physical body being simulated. The available values are `"static"`, `"dynamic"`, and `"kinematic"`:

- `static` bodies don't move or interact with each other. Examples of static objects would include the ground or the walls of a maze.
- `dynamic` bodies are affected by gravity and collisions with other body types.
- `kinematic` objects are affected by forces but not by gravity. Bodies that are draggable objects should be set to `"kinematic"` for the duration of the drag event.

The default body type is `"dynamic"`.

```
newBody.bodyType = "kinematic"
local currentBodyType = newBody.bodyType
```

Time for action – creating the egg collision

We have handled collisions in the previous sample games we created. Handling post-collisions requires the introduction of force to execute the completion of a post-collision event.

1. Create a new local function called `onEggCollision()` with two parameters called `self` and `event`.

```
local onEggCollision = function( self, event )
```

2. Create an `if` statement when force is greater than 1 and `not self.isHit`. Add in the `eggCaughtSound` sound effect.

```
if event.force > 1 and not self.isHit then
    audio.play( eggCaughtSound )
```

3. Make `self` invisible and inactive and replace it with the `friedEgg` display object.

```
self.isHit = true
print( "Egg destroyed!")
self.isVisible = false
friedEgg.x = self.x; friedEgg.y = self.y
friedEgg.alpha = 0
friedEgg.isVisible = true
```

4. Create a function that transitions the `friedEgg` display object and makes it fade on the stage using the `onComplete` command.

```
local fadeEgg = function()
    transition.to( friedEgg, { time=500, alpha=0 } )
end
transition.to( friedEgg, { time=50, alpha=1.0,
    onComplete=fadeEgg } )
self.parent:remove( self )
self = nil
```

5. Using `if event.other.myName == "character"`, update the `eggCount` when the main character catches the eggs. Also update the `gameScore` by 500 points for every collision. If the egg hits the ground, use `elseif event.other.myName == "ground"` and decrement the lives using `livesCount()`.

```
if event.other.myName == "character" then
    eggCount = eggCount + 1
    eggText.text = "Caught: " .. eggCount
    eggText.xScale = 0.5; eggText.yScale = 0.5  --> for
        clear retina display text
```

```
        eggText.x = (480 - (eggText.contentWidth * 0.5)) - 15
        eggText.y = 305
        print("egg caught")
        local newScore = gameScore + 500
        setScore( newScore )
      elseif event.other.myName == "ground" then
        livesCount()
        print("ground hit")
      end
    end
  end
```

What just happened?

Using onEggCollision(self, event), we set up the function with the if statement for event.force > 1 and not self.isHit. When both statements return true, the sound effect for the egg plays. The initial egg falling from the sky is removed from the scene upon collision and replaced by the friedEgg display object in the same location using friedEgg.x = self.x; friedEgg.y = self.y.

The function fadeEgg() makes the newly replaced egg object appear in 50 milliseconds by transition.to(eggCrack, { time=50, alpha=1.0, onComplete=fadeCrack }) and then with the onComplete command, returns the object to an invisible state with transition.to(eggCrack, { time=500, alpha=0 }).

When the name "character" is called from event.other.myName, every collision is assigned to that name increments eggCount + 1. Therefore, the eggText is updated with eggCount value. setScore(newScore) increments the score by 500 with every collision made to "character". When a collision is made to "ground", the livesCount() function is called, which subtracts a life by 1.

Making the display objects fall

We're going to apply the main asset by learning how to add physical objects to the scene and have them fall in random areas in the game. The physics engine will take into account a dynamic physics body that we will create for the egg display object.

Time for action – adding the egg object

Imagine a world full of falling eggs. It's not entirely too realistic, but in this game, we're creating this element. At least we'll be making sure that the gravity and real-world physics will be applied.

1. Create a new local function called eggDrop().

   ```
   local eggDrop = function()
   ```

2. Add in the egg display object properties.

   ```
   local egg = display.newImageRect( "egg.png", 26, 30 )
   egg.x = 240 + mRand( 120 ); egg.y = -100
   egg.isHit = false
   physics.addBody( egg, "dynamic",{ density=eggDensity,
     bounce=0,friction=0.5, shape=eggShape } )
   egg.isFixedRotation = true
   gameGroup:insert( egg )
   ```

3. Add in the postCollision event for the egg display object.

   ```
   egg.postCollision = onEggCollision
   egg:addEventListener( "postCollision", egg )
   end
   ```

What just happened?

We have set the egg value for x to `240 + mRand( 120 )`. The `mRand` function equals to `math.random`, which will allow the egg to appear in randomized places in an area of `120` pixels starting at 50 in the x-direction.

It is vital to make sure `egg.isHit = false` for the collision event to apply correctly. The physics body is set to `"dynamic"` so it reacts to gravity and makes the object fall. There is a customized density and shape made for the egg that we created, which is already made at the beginning of the code.

The last important detail for the collision to work is adding egg to the `onEggCollision()` function with `egg.postCollision = onEggCollision` and then making the event listener use the `"postCollision"` event with `egg:addEventListener( "postCollision", egg )`.

Time for action – making the egg drop

We're going to execute the timer for the egg so they can start dropping them on the screen.

1. Create a local function called `eggTimer()` and use `timer.performWithDelay` to drop an egg every 1 second (`1000` milliseconds) repeatedly. Use `eggDrop()` to activate the drop.

```
local eggTimer = function()
  startDrop = timer.performWithDelay( 1000, eggDrop, 0 )
end
```

2. Within the first `if` statement in the `onEggCollision()` function, cancel the timer using the `timerID`, `startDrop`. Add the statement `if gameLives < 1` to stop the eggs from falling.

```
if gameLives < 1 then
  timer.cancel( startDrop )
  print("timer cancelled")
end
```

What just happened?

In order for the eggs to start dropping from the sky, we created a function called `eggTimer()`. It activates the `eggDrop()` function by letting an egg drop after `1000` milliseconds (1 second) every time infinitely using `startDrop = timer.performWithDelay( 1000, eggDrop, 0 )`.

Backtracking to `onEggCollision()`, we want to check that `gameLives` has reached less than 1. When this statement is true, the eggs will stop dropping. This is done by `timer.cancel( startDrop )`. `startDrop` is the `timerID` we set in `eggTimer()`.

Ending the gameplay

Every start of a game always has an ending. Whether it is a simple *You Win* or *You lose* or just a *Game Over* it gives closure for the player. It's important to notify a player of such events so that they can reflect on the achievements earned.

Time for action – calling game over

We are going to make sure that when a **Game Over** display screen pops up, any of our display objects currently in motion stop moving and the event listeners are deactivated. Aside from the visual display of our **Game Over** screen, we'll be adding a sound notification that will also help to trigger the event.

1. Create a new local function called `callGameOver()` and place it after the `setScore()` function and before the `drawBackground()` function.

```
local callGameOver = function()
```

2. Introduce the sound effects when the **Game Over** display pops up. Have `gameIsActive` set to `false` and pause the physics in the game.

```
audio.play( gameOverSound )
gameIsActive = false
physics.pause()
```

3. Create a shade that overlays over the current background.

```
shade = display.newRect( 0, 0, 570, 320 )
shade:setFillColor( 0, 0, 0, 255 )
shade.x = 240; shade.y = 160
shade.alpha = 0
```

4. Display the **Game Over** window and reiterate the final score.

```
gameOverScreen = display.newImageRect( "gameOver.png", 400,
  300 )
local newScore = gameScore
setScore( newScore )
gameOverScreen.x = 240; gameOverScreen.y = 160
gameOverScreen.alpha = 0
gameGroup:insert( shade )
gameGroup:insert( gameOverScreen )
transition.to( shade, { time=200, alpha=0.65 } )
transition.to( gameOverScreen, { time=500, alpha=1 } )
```

5. Have the **Score** displayed on the **Game Over** screen.

```
scoreText.isVisible = false
scoreText.text = "Score: " .. gameScore
scoreText.xScale = 0.5; scoreText.yScale = 0.5  --> for
  clear retina display text
scoreText.x = 240
scoreText.y = 160
scoreText:toFront()
timer.performWithDelay( 0,
  function() scoreText.isVisible = true; end, 1 )
end
```

What just happened?

Our `gameOver()` function triggers our `gameOverSound` sound effect that we pre-loaded at the beginning of our code. We made sure no events such as the motion from the accelerometer are disabled through `gameIsActive = false`.

The elements of our display objects appear at this point in time with `shade`, `gameOverScreen`, and `scoreText`.

If you notice, `scoreText` disappears when gameplay has ended by `scoreText. isVisible = false` and then reappears in a different area of the screen using `timer. performWithDelay( 0, function() scoreText.isVisible = true; end, 1 )`.

Starting the game

We're going to activate all the remaining functions and have them run accordingly.

Time for action – activating the game

With all the gameplay elements set in place, it is time to get the application started.

1. Create a new local function called `gameActivate()` and insert `gameIsActive = true`. Place the function above the `moveChar()` function.

```
local gameActivate = function()
  gameIsActive = true
end
```

2. Initialize all the game actions by making a new function called `gameStart()`.

```
local gameStart = function()
```

3. Start the physics property and set the gravity for the falling object.

```
physics.start( true )
physics.setGravity( 0, 9.8 )
```

4. Activate all the functions instantiated. Add an event listener for the `charObject` using the `"touch"` for the `moveChar()` function.

```
drawBackground()
createChar()
eggTimer()
hud()
gameActivate()
Runtime:addEventListener("accelerometer", moveChar)
end
```

5. Instantiate the `gameStart()` function and return the group `gameGroup`.

```
gameStart()
return gameGroup
```

What just happened?

If you remember, in the beginning of our code, we set `gameIsActive = false`. We then changed that status through the `gameActivate()` function and made `gameIsActive = true`. We made the `gameStart()` function apply all the initial gameplay elements. This included the start of the physics engine and gravity. At the same time, we took the remainder of all the functions and initialize them.

Once all the functions are activated, `gameGroup` needs to be returned so that all the display objects appear during the gameplay.

To make sure that your physical object boundaries for your display objects are in the right place, use `physics.setDrawMode( "hybrid" )` in the `gameStart()` function.

Pop quiz – animating the graphics

1. What retrieves or sets the text string of a text object?

    a. `object.text`

    b. `object.size`

    c. `object:setTextColor()`

    d. None of the above

2. What function converts any argument into a string?

    a. `tonumber()`

    b. `print()`

    c. `tostring()`

    d. `nil`

3. What body type is affected by gravity and collisions with other body types?

    a. Dynamic

    b. Kinematic

    c. Static

    d. None of the above

Summary

The gameplay construction of our application is now completed. Now that we're familiar with a variety of ways to use the physics engine, it goes to show the ease of using Box2D and designing other games that involve physics bodies.

We have a better idea of:

◆ Applying the uses of dynamic and static physics bodies

◆ Constructing a customized shape for the physical properties of our display objects

◆ Tracking the number of objects caught using values from variables that are given

◆ Using post-collisions to switch out images

In the next chapter, we will complete the gaming experience by creating versatile menu screens using **Storyboard API**. We will also learn how to add the pause action, save high scores, and understand more about data saving and unloading files.

Using Corona SDK has helped us design and develop games in a minimal amount of time. Let us continue adding the final touches to our game!

8
Operation Storyboard

We've taken our game Egg Drop and explored ways to create game physics to react with collision detection and tracking other useful data such as lives and a points system. We also worked with customizing physical bodies and creating names for our display objects that apply to the game score count.

Next, we'll be adding a menu system that incorporates an introduction to the game and also applying a pause menu during gameplay and saving high scores when the game is over.

We're on our way to completing an application that has the necessary elements that will be ready for the App Store or Google Play Store.

In this chapter, we will learn the following topics:

- Saving high scores
- Adding a pause menu
- Changing scenes with Storyboard API
- Adding a loading screen
- Adding a main menu and options menu

So let's keep on going!

Continuation of Egg Drop

We have finished the main game portion of Egg Drop as the base of our application. Now it's time for us to include how to pause action mid-game and also how to save high scores. We're also going to add some new scenes that will help us introduce and transition to the game in an easy and quick fashion.

In the Chapter 8 `Resources` folder, grab all the image and file assets inside and copy them to your current `Egg Drop` project folder. You can download the project files accompanying this book from the Packt website. We'll be using these files to add the final touches to our game.

Data saving

Saving file information is used in many aspects of game development. We use it to save high scores, game settings such as sound on/off, locking/unlocking levels, and so on. They're not necessary to have, but good to have if you'd like to have those features included in your applications.

In Corona SDK, applications are sandboxed, meaning that your files (application images, data, and preferences) are stored in a location that no other application can access. Your files will reside in an app-specific directory for documents, resources, or temporary files. This restriction is related to the files on your device, not when you are coding on your Mac or PC.

BeebeGames Class for saving and loading values

We'll be using BeebeGames Class, created by Jonathan Beebe. It provides many easy and useful functions to use for games. Some of the notable functions included incorporate a simple way of saving and loading data that we'll be able add into our game. More information on BeebeGames Class can be found at: `http://developer.anscamobile.com/code/beebegames-class`. You can download the file from the link and take a look at other methods relating to animation, transitions, timers, and so on, incase you would like to use them for future use. For now, we'll be focusing on the methods for easy saving and loading values for our game.

Example of saving and loading values:

```
-- Public Method: saveValue()  --> save single-line file (replace
contents)

function saveValue( strFilename, strValue )
  -- will save specified value to specified file
  local theFile = strFilename
```

```
   local theValue = strValue

   local path = system.pathForFile( theFile, system.DocumentsDirectory
)

   -- io.open opens a file at path. returns nil if no file found
   -- "w+": update mode, all previous data is erased
   local file = io.open( path, "w+" )
   if file then
      -- write game score to the text file
      file:write( theValue )
      io.close( file )
   end
end

-- Public Method: loadValue()   --> load single-line file and store it
into variable

function loadValue( strFilename )
   -- will load specified file, or create new file if it doesn't exist

   local theFile = strFilename

   local path = system.pathForFile( theFile, system.DocumentsDirectory
)

   -- io.open opens a file at path. returns nil if no file found
   -- "r": read mode
   local file = io.open( path, "r" )
   if file then
      -- read all contents of file into a string
     -- "*a": reads the whole file, starting at the current position
      local contents = file:read( "*a" )
      io.close( file )
      return contents
   else
      -- create file b/c it doesn't exist yet
     -- "w": write mode
      file = io.open( path, "w" )
      file:write( "0" )
      io.close( file )
      return "0"
   end
end
```

Getting paths to files

The paths to these files are unique to your application. To create file paths, you use the `system.pathForFile` function. The following generates an absolute path to the icon file for your application using the application's resource directory as the base directory for `Icon.png`:

```
local path = system.pathForFile( "Icon.png", system.ResourceDirectory )
```

In general, your files must reside in one of three possible base directories:

◆ `system.DocumentsDirectory` should be used for files that need to persist between application sessions.

◆ `system.TemporaryDirectory` is a temporary directory. Files written to this directory are not guaranteed to exist in subsequent application sessions. They may or may not exist.

◆ `system.ResourceDirectory` is the directory where all application assets exist. Note that you should never create, modify, or add files to this directory.

> More information on files can be found at: `http://developer.anscamobile.com/content/files`.

Reading files

To read files, the `io` library is used. This library allows you to open files given an absolute path.

Writing files

To write files, you follow many of the same steps as reading a file. Instead of using a read method, you write data (strings or numbers) to a file.

Time for action – saving and loading the high score

When the **Game Over** screen displays, we're going to save and load the values of our final score and highest score.

1. Open up your `main.lua` file that we created for Egg Drop. We'll continue using the same file and add in more code with the new alterations to the game.

2. Add in two new variables, `local highScoreText` and `local highScore` where all the other initialised variables are located near the top of the code.

```
local highScoreText
local highScore
```

3. Introduce the `saveValue()` function after the pre-loaded sound files.

```
local saveValue = function( strFilename, strValue )
   -- will save specified value to specified file
   local theFile = strFilename
   local theValue = strValue

   local path = system.pathForFile( theFile, system.
DocumentsDirectory )

   -- io.open opens a file at path. returns nil if no file found
   local file = io.open( path, "w+" )
   if file then
      -- write game score to the text file
      file:write( theValue )
      io.close( file )
   end
end
```

4. Add in the `loadValue()` function.

```
local loadValue = function( strFilename )
   -- will load specified file, or create new file if it doesn't
exist

   local theFile = strFilename

   local path = system.pathForFile( theFile, system.
DocumentsDirectory )

   -- io.open opens a file at path. returns nil if no file found
   local file = io.open( path, "r" )
   if file then
      -- read all contents of file into a string
      local contents = file:read( "*a" )
      io.close( file )
      return contents
   else
```

```
    -- create file b/c it doesn't exist yet
    file = io.open( path, "w" )
    file:write( "0" )
    io.close( file )
    return "0"
  end
end
```

5. At the end of the `callGameOver()` function, create an `if` statement to compare the `gameScore` and `highScore`. Save the highest score using the `saveValue()` function.

```
if gameScore > highScore then
  highScore = gameScore
  local highScoreFilename = "highScore.data"
  saveValue( highScoreFilename, tostring(highScore) )
end
```

6. Next, add in the `highScoreText` display text in the same `callGameOver()` function to show the high score at the end of the game.

```
highScoreText = display.newText( "Best Game Score: " ..
tostring( highScore ), 0, 0, "Arial", 30 )
  highScoreText:setTextColor( 255, 255, 255, 255 )
  highScoreText.xScale = 0.5; highScoreText.yScale = 0.5
  highScoreText.x = 240
  highScoreText.y = 120

  gameGroup:insert( highScoreText )
```

7. At the end of the `gameStart()` function, have the high score loaded using the `loadValue()` function.

```
    local highScoreFilename = "highScore.data"
    local loadedHighScore = loadValue( highScoreFilename )

    highScore = tonumber(loadedHighScore)
```

What just happened?

After initializing the `saveValue()` and `loadValue()` functions in the game level, we created an `if` statement to compare the `gameScore`, which is the current score during gameplay and the `highScore`, which is the highest score accrued so far. When the outcome of `gameScore` is higher, then it replaces the `highScore` data saved.

In order to save the value, a data file needs to be created. We created a variable called `local highScoreFilename = "highscore.data"`. We called the `saveValue()` function using `highScoreFilename` as a parameter. `tostring(highScore)` will be converted to a string.

When the **Game Over** screen is visible, `highScoreText` displays the value saved from `highScore` above the `gameScore` that is achieved. Adding a high score gives the player an incentive to top the highest score and to add the replay value to the game.

In the `gameStart()` function, it's important to have the value of `highScore.data` loaded at the start of gameplay. By using the same data file we created to save `highScore`, we can also use it to load the value throughout the game. To load the value, `local highScore` calls `loadValue(highScoreFileName)`. This takes the information from `highScore.data`. To obtain the value, `tonumber(loadedHighScore)` converts it to an integer from a string and can be used to display the value of `highScore`.

Pausing the game

Have you ever found yourself in the middle of playing a game and all of sudden you have to take a bathroom break or your hand cramps up? Obviously, any of those situations require you to avert your attention from your game progress and you need to stop the current action temporarily to attend to those needs. This is when a pause button comes in handy so you can stop the action in that moment in time and continue where you left off when you're ready to play again.

Time for action – pausing the game

It's more than just making a button, it's also pausing all the action onscreen, including physics and timers.

1. Add in the variables `local pauseBtn` and `local pauseBG` where all the other variables are initialized near the beginning of the code. Preload the `btnSound` audio after `gameOverSound` near the top of the script.

```
-- Place near other game variables
local pauseBtn
local pauseBG

-- Place after gameOverSound
local btnSound = audio.loadSound( "btnSound.wav" )
```

2. Within the `hud()` function and after the `scoreText` chunk, create another function that will run the event for the pause button. Call the function `onPauseTouch(event)`. Pause the physics in the game by setting `gameIsActive` to `false` and have the pause elements appear on screen.

```
local onPauseTouch = function( event )
  if event.phase == "release" and pauseBtn.isActive then
    audio.play( btnSound )

    -- Pause the game

    if gameIsActive then

      gameIsActive = false
      physics.pause()

      local function pauseGame()
              timer.pause( startDrop )
              print("timer has been paused")
```

```
                end
                timer.performWithDelay(1, pauseGame)


        -- SHADE
        if not shade then
          shade = display.newRect( 0, 0, 570, 380 )
          shade:setFillColor( 0, 0, 0, 255 )
          shade.x = 240; shade.y = 160
          gameGroup:insert( shade )
        end
        shade.alpha = 0.5


        -- SHOW MENU BUTTON
        if pauseBG then
          pauseBG.isVisible = true
          pauseBG.isActive = true
          pauseBG:toFront()
        end


        pauseBtn:toFront()
```

3. When the game is unpaused, have the physics become active again and remove all pause display objects.

```
        else

          if shade then
            display.remove( shade )
            shade = nil
          end


          if pauseBG then
            pauseBG.isVisible = false
            pauseBG.isActive = false
          end

          gameIsActive = true
          physics.start()

          local function resumeGame()
                    timer.resume( startDrop )
```

```
                    print("timer has been resumed")
                end
                timer.performWithDelay(1, resumeGame)

        end
      end
    end
```

4. Add the `pauseBtn` UI button and `pauseBG` display object after the
    `onPauseTouch()` function.

```
pauseBtn = ui.newButton{
  defaultSrc = "pausebtn.png",
  defaultX = 44,
  defaultY = 44,
  overSrc = "pausebtn-over.png",
  overX = 44,
  overY = 44,
  onEvent = onPauseTouch,
  id = "PauseButton",
  text = "",
  font = "Helvetica",
  textColor = { 255, 255, 255, 255 },
  size = 16,
  emboss = false
}

pauseBtn.x = 38; pauseBtn.y = 288
pauseBtn.isVisible = false
pauseBtn.isActive = false

gameGroup:insert( pauseBtn )

pauseBG = display.newImageRect( "pauseoverlay.png", 480, 320 )
pauseBG.x = 240; pauseBG.y = 160
pauseBG.isVisible = false
pauseBG.isActive = false

gameGroup:insert( pauseBG )
```

5. In order for `pauseBtn` to display during gameplay, make it visible and active in the
    `gameActivate()` function.

```
pauseBtn.isVisible = true
pauseBtn.isActive = true
```

6. When the game is over, disable `pauseBtn` in the `callGameOver()` function. Place the code right after the `physics.pause()` line.

```
pauseBtn.isVisible = false
pauseBtn.isActive = false
```

What just happened?

We created the `onPauseTouch(event)` function to control all pause events that occur within gameplay. To pause all the motion in game, we changed the boolean of `gameIsActive` to `false` and `physics.pause()` to stop all the eggs that are falling from moving. Next, the timer is paused for `startDrop` so any eggs falling from the sky won't accumulate over time as long as the pause function is still active.

A slightly transparent overlay called `shade` is called to appear when the pause button is pressed. This will avert the attention of the user from the game scene and allow the user to differentiate when the gameplay is not active.

The **Game Paused** banner also displays on top of the screen by making it visible and active. `pauseBG` is pushed ahead of the display hierarchy by `pauseBG:toFront()`.

To unpause, we reversed the process of how the pause display items appear. When `pauseBtn` is pressed for the second time, `shade` is taken away by `display.remove(shade); shade = nil. pauseBG.isVisible` and `pauseBG.isActive` are both set to `false`.

Remember when we set `gameIsActive` to `false`? Well, it's time to set it back to `true`. This also means resuming physics with `physics.start()`. The timer is resumed by local function `resumeGame()` and calls `timer.resume(startDrop)` within the function.

The `pauseBtn` and `pauseBG` display objects are inserted at the end of the `if` statement block. `pauseBtn` is then shown as visible and active once the game is playable. It is invisible and inactive when the **Game Over** screen appears. This is because there are no other touch events that interfere when the game is over.

Storyboard API

The Storyboard API provides an easy solution for developers to control scenes with or without transitions. This is a great scene-management library for displaying menu systems and even managing multiple levels in a game. Storyboard also comes with a variety of transition effects. A listing of them can be found on the `storyboard.gotoScene()` API reference page at: `http://developer.anscamobile.com/reference/index/storyboardgotoscene`.

More information on the Storyboard API can be found on the *Anscamobile* website at: `http://developer.anscamobile.com/content/storyboard`.

Our scene management will look similar to the scene template displayed at: `http://developer.anscamobile.com/reference/index/scene-template`.

You can also download the *Storyboard Sample Code* from `https://github.com/ansca/Storyboard-Sample` and run the project file in the Corona simulator to get familiar with how it works.

Game development with Storyboard API

You may wonder how we're going to apply Storyboard with Egg Drop. It's really simple actually. We'll have to alter some lines in our game code to make it compatible with Storyboard and create some new scenes for the menu system that is applied before gameplay.

Time for action – altering the game file

We're going to rename our current `main.lua` file to `maingame.lua` and put some additional lines into our game code.

 Be sure to change the filename within your Egg Drop project folder.

1. Remove the following lines near the top of the code. We'll hide the status bar in another scene that we'll create later on in this chapter. The `gameGroup` display group will be altered to fit within the Storyboard parameters.

```
display.setStatusBar( display.HiddenStatusBar )

local gameGroup = display.newGroup()
```

2. At the very top of the code, implement Storyboard by adding `local storyboard = require( "storyboard" )` and `local scene = storyboard.newScene()` so we can call scene events.

```
local storyboard = require( "storyboard" )
local scene = storyboard.newScene()
```

3. After `local loadValue = function( strFilename )`, add in the `createScene()` event. We will also add back in our `gameGroup` display group, but under the scene's view property. Also, add in `storyboard.removeScene( "loadgame" )`. The `"loadgame"` scene will be introduced later on in this chapter.

```
-- Called when the scene's view does not exist:
function scene:createScene( event )
  local gameGroup = self.view

  -- completely remove loadgame's view
  storyboard.removeScene( "loadgame" )

  print( "\nmaingame: createScene event")
end
```

4. After the `createScene()` event, create the `enterScene()` event and add it before the `gameActivate()` function. `enterScene()` will transition all our gameplay functions onscreen. Include `gameGroup` in the scene's view property as well.

```
-- Called immediately after scene has moved onscreen:
function scene:enterScene( event )
  local gameGroup = self.view
```

5. After the `gameStart()` function, remove the `return gameGroup` line.

```
return gameGroup -- Code will not run if this line is not removed
```

6. Next, close `function scene: enterScene( event )` with `end`.

```
  print( "maingame: enterScene event" )

end
```

7. Create the `exitScene()` and `destroyScene()` events.

```
-- Called when scene is about to move offscreen:
function scene:exitScene( event )

    print( "maingame: exitScene event" )

end


-- Called prior to the removal of scene's "view" (display group)
function scene:destroyScene( event )

    print( "((destroying maingame's view))" )

end
```

8. Lastly, create event listeners for all the scene events and add `return scene` at the end of the code.

```
-- "createScene" event is dispatched if scene's view does not
exist
scene:addEventListener( "createScene", scene )

-- "enterScene" event is dispatched whenever scene transition has
finished
scene:addEventListener( "enterScene", scene )

-- "exitScene" event is dispatched before next scene's transition
begins
scene:addEventListener( "exitScene", scene )

-- "destroyScene" event is dispatched before view is unloaded,
which can be
-- automatically unloaded in low memory situations, or explicitly
via a call to
-- storyboard.purgeScene() or storyboard.removeScene().
scene:addEventListener( "destroyScene", scene )

return scene
```

What just happened?

Using Storyboard API will help us transition scenes a lot easily and quickly. Every time you want to load a new scene into view, `require("storyboard")` needs to be added. `local scene = storyboard.newScene()` will allow us to call the scene events: `createScene()`, `enterScene()`, `exitScene()`, and `destroyScene()`.

At the very end of the game code, we added event listeners to all the scene events and `return scene`.

The format for how each scene is managed with Storyboard will look similar to the preceding code. Most of the game code will be dispatched during a scene is displayed by the `createScene()` and `enterScene()` events. When you want to clean or unload listeners, audio, assets, and so on, the `exitScene()` and `destroyScene()` events are used.

Organizing the game

We've been used to having the `main.lua` as our main source file to show every detail of our game code. It's time to organize it efficiently with the help of Storyboard API.

Time for action – adding the new main.lua file

While using Storyboard, our `main.lua` file is still vital since it is the first thing that Corona SDK looks at to launch an application in the simulator. We're going add some lines of code that will change scenes for our game.

1. Create a brand new file called `main.lua` and let's add back in our status bar.

   ```
   display.setStatusBar( display.HiddenStatusBar )
   ```

2. Import Storyboard and load the first scene called `loadmainmenu`. We will create this scene in the next couple of sections.

   ```
   -- require controller module
   local storyboard = require ( "storyboard" )

   -- load first screen
   storyboard.gotoScene( "loadmainmenu" )
   ```

What just happened?

In order to incorporate Storyboard throughout the application, we called the `local storyboard = require ( "storyboard" )` module. The scene will be changed with `storyboard.gotoScene( "loadmainmenu" )`, which is a loading screen directing the user to the main menu screen.

New game transitions

Now that we have introduced Storyboard API, we can apply some long-awaited transitions that will be helpful to our game. One way to approach this is by transitioning out of the game once it is over.

Time for action – changing screens after the game is over

Now that we have renamed our game file, let's add in a scene transition so that our game is not stuck on the **Game Over** screen once gameplay is over.

In our `maingame.lua` file, add in a new variable called `local menuBtn` where all the other variables are initialized in the beginning of the code. Inside the `callGameOver()` function, add the following lines after the `highScoreText` code:

```lua
local onMenuTouch = function( event )
  if event.phase == "release" then

    audio.play( btnSound )
    storyboard.gotoScene( "mainmenu", "fade", 500  )


  end
end

menuBtn = ui.newButton{
  defaultSrc = "menubtn.png",
  defaultX = 60,
  defaultY = 60,
  overSrc = "menubtn-over.png",
  overX = 60,
  overY = 60,
  onEvent = onMenuTouch,
  id = "MenuButton",
  text = "",
  font = "Helvetica",
  textColor = { 255, 255, 255, 255 },
  size = 16,
  emboss = false
}

menuBtn.x = 100; menuBtn.y = 260

gameGroup:insert( menuBtn )
```

What just happened?

In order to transition out of the **Game Over** screen, a menu button was created to change scenes. Inside the `onMenuTouch()` function, upon `"release"` of the button, we called `storyboard.gotoScene( "mainmenu", "fade", 500  )`. This will allow the application to transition to the main menu, which we will create later on in this chapter.

Have a go hero – restarting the game

Now that you're well aware of how Storyboard API works with changing scenes and using UI buttons to transition between them, how about creating a button that restarts the game after the **Game Over** screen appears. So far, the application allows the user to go back to the menu screen once the game has reached an end.

Within the `callGameOver()` function, a new local function needs to be created that will run an event using the UI button system to change scenes with Storyboard. Hint: You can't call the same scene over if you're currently in it.

Creating a loading screen

Loading screens provide feedback that the program is in the process of loading. This is helpful by informing the user that the next screen is underway so they don't assume the application crashed, especially if the next screen is loading a large amount of data.

Time for action – adding the loading screen

We'll be placing loading screens when the application launches and before the game level starts. This tells the user that more content or information is on its way.

1. Create a new file called `loadmainmenu.lua` in your project folder.

2. Import Storyboard and add in the `storyboard.newScene()` function.

```
local storyboard = require( "storyboard" )
local scene = storyboard.newScene()
```

3. Create two local variables called `myTimer` and `loadingImage`. Add in the `createScene()` event and a `screenGroup` display group.

```
local myTimer
local loadingImage

-- Called when the scene's view does not exist:
function scene:createScene( event )
  local screenGroup = self.view

  print( "\nloadmainmenu: createScene event" )
end
```

4. Create the `enterScene()` event and add in a `screenGroup` display group.

```
-- Called immediately after scene has moved onscreen:
function scene:enterScene( event )
  local screenGroup = self.view

  print( "loadmainmenu: enterScene event" )
```

5. Introduce the `loadingImage` display object.

```
loadingImage = display.newImageRect( "loading.png", 480, 320 )
loadingImage.x = 240; loadingImage.y = 160
screenGroup:insert( loadingImage )
```

6. Create another local function called `goToMenu()` and call `storyboard.gotoScene( "mainmenu", "zoomOutInFadeRotate", 500 )` to change the scene to `"mainmenu"`.

```
    local goToMenu = function()
      storyboard.gotoScene( "mainmenu", "zoomOutInFadeRotate", 500
)
    end
```

7. Use the timer function and have it call `goToMenu()` in 1000 milliseconds once. Define it with the timerID, `myTimer`. Close the `enterScene()` event with `end`.

```
    myTimer = timer.performWithDelay( 1000, goToMenu, 1 )
end
```

8. Call the `exitScene()` and the `destroyScene()` events. In the `exitScene()` event, cancel `myTimer`.

```
-- Called when scene is about to move offscreen:
function scene:exitScene()

   if myTimer then timer.cancel( myTimer ); end

   print( "loadmainmenu: exitScene event" )

end


-- Called prior to the removal of scene's "view" (display group)
function scene:destroyScene( event )

   print( "((destroying loadmainmenu's view))" )
end
```

9. Add event listeners for all the scene events and `return scene`. Save and close the file.

```
-- "createScene" event is dispatched if scene's view does not
exist
scene:addEventListener( "createScene", scene )

-- "enterScene" event is dispatched whenever scene transition has
finished
scene:addEventListener( "enterScene", scene )

-- "exitScene" event is dispatched before next scene's transition
begins
scene:addEventListener( "exitScene", scene )

-- "destroyScene" event is dispatched before view is unloaded,
which can be
scene:addEventListener( "destroyScene", scene )

return scene
```

10. Create a new file called `loadgame.lua` in your project folder. We'll be making another loading screen that occurs right before the game scene, `maingame.lua`. Use `storyboard.gotoScene( "maingame", "flipFadeOutIn", 500 )` to transition scenes. Save and close your file.

```lua
local storyboard = require( "storyboard" )
local scene = storyboard.newScene()

local myTimer
local loadingImage

-- Called when the scene's view does not exist:
function scene:createScene( event )
  local screenGroup = self.view

  -- completely remove mainmenu
  storyboard.removeScene( "mainmenu" )

  print( "\nloadgame: createScene event" )
end

-- Called immediately after scene has moved onscreen:
function scene:enterScene( event )
  local screenGroup = self.view

  print( "loadgame: enterScene event" )

  loadingImage = display.newImageRect( "loading.png", 480, 320 )
  loadingImage.x = 240; loadingImage.y = 160
  screenGroup:insert( loadingImage )

  local changeScene = function()
    storyboard.gotoScene( "maingame", "flipFadeOutIn", 500 )
  end
  myTimer = timer.performWithDelay( 1000, changeScene, 1 )

end

-- Called when scene is about to move offscreen:
function scene:exitScene()

  if myTimer then timer.cancel( myTimer ); end
```

```
    print( "loadgame: exitScene event" )

end

-- Called prior to the removal of scene's "view" (display group)
function scene:destroyScene( event )

  print( "((destroying loadgame's view))" )
end

-- "createScene" event is dispatched if scene's view does not
exist
scene:addEventListener( "createScene", scene )

-- "enterScene" event is dispatched whenever scene transition has
finished
scene:addEventListener( "enterScene", scene )

-- "exitScene" event is dispatched before next scene's transition
begins
scene:addEventListener( "exitScene", scene )

-- "destroyScene" event is dispatched before view is unloaded,
which can be
scene:addEventListener( "destroyScene", scene )

return scene
```

What just happened?

In the `loadmainmenu.lua` file, once `loadingImage` is added to the screen, we created the `goToMenu()` function to change scenes to `"mainmenu"` and use the transition `"zoomOutInFadeRotate"` that zooms out and rotates the loading screen image as it fades to the background. `myTimer = timer.performWithDelay( 1000, goToMenu, 1 )` performs the function in 1000 milliseconds (one second) and runs it once. This is long enough to view the image and have it fade out.

All display objects enter the scene by `function scene:enterScene( event )`. `loadingImage` is placed in `screenGroup`. To make sure we have no timers running after the scene change, `myTimer` stops running with the use of `timer.cancel(myTimer)` under `function scene:exitScene()`.

The code for `loadgame.lua` is similar to `loadmainmenu.lua`. For this file, Storyboard transitions scenes to `maingame.lua`, the gameplay file.

Creating a main menu

A main menu or title screen is one of the first impressions a player sees before playing the game. It usually shows small snippets of images or scenery that correlate with the actual game and also displays the title of the application.

There are buttons such as **Start** or **Play** that urge the player to go into the game if they choose to and some secondary buttons such as **Options** to view settings and other information that may be included in relation to the app.

Time for action – adding a main menu

We're going to create the frontend of our game by introducing the game title, **Play** button, and **Options** button that will transition throughout different scenes in the application with ease.

1. Create a new file called `mainmenu.lua` and import Storyboard and UI modules, the `storyboard.newScene()` function, and the variables for timer and audio.

```
local storyboard = require( "storyboard" )
local scene = storyboard.newScene()

local ui = require("ui")

local btnAnim

local btnSound = audio.loadSound( "btnSound.wav" )
```

2. Create the `createScene()` event. Add in the line, `storyboard.removeScene( "maingame" )` and `storyboard.removeScene( "options" )`, which will remove the `"maingame"` and `"options"` scene. Removing `"maingame"` will occur after the player has transitioned from the main game screen and is sent to the main menu screen. Removing `"options"` will occur after the player has transitioned from the options screen and is sent to the main menu screen.

```
-- Called when the scene's view does not exist:
function scene:createScene( event )
  local screenGroup = self.view

    -- completely remove maingame and options
    storyboard.removeScene( "maingame" )
    storyboard.removeScene( "options" )

    print( "\nmainmenu: createScene event" )

end
```

3. Add in the `enterScene()` event and the `backgroundImage` display object.

```
-- Called immediately after scene has moved onscreen:
function scene:enterScene( event )
  local screenGroup = self.view

    print( "mainmenu: enterScene event" )

    local backgroundImage = display.newImageRect( "mainMenuBG.png",
480, 320 )
    backgroundImage.x = 240; backgroundImage.y = 160
    screenGroup:insert( backgroundImage )
```

4. Introduce the `playBtn` display object and create a function called `onPlayTouch(event)` that uses `storyboard.gotoScene()` to change the scene to `"loadgame"`. Use the `"fade"` effect to change scenes.

```
    local playBtn

    local onPlayTouch = function( event )
      if event.phase == "release" then

        audio.play( btnSound )
        storyboard.gotoScene( "loadgame", "fade", 300  )

      end
```

```
      end

      playBtn = ui.newButton{
        defaultSrc = "playbtn.png",
        defaultX = 100,
        defaultY = 100,
        overSrc = "playbtn-over.png",
        overX = 100,
        overY = 100,
        onEvent = onPlayTouch,
        id = "PlayButton",
        text = "",
        font = "Helvetica",
        textColor = { 255, 255, 255, 255 },
        size = 16,
        emboss = false
      }

      playBtn.x = 240; playBtn.y = 440
        screenGroup:insert( playBtn )
```

5. Transition the `playBtn` display object to $y = 260$ in 500 milliseconds using the `easing.inOutExpo` transition. Have it initialized through `btnAnim`.

```
btnAnim = transition.to( playBtn, { time=500, y=260,
transition=easing.inOutExpo } )
```

6. Introduce the `optBtn` display object and create a function called `onOptionsTouch(event)`. Use `storyboard.gotoScene()` to transition the scene to `"options"` using the `"crossFade"` effect.

```
local optBtn

      local onOptionsTouch = function( event )
        if event.phase == "release" then

          audio.play( btnSound )
          storyboard.gotoScene( "options", "crossFade", 300   )

        end
      end

      optBtn = ui.newButton{
        defaultSrc = "optbtn.png",
        defaultX = 60,
```

```
          defaultY = 60,
          overSrc = "optbtn-over.png",
          overX = 60,
          overY = 60,
          onEvent = onOptionsTouch,
          id = "OptionsButton",
          text = "",
          font = "Helvetica",
          textColor = { 255, 255, 255, 255 },
          size = 16,
          emboss = false
      }

    optBtn.x = 430; optBtn.y = 440
      screenGroup:insert( optBtn )
```

7. Transition the `optBtn` display object to `y = 280` in 500 milliseconds using the `easing.inOutExpo` transition. Have it initialized through `btnAnim`. Close the `scene:enterScene( event )` function with `end`.

```
  btnAnim = transition.to( optBtn, { time=500, y=280,
transition=easing.inOutExpo } )
```

```
end
```

8. Create the `exitScene()` event and cancel the `btnAnim` transition. Also, create the `destroyScene()` event.

```
-- Called when scene is about to move offscreen:
function scene:exitScene()

  if btnAnim then transition.cancel( btnAnim ); end

  print( "mainmenu: exitScene event" )

end
```

```
-- Called prior to the removal of scene's "view" (display group)
function scene:destroyScene( event )

  print( "((destroying mainmenu's view))" )
end
```

9. Add the event listeners for all the scene events and `return scene`. Save and close your file.

```
-- "createScene" event is dispatched if scene's view does not
exist
scene:addEventListener( "createScene", scene )

-- "enterScene" event is dispatched whenever scene transition has
finished
scene:addEventListener( "enterScene", scene )

-- "exitScene" event is dispatched before next scene's transition
begins
scene:addEventListener( "exitScene", scene )

-- "destroyScene" event is dispatched before view is unloaded,
which can be
scene:addEventListener( "destroyScene", scene )

return scene
```

What just happened?

On the main menu screen, we added an image that displays the game title, a **Play** button, and an **Options** button. The **Options** button is still not functional at this time. The `onPlayTouch()` function transitions the scene to `"loadgame"`. This will change scenes to `loadgame.lua`. The **Play** button is placed at x = 240; y = 440, (middle and offscreen). When the scene loads, `playBtn` transitions to y = 260 so it pops up from the bottom of the screen in 500 milliseconds.

The **Options** button does a similar thing. optBtn is placed towards the right side of the stage and pops up at y = 280 in 500 milliseconds.

The btnAnim transition is cancelled by transition.cancel(btnAnim) through the scene:exitScene() function. Cleaning timers, transitions, and event listeners is important to do every time you change scenes so potential memory leaks do not occur while in the application.

Creating an options menu

An options menu allows users to change various settings in the game or include other information that can't be displayed in the main menu. Games can vary from having many options to only having a few. Sometimes an options menu can be called a settings menu, which offers the same type of customization to the player's experience.

Time for action – adding an options menu

We'll be adding an options menu that can be accessed through the main menu. We're going to add a new UI button called **Credits**, which will direct the user to the credits screen once it is pressed.

1. Create a new file called options.lua and import Storyboard and UI modules, the storyboard.newScene() function, and the variables for timer and audio.

```
local storyboard = require( "storyboard" )
local scene = storyboard.newScene()

local ui = require("ui")

local btnAnim

local btnSound = audio.loadSound( "btnSound.wav" )
```

2. Create the createScene() event. Add in, storyboard.removeScene ("mainmenu"), which will remove the "mainmenu" scene. This will occur after the player has transitioned from the main menu screen and is sent to the options screen. Next, add in storyboard.removeScene("creditsScreen"). This will remove the "creditsScreen" after the player has transitioned from the credits screen back to the options screen.

```
-- Called when the scene's view does not exist:
function scene:createScene( event )
  local screenGroup = self.view
```

```
     -- completely remove mainmenu and creditsScreen
     storyboard.removeScene( "mainmenu" )
     storyboard.removeScene( "creditsScreen" )

     print( "\noptions: createScene event" )
end
```

3. Add in the `enterScene()` event and the `backgroundImage` display object.

```
-- Called immediately after scene has moved onscreen:
function scene:enterScene( event )
     local screenGroup = self.view

     print( "options: enterScene event" )

     local backgroundImage = display.newImageRect( "optionsBG.png",
480, 320 )
     backgroundImage.x = 240; backgroundImage.y = 160
     screenGroup:insert( backgroundImage )
```

4. Create a button for the credits screen. Transition the `creditsBtn` display object to y = 260 in 500 milliseconds using the `easing.inOutExpo` transition. Have it initialized through `btnAnim`.

```
local creditsBtn

local onCreditsTouch = function( event )
  if event.phase == "release" then

    audio.play( btnSound )
    storyboard.gotoScene( "creditsScreen", "crossFade", 300 )

  end
end

creditsBtn = ui.newButton{
  defaultSrc = "creditsbtn.png",
  defaultX = 100,
  defaultY = 100,
  overSrc = "creditsbtn-over.png",
  overX = 100,
  overY = 100,
  onEvent = onCreditsTouch,
  id = "CreditsButton",
  text = "",
```

```
      font = "Helvetica",
      textColor = { 255, 255, 255, 255 },
      size = 16,
      emboss = false
   }

   creditsBtn.x = 240; creditsBtn.y = 440
   screenGroup:insert( creditsBtn )

   btnAnim = transition.to( creditsBtn, { time=500, y=260,
transition=easing.inOutExpo } )
```

5. Create the **Close** button that loads the main menu. Close the `scene:enterScene` (`event`) **with** end.

```
   local closeBtn

   local onCloseTouch = function( event )
      if event.phase == "release" then
         audio.play( tapSound )
         storyboard.gotoScene( "mainmenu", "zoomInOutFadeRotate", 500
)
      end
   end

   closeBtn = ui.newButton{
      defaultSrc = "closebtn.png",
      defaultX = 60,
      defaultY - 60,
      overSrc = "closebtn-over.png",
      overX = 60,
      overY = 60,
      onEvent = onCloseTouch,
      id = "CloseButton",
      text = "",
      font = "Helvetica",
      textColor = { 255, 255, 255, 255 },
      size = 16,
      emboss = false
   }

   closeBtn.x = 50; closeBtn.y = 280
   screenGroup:insert( closeBtn )
end
```

6. Create the `exitScene()` event and cancel the `btnAnim` transition. Also, create the `destroyScene()` event. Add the event listeners to all the scene events and return `scene`. **Save and close your file.**

```
-- Called when scene is about to move offscreen:
function scene:exitScene()

   if btnAnim then transition.cancel( btnAnim ); end

   print( "options: exitScene event" )

end


-- Called prior to the removal of scene's "view" (display group)
function scene:destroyScene( event )

   print( "((destroying options's view))" )
end


-- "createScene" event is dispatched if scene's view does not
exist
scene:addEventListener( "createScene", scene )

-- "enterScene" event is dispatched whenever scene transition has
finished
scene:addEventListener( "enterScene", scene )

-- "exitScene" event is dispatched before next scene's transition
begins
scene:addEventListener( "exitScene", scene )

-- "destroyScene" event is dispatched before view is unloaded,
which can be
scene:addEventListener( "destroyScene", scene )

return scene
```

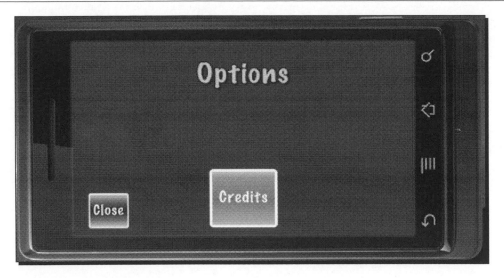

What just happened?

In this scene, `creditsBtn` will operate in a similar fashion like how our main menu was created. The **Credits** button is still not functional at this time. In the `onCreditsTouch()` function, the scene is transitioned to `"creditsScreen"` and uses `"crossFade"` as the effect. From the offscreen position, `creditsBtn` transitions to y=260 in 500 milliseconds when the scene is loaded.

A **Close** button is created for this scene so the user will have a way to go back to the previous screen. With the `onCloseTouch()` function, Storyboard changes the scene to `"mainmenu"` upon `"release"` of `closeBtn`. The main menu screen will display upon pressing the **Close** button. The `btnAnim` transition is cancelled through the `scene:exitScene()` function.

Creating a credits screen

A credits screen usually shows and lists all the people involved in the production of the game. It can include other information in the form of thanking certain individuals and programs used to create the final project.

Time for action – adding a credits screen

The credits screen we'll be creating will be based on a touch event that transitions to the previous screen from which it was introduced.

1. Create a new file call `creditsScreen.lua` and import Storyboard, the `storyboard.newScene()` function, and the `backgroundImage` variable.

```
local storyboard = require( "storyboard" )
local scene = storyboard.newScene()

local backgroundImage
```

2. Create the `createScene()` event. Add in the line, `storyboard.removeScene ( "options" )`, which will remove the `"options"` scene. This will occur after the player has transitioned from the options screen and is sent to the credits screen.

```
-- Called when the scene's view does not exist:
function scene:createScene( event )
  local screenGroup = self.view

  -- completely remove options
  storyboard.removeScene( "options" )


  print( "\ncreditsScreen: createScene event" )
end
```

3. Add in the `enterScene()` event and `backgroundImage` display object.

```
-- Called immediately after scene has moved onscreen:
function scene:enterScene( event )
  local screenGroup = self.view

  print( "creditsScreen: enterScene event" )

  backgroundImage = display.newImageRect( "creditsScreen.png",
480, 320 )
  backgroundImage.x = 240; backgroundImage.y = 160
  screenGroup:insert( backgroundImage )
```

4. Create a local function called `changeToOptions()` with an event parameter. Have the function change the scene with Storyboard back to the options screen using a touch event on `backgroundImage`. Close the `scene:enterScene( event )` function with `end`.

```
local changeToOptions = function( event )
   if event.phase == "began" then

      storyboard.gotoScene( "options", "crossFade", 300  )

    end
  end


  backgroundImage:addEventListener( "touch", changeToOptions)
end
```

5. Create the `exitScene()` and `destroyScene()` events. Add the event listeners to all the scene events and `return` scene. Save and close your file.

```
-- Called when scene is about to move offscreen:
function scene:exitScene()

  print( "creditsScreen: exitScene event" )

end



-- Called prior to the removal of scene's "view" (display group)
function scene:destroyScene( event )

  print( "((destroying creditsScreen's view))" )
end

-- "createScene" event is dispatched if scene's view does not
exist
scene:addEventListener( "createScene", scene )

-- "enterScene" event is dispatched whenever scene transition has
finished
scene:addEventListener( "enterScene", scene )
```

```
            -- "exitScene" event is dispatched before next scene's transition
            begins
            scene:addEventListener( "exitScene", scene )

            -- "destroyScene" event is dispatched before view is unloaded,
            which can be
            scene:addEventListener( "destroyScene", scene )

            return scene
```

What just happened?

The credits screen works with an event listener. The changeToOptions(event) function
will tell Storyboard to change the scene to "options" using storyboard.gotoScene
("options", "crossFade", 500). At the end of the function, backgroundImage
will activate the event listener when the screen is touched. backgroundImage is inserted
into the screenGroup under the scene:enterScene(event) function. Egg Drop
is now fully operable using Storyboard. Run the game in the simulator. You'll be able to
transition to all the scenes we have created in this chapter as well as play the game.

Have a go hero – adding more levels

Now that Egg Drop is completed and has a working menu system, challenge yourself by
creating more levels. Minor alterations will have to be added to incorporate some placement
for additional levels. Remember to apply Storyboard when changing scenes.

Try creating the following:

- Level select screen
- Level number buttons to add additional levels

When creating new levels, refer to the format as shown in `maingame.lua`. New levels can be altered by changing the interval of how fast the egg falls from the sky or maybe adding other game assets that fall but have to be avoided so there is no penalty during gameplay. There are so many possibilities on adding your own spin with this game framework. Give it a try!

Pop quiz – game transitions and scenes

1. Which function do you call to change scenes with Storyboard?

    a. `storyboard()`

    b. `storyboard.gotoScene()`

    c. `storyboard(changeScene)`

    d. None of the above

2. Which function converts any argument into a number?

    a. `tonumber()`

    b. `print()`

    c. `tostring()`

    d. nil

3. How do you pause a timer?

    a. `timer.cancel()`

    b. `physics.pause()`

    c. `timer.pause( timerID )`

    d. None of the above

4. How do you resume a timer?

    a. `resume()`

    b. `timer.resume( timerID )`

    c. `timer.performWithDelay()`

    d. None of the above

Summary

Congratulations! We have a game that is complete enough to go into the App Store or Google Play Store. Of course not using this exact game, but we have learned enough material to create one. It's a great accomplishment to have completed game framework, especially in the short amount of time it took to create something so simple.

Here are some skills you learned:

◆ Saving high scores using `saveValue()` and `loadValue()`

◆ Understanding how to pause physics/timers

◆ Displaying the pause menu

◆ Changing scenes with the Storyboard API

◆ Creating transitions between scenes using loading screens

◆ Using a main menu to introduce the game title and submenus

This chapter was an important milestone to achieve. Everything that we have gone over in the previous chapters was applied to this sample game. The great thing about it is that it took only less than a day's worth of development to code. The art assets on the other hand are a different story.

We still have quite a few more things to learn of what Corona SDK is capable of. In the next chapter, we'll go over more in detail on how to optimize our game assets for high-resolution devices. We're also going to go over how to post messages on Facebook and Twitter and sync our applications with Openfeint!

9

Handling Multiple Devices and Networking your Apps

Allowing your application to integrate with social networks is a great way to promote your finished product. Many games enable the player to upload their high scores and share them among other users playing the same title. Some provide challenges that need to be completed successfully in order to unlock achievements. Social networks enhance the gaming experience and provide great exposure for the developer.

We'll also go into more detail about build configuration since we're getting more accustomed to programming. Understanding the importance of configuring your device builds is mandatory for cross-platform development. This is a capability that Corona SDK can handle with ease across iOS and Android devices.

In this chapter, we will learn the following topics:

◆ Revisiting configuration settings

◆ Posting messages to Twitter

◆ Posting messages to Facebook

◆ Adding achievements and leaderboards with OpenFeint

Let's add in these finishing touches!

Return to configuration

Build settings and runtime configuration were briefly discussed in *Chapter 2, Lua Crash Course and the Corona Framework*. Let's get into more specific details on handling a variety of devices on the iOS and Android platform.

Build configuration

There are a variety of ways to handle device orientation to match the settings your game design requires.

Orientation support (iOS)

There are scenarios in which you want the native UI elements to autorotate, or to be oriented in a certain way, but you also want to maintain a fixed coordinate system within Corona.

To lock Corona's orientation while allowing native iPhone UI elements to rotate, add a content parameter in `build.settings` as follows:

```
settings =
{
        orientation =
        {
                default = "portrait",
                content = "portrait",
                supported =
                {
                        "landscapeLeft", "landscapeRight", "portrait",
"portraitUpsideDown",
                },
        },
}
```

To lock Corona's internal coordinate system to portrait orientation while locking iPhone UI elements to landscape orientation, you could do the following in `build.settings`:

```
settings =
{
        orientation =
        {
                default ="landscapeRight",
                content = "portrait",
                supported =
```

```
                            {
                                    "landscapeRight", "landscapeLeft",
                            },
                    },
        }
```

Orientation support (Android)

The Android platform supports two orientations: `portrait` and `landscapeRight`. The orientations *landscapeLeft* and *portraitUpsideDown* have no effect on Android. Also, autorotation is not currently supported on Android. The default orientation doesn't affect Android devices. The orientation is initialized to the actual orientation of the device (unless only one orientation is specified).

Here is an example of an Android-specific `build.settings` file (you may also combine Android and iPhone settings in the same file):

```
        settings =
        {
                android =
                {
                        versionCode = "2",
                    versionName = "2.0"
                },

                androidPermissions =
                {
                                "android.permission.INTERNET"
                },

                orientation =
                {
                        default = "portrait"
                },
        }
```

Version code and version name (Android)

The `versionCode` and `versionName` can be set within an optional `"android"` table in `build.settings`.

The `versionCode` field is defaulted to `"1"`, while the `versionName` field is defaulted at `"1.0"` if it's not set in the `build.settings` file. When an updated version of an application is submitted to the Google Play Store, the `versionCode` and `versionName` also have to be updated. All version numbers for `versionCode` have to be whole numbers. The `versionCode` cannot contain any decimal numbers. The `versionName` can contain decimals.

For more information, see *android:versionCode* and *android:versionName*: `http://developer.android.com/guide/topics/manifest/manifest-element.html#vcode`.

 The `versionCode` is an internal number used to distinguish application releases for the Google Play Store. It is not the same as the version provided by the Corona build dialog. The `versionName` is the version number shown to users.

Application permissions (Android)

An optional `"androidPermissions"` table can be used to specify permissions, using string values as given in the *Android Manifest Reference*: `http://developer.android.com/reference/android/Manifest.permission.html`.

Developers should use permissions that match their application requirements. For example, if network access is required, the Internet permission needs to be set.

Content scaling on an easier level

Content scaling throughout multiple devices can be frustrating at times if you've never addressed them before. While the iPhone and iPhone 4 are easy to scale across evenly, it takes some other individual sizes to manipulate screen sizes with the iPad, which is at 768 x 1024. The Droid is 480 x 854 and Samsung Galaxy tablet is 600 x 1024 just to name a few.

When setting up your `config.lua` like we've done in the previous chapters, we had our content set to `width = 320`, `height = 480`, and `scale = "letterbox"`. If building for Android devices, `"zoomStretch"` works best to accommodate varying screen sizes on the platform. This helps to build between iOS/Android devices together and present display images that are large enough to fit on a variety of screen sizes.

If you want to scale for larger screen sizes and then scale down, use the screen size of the iPad. Your `config.lua` would look similar to the following code:

```
application =
{
    content =
    {
```

```
            width = 768,
            height = 1024,
            scale = "letterbox"
        }
    }
```

While the preceding example is another solution to scale content, it's important to remember the limitations in texture memory involved with larger (high resolution) images. While devices such as the iPad, iPhone 4, and the Samsung Galaxy tablet will handle this just fine, the iPhone 3GS and older devices will have far less texture memory available to handle large graphics.

A way to resolve this potential problem is to use *Dynamic Image Resolution* to substitute assets that are better suited for low-end devices and high-end devices. We will discuss this topic in more detail later in this section.

The best of both worlds

As you may have noticed, some of the background images we used in our sample apps are scaled at 380 x 570. This happens to be the size that fills the entire screen on all common devices for both iOS and Android. And better yet, it is a middle ground for compensating for higher- and lower-resolution images on any device.

In order for your content to be displayed as evenly as possible, the following must be set up accordingly:

Settings for the config.lua are as follows:

```
    application =
    {
        content =
        {
            width = 320,
            height = 480,
            scale = "letterbox"
        }
    }
```

In any file that contains any of your display images, a typical background would be displayed as follows:

```
    local backgroundImage = display.newImage( "bg.png", true )
    backgroundImage.x = display.contentWidth / 2
    backgroundImage.y = display.contentHeight / 2
```

Any content with a size of 320 x 480 is considered the focus area. Anything outside of the area is cropped, but will fill the screen with content on any device.

The deeper meaning of dynamic image resolutions

We know we can swap base images `"image.png"` used for iOS devices (3GS and lower) and double-resolution images `"image@2x.png"` (for the iPhone 4 which has retina display). This only occurs since Apple devices can tell when the screen size is twice the resolution size of the original content.

A naming scheme is available for use to handle devices such as the iPad and Android handsets. Knowing how to handle the scaling of assets affected for the device proposed is half the battle. We'll have to define what resolution scale needs to be addressed for Corona to access the assets they're directed towards.

By using the line: `display.newImageRect( [parentGroup,] filename [, baseDirectory] w, h )` will call out your dynamic resolution images.

Typically, we've used `["@2x"] = 2` to call out the higher resolution image when available in our project for iOS devices:

```
application =
{
    content =
    {
        width = 320,
        height = 480,
        scale = "letterbox",

        imageSuffix =
        {
            ["@2x"] = 2,
        },
    },
}
```

The preceding example will only work for iPhone 4 and iPad since it surpasses the base size of 320 x 480 on both devices. If we wanted to make it accessible to the Droid, the scale threshold would be 1.5. For an Android tablet to work, such as the Samsung Galaxy tablet, the scale threshold is 1.875. So how do we figure out these numbers? Simple. Take the width of the higher-end device and divide it by 320 (the base size). For example:

The Droid dimensions are 480 x 854. Divide 480 by 320 and it equals 1.5.

The Samsung Galaxy tablet dimensions are 600 x 1024. Divide 600 by 320 and it equals 1.875.

If trying to manage both iOS and Android devices in the same project, you can change your imageSuffix in the config.lua as follows:

```
        imageSuffix =
        {
              ["@2x"] = 1.5, -- this will handle most Android devices
   such as the Droid, Nexus, Galaxy Tablet, etc...
        }
```

-- or

```
        imageSuffix =
        {
              ["@2x"] = 1.8, -- this will handle the Galaxy Tablet and
   similar sized devices
        }
```

Using either of the preceding examples will trigger the proposed Android devices to display the higher resolution image.

The imageSuffix doesn't necessarily have to be "@2x", it can be anything like "@2", "_lrg", or even "-2x". As long as your higher-resolution image has the intended suffix after the primary image name, it'll work just fine.

High-resolution sprite sheets

High-resolution sprite sheets are not handled the same way as dynamic image resolutions. While you can continue using the same naming convention to differentiate your high-resolution images from your basic images, the image will not be able to use display.newImageRect() when referring to sprite sheets.

If your current content scale is width = 320, height = 480, and scale = "letterbox" in your config.lua file, then the scale output for the following devices will demonstrate the following:

- iPhone = 1
- iPhone 4 = 0.5
- Droid = 0.666666668653488
- iPad = 0.46875

Applying a basic sprite sheet that matches the scale for an iPhone will display sharp and clean images. When the same sprite sheet is applied to the iPhone 4, the display will match the content scale of the device, but the sprite sheet will look slightly pixilated and blurry around the edges. Using `display.contentScaleX` and calling some methods will solve that problem for you. Notice that `displayScale < 1` will access the high-resolution sprite sheet based on the preceding device scale.

```
local spriteSheet
local myObject

local displayScale = display.contentScaleX -- scales sprite sheets
down
    if displayScale < 1 then -- pertains to all high-res devices

        spriteSheet = sprite.newSpriteSheet( "mySprite@2x.png", 512, 512
)
    else
        spriteSheet = sprite.newSpriteSheet( "mySprite.png", 256, 256 )
    end


    local spriteSet = sprite.newSpriteSet(spriteSheet, 1, 4)
    sprite.add( spriteSet, "walk", 1, 4, 300, 0 ) -- play 4 frames
every 300 ms


    myObject = sprite.newSprite( spriteSet )

    if displayScale < 1 then --scale the high-res sprite sheet if
you're on a high-res device.
        myObject.xScale = .5; myObject.yScale = .5
    end

    myObject.x = display.contentWidth / 2
    myObject.y = display.contentHeight / 2

    myObject.x = 150; myObject.y = 195

    myObject:prepare("walk")
    myObject:play()
```

Networking your apps

When you have completed developing your main game framework, it's good to think about how to network it if you decide to do so.

We all have used some kind of networking tool during some point in our lives, such as Twitter and Facebook. Maybe you currently use these applications, but the point is you've read updates from other users about a new game that came out or someone is spreading the word to download a game and compete with them. You can be that developer and develop the game they're talking about!

Incorporating networking mechanisms in your game does not have to be a hassle. It only takes several lines of code to get it working.

Posting to Twitter

Tweet, tweet, tweet... Twitter is a networking tool that connects you to the latest information that appeals to your interests. It is also a great tool to share information with others about your business and of course your game. Reach out to the game development audience by promoting your application.

In order for posting on Twitter to work, you need to create a Twitter account at: `http://twitter.com/` and make sure that you're logged in.

Time for action – adding Twitter in your apps

We're going to implement Twitter in our apps by accessing a web service through UI buttons.

1. In the `Chapter 9` folder, copy the `Twitter Web Pop-Up` project folder to your desktop. All the configuration, libraries, and assets needed are already included. You can download the project files accompanying this book from the Packt website.

2. Create a new `main.lua` file and save it to the project folder.

3. Set the following variables at the beginning of the code:
   ```
   display.setStatusBar( display.HiddenStatusBar )

   local ui = require("ui")

   local openBtn
   local closeBtn
   local score = 100
   ```

4. Create a local function called onOpenTouch() with an event parameter. Add in an if statement so the event receives a "release" action.

```
local onOpenTouch = function( event )
  if event.phase == "release" then
```

5. Using the local variable called message, add in the following string statement and concatenate score.

```
local message = "Posting to Twitter from Corona SDK and got a
final score of " ..score.. "."
```

6. Add in local myString and apply a string.gsub() for message to replace space instances.

```
local myString = string.gsub(message, "( )", "%%20")
```

7. Introduce the native.showWebPopup() function that links to the Twitter account. Concatenate myString to include the pre-loaded message. Close the function.

```
    native.showWebPopup(0, 0, 320, 300, "http://twitter.com/
intent/tweet?text="..myString)

  end
end
```

8. Set up the openBtn UI function.

```
    openBtn = ui.newButton{
    defaultSrc = "openbtn.png",
    defaultX = 90,
    defaultY = 90,
    overSrc = "openbtn-over.png",
    overX = 90,
    overY = 90,
    onEvent = onOpenTouch,
}

openBtn.x = 110; openBtn.y = 350
```

9. Create a local function called onCloseTouch() with an event parameter. Add an if statement with event.phase == "release" to activate native. cancelWebPopup().

```
local onCloseTouch = function( event )
  if event.phase == "release" then

    native.cancelWebPopup()

  end
end
```

10. Set up the `closeBtn` UI function.

```
closeBtn = ui.newButton{
defaultSrc = "closebtn.png",
defaultX = 90,
defaultY = 90,
overSrc = "closebtn-over.png",
overX = 90,
overY = 90,
onEvent = onCloseTouch,
}

closeBtn.x = 210; closeBtn.y = 350
```

11. Save the file and run the project in the simulator. Make sure you're connected to the Internet to see the results.

 If you're currently not logged in to your Twitter account, you'll be asked to log in before you see the results of the tweet from our code.

What just happened?

Near the top of the code we set a variable, `local score = 100`. This will be used in our Twitter message.

In the `onOpenTouch(event)` function, a web pop-up will load upon the release of `openBtn`. The text that will be posted is displayed in a string format under the variable, local message. You will notice that we concatenate `score` into the string so it displays the value in the message post.

`local myString, string.gsub()` is used to replace all the instances indicated in a pattern inside the string. In this case, it takes the string inside message and searches for every empty space between each word and replaces it with `%20`. `%20` encodes URL parameters to indicate spaces. The extra `%` acts as an escape character.

The `native.showWebPopup()` function displays at dimensions 320 x 300; about half the screen size on a device. The URL to display the Twitter message dialog is added and concatenates `myString`.

When the web pop-up no longer needs to be used and needs to be closed, `onCloseTouch(event)` is called by `closeBtn`. This will take the `event` parameter `"release"` and call the `native.cancelWebPopup()`. This particular function will dismiss the current web pop-up.

Posting to Facebook

Another social networking tool that can be used to share information about your game is Facebook. You can easily customize a post to link information about your game or share messages about high scores and insist upon other users downloading it.

In order to post messages to Facebook, you need to be logged in to your Facebook account or create one at: `http://www.facebook.com/`. You will have to obtain an App ID from the *Facebook Developer* website at: `https://developers.facebook.com/`. The App ID is a unique identifier for your site that determines what the right level of security is in place between the user and the app page/website.

Once you have created an App ID, you will also need to edit the app information and choose how you want it to integrate with Facebook. You are given several choices, such as: Website, Native iOS App, and Native Android App, just to name a few. The website integration must be selected and filled in with a valid URL in order for Facebook to redirect to the specified URL for posts dealing with web pop-ups.

Time for action – adding Facebook to your apps

Similar to our Twitter example, we'll be incorporating Facebook posts with a web pop-up as well.

1. In the `Chapter 9` folder, copy the `Facebook Web Pop-Up` project folder to your desktop. All the configuration, libraries, and assets needed are already included. You can download the project files accompanying this book from the Packt website.

2. Create a new `main.lua` file and save it to the project folder.

3. Set the following variables at the beginning of the code:
   ```
   display.setStatusBar( display.HiddenStatusBar )

   local ui = require("ui")

   local openBtn
   local closeBtn
   local score = 100
   ```

4. Create a local function called `onOpenTouch()` with an event parameter. Add in an `if` statement when the event receives a `"release"` action.
   ```
   local onOpenTouch = function( event )
     if event.phase == "release" then
   ```

5. Add in the following local variables that include the strings we'll be implementing into the Facebook post.
   ```
   local appId = "0123456789" -- Your personal FB App ID from the
   facebook developer's website

   local message1 = "Your App Name Here"
   local message2 = "Posting to Facebook from Corona SDK and got
   a final score of " ..score.. "."
   local message3 = "Download the game and play!"

   local myString1 = string.gsub(message1, "( )", "%%20")
   local myString2 = string.gsub(message2, "( )", "%%20")
   local myString3 = string.gsub(message3, "( )", "%%20")
   ```

6. Introduce the native web pop-up function that links to the Facebook account. Include parameters for the Facebook Dialog box that redirects the URL of your preferred website, the display with a touch mode that connects to your app URL, and an image URL that presents your app icon or company logo. Concatenate all variables with string methods to output all messages. Close the function. Add in the openBtn UI function. (You will need to replace all the URL information below with your own).

```
    native.showWebPopup(0, 0, 320, 300, "http://www.facebook.
com/dialog/feed?app_id=" .. appId .. "&redirect_uri=http://
www.yourwebsite.com&display=touch&link=http://www.yourgamelink.
com&picture=http://www.yourwebsite.com/image.png&name="
..myString1.. "&caption=" ..myString2.. "&description="..
myString3)

  end
end

  openBtn = ui.newButton{
  defaultSrc = "openbtn.png",
  defaultX = 90,
  defaultY = 90,
  overSrc = "openbtn-over.png",
  overX = 90,
  overY = 90,
  onEvent = onOpenTouch,
}
openBtn.x = 110; openBtn.y = 350
```

 More information pertaining to the Facebook Dialog can be found on the *Facebook Developers* website at: http://developers.facebook.com/docs/reference/dialogs/.

7. Create a local function called onCloseTouch() with an event parameter. Add an if statement with event.phase == "release" to activate native.cancelWebPopup(). Set up the closeBtn UI function.

```
local onCloseTouch = function ( event )
  if event.phase == "release" then

    native.cancelWebPopup()

  end
end
```

```
closeBtn = ui.newButton{
defaultSrc = "closebtn.png",
defaultX = 90,
defaultY = 90,
overSrc = "closebtn-over.png",
overX = 90,
overY = 90,
onEvent = onCloseTouch,
}

closeBtn.x = 210; closeBtn.y = 350
```

8. Save the file and run the project in the simulator. Make sure you're connected to the Internet and your Facebook account to see the results.

What just happened?

Within the `onOpenTouch(event)` function, several variables are called when `openBtn` is pressed and released. Notice that `local appId` indicates a string of numbers that you can obtain after creating an app on the Facebook Developers website.

`message1`, `message2`, and `message3` are the strings that display the message post. `myString1`, `myString2`, and `myString3` help replace the spaces indicated in `message1`, `message2`, and `message3`.

The `native.showWebPopup()` function displays with a dimension of 320 x 300 and presents the dialog URL to Facebook. The following parameters display accordingly:

- `app_id`—Example: `"1234567"` (This is your unique ID created on the Facebook Developer website).
- `redirect_uri`—The URL to redirect to after the user clicks a button on the dialog. This is required in the parameters.
- `display`—Displays the mode to render the dialog.
    - `touch`—Used on smart phone devices like iPhone and Android. Fits the dialog screen within small dimensions.
- `link`—The link attached to the post.
- `picture`—The URL of a picture to the post.
- `name`—name of the link attachment.
- `caption`—Caption of the link (appears beneath the link name).
- `description`—Description of the link (appears beneath the link caption).

When the web pop-up no longer needs to be used and needs to be closed, `onCloseTouch(event)` is called by `closeBtn`. This will take the event parameter `"release"` and call `native.cancelWebPopup()`. This particular function will dismiss the current web pop-up.

Facebook Connect

This library supplies a number of functions that interface to `http://www.facebook.com` through the official Facebook Connect interface.

Time for action – posting scores using Facebook Connect

Facebook Connect is another way to post on the wall feed by using the native Facebook UI features. We'll be creating a different way to post messages and scores to the newsfeed. In order to see how Facebook Connect operates, you need to load the build to a device to view the results. It will not run in the simulator.

1. In the `Chapter 9` folder, copy the `Facebook Connect` project folder to your desktop. All the configuration, libraries, and assets needed are already included. You can download the project files accompanying this book from the Packt website.

2. Create a new `main.lua` file and save it to the project folder.

3. Set up the following variables at the beginning of the code:

```
display.setStatusBar( display.HiddenStatusBar )

local ui = require("ui")
local facebook = require "facebook"

local fbBtn
local score = 100
```

4. Create a local function called `onFBTouch()` with an event parameter. Add in an `if` statement containing `event.phase == release`. Also include your Facebook app ID in a string format.

```
local onFBTouch = function( event )
  if event.phase == "release" then

    local fbAppID = "0123456789" -- Your FB App ID from facebook
developer's panel
```

5. Create another local function within `onFBTouch(event)` called `facebookListener()` with an event parameter as well. Include an `if` statement that refers to `"session" == event.type`.

```
    local facebookListener = function( event )
      if ( "session" == event.type ) then
```

6. Add in another `if` statement where `"login" == event.phase`. Include a local variable called `theMessage` to display the message you want to share with other Facebook users.

```
      if ( "login" == event.phase ) then

        local theMessage = "Got a score of " .. score .. " on
Your App Name Here!"
```

7. Add in the `facebook.request()` function that will post the following messages to the user's Facebook wall. Close any remaining `if` statements with `end` in the `facebookListener(event)` function.

```
            facebook.request( "me/feed", "POST", {
                message=theMessage,
                name="Your App Name Here",
                caption="Download and compete with me!",
                link="http://itunes.apple.com/us/app/your-app-name/
    id382456881?mt=8",
                picture="http://www.yoursite.com/yourimage.png"} )
        end
      end
    end
```

> The `link` parameter demonstrates a URL for an iOS application. You can direct the URL to an Android application that will look something like: `https://play.google.com/store/apps/details?id=com.yourcompany.yourappname` or a general website URL of your choosing.

8. Call the `facebook.login()` that includes your appID, listener, and permissions to post on the user's Facebook wall. Close the remainder of the `onFBTouch(event)` function.

```
    facebook.login( fbAppID, facebookListener, { "publish_stream"
} )

  end
end
```

9. Enable the `fbBtn` UI function and save your file.

```
fbBtn = ui.newButton{
  defaultSrc = "facebookbtn.png",
  defaultX = 100,
  defaultY = 100,
  overSrc = "facebookbtn-over.png",
  overX = 100,
  overY = 100,
  onEvent = onFBTouch,
}

fbBtn.x = 160; fbBtn.y = 160
```

10. Create a new device build for either iOS or Android. Load the build to your device and run the application. You will be asked to log in to your Facebook account before you can see the results from the application.

What just happened?

One of the most important things that needs to be done is `require "facebook"` in order to have the Facebook API to work. We also created a local variable called `score` with the value of 100.

The `onFBTouch(event)` function will initiate the event parameter upon `"release"` of `fbBtn`. Within the function, `fbAppID` is included with characters in a string format. This will be a unique set of numbers that you must obtain from the Facebook Developers website. The App ID will be created for you when you make an App page on the site.

Another function, `facebookListener(event)`, is created and it will initiate all `fbConnect` events. Under the `if` statement containing (`"login" == event.phase`) will request to post a message to your feed through `"me/feed, "POST"`. The feed contains the following:

- `message=theMessage`—Refers to the string belonging to the variable. It also concatenates scores so it displays the value as well.

- `name`—A message that includes your app name or subject matter.

- `caption`—A short persuasive message to catch other users attention about playing the game.

- `link`—The URL to download the game from either the App Store or Google Play Store.

- `picture`—A URL containing your image that displays your app icon or visual representation of the game.

After the parameters are set, `facebook.login()` will refer to `fbAppID` and `facebookListener()` to see if a valid application ID is being used to post on Facebook. Upon success, the post is published through `"publish_stream"`.

Have a go hero – create a dialog box

See if you can figure out how to display a dialog box using Facebook Connect and using the same setup as the preceding example. The following line will display this as:

```
facebook.showDialog( {action="stream.publish"} )
```

Now see where in the code `facebook.showDialog()` can be accessed. This is another way of posting messages to Facebook.

The wonders of OpenFeint

OpenFeint is a third-party library that enables social gaming features such as public leaderboards and achievements. For more information, see `http://www.openfeint.com/`.

It is very simple to implement leaderboards and achievements once you are ready to network your mobile game to the public.

You will need to create a user account on the OpenFeint Developer site at: `http://www.openfeint.com/developers` to integrate its features in your application.

Game network API

Game network allows access to third-party libraries such as OpenFeint, Papaya, and Game Center which enable social gaming features such as public leaderboards and achievements. The API will be able to access those libraries once you implement them in your application. We'll be focusing on the easy-to-use OpenFeint library, which will implement the following features from the game network API.

The following line makes the game network features available under the OpenFeint namespace:

```
local gameNetwork = require "gameNetwork"
```

gameNetwork.init()

Initializes an app with the parameters (product key, secret, display name, and so on) required by the game network provider. After you have logged in to your OpenFeint developer account, you'll need to select the **Add New Game** button and create a new application name. The **App ID**, **Product Key**, and **Product Secret** can be found in the **Application Information** section of your application name.

Syntax:

```
gameNetwork.init( providerName [, parms ...] )
```

Parameters:

- ◆ `providerName`—The string of the game network provider (`"openfeint"`)
- ◆ `parms`—Additional parameters required by the `"openfeint"` provider
    - ❑ `Product Key`—The string of your application's OpenFeint product key (provided by OpenFeint)
    - ❑ `Product Secret`—The string of your application's product secret (provided by OpenFeint)
    - ❑ `Display Name`—The string of the name to display in OpenFeint leaderboards and other views
    - ❑ `App ID`—The string of the application ID (provided by OpenFeint)

Example:

```
gameNetwork.init( "openfeint", "<OpenFeint Product Key>", "<OpenFeint
Product Secret>", "Display Name", "<App ID>" )
```

Initializes an app with the specified product key, secret, and display name. This should only be called once.

gameNetwork.show()

Shows information from the game network provider on the screen.

For the OpenFeint provider, launch the OpenFeint dashboard in one of the following configurations: leaderboards, challenges, achievements, friends, playing, or high score.

Syntax:

```
gameNetwork.show( name [, data]  )
```

Parameters:

- ◆ `name`—Strings supported by the OpenFeint provider:
    - ❑ `gameNetwork.show()`—Launches the OpenFeint dashboard
    - ❑ `gameNetwork.show( "leaderboards" )`—Opens the user's Leaderboard dashboard

- ❑ gameNetwork.show("challenges")—Opens the user's Challenge dashboard (not supported in Android)

- ❑ gameNetwork.show("achievements")—Opens the user's Achievements dashboard

- ❑ gameNetwork.show("friends")—Opens the user's Friends dashboard (not supported in Android)

- ❑ gameNetwork.show("playing ")—Opens the user's Playing dashboard (not supported in Android)

- ❑ gameNetwork.show("highscore", "LeaderboardID")—Opens the user's High Score dashboard for a particular item

- ◆ data-String—When the OpenFeint dashboard view is "highscore", the string should contain the "leaderboardID" property whose value is the corresponding OpenFeint leaderboard ID.

gameNetwork.request()

Send or request information to/from the game network provider.

Syntax:

```
gameNetwork.request( command [, parms ...] )
```

Parameters:

- ◆ command—Strings supported by the OpenFeint provider:

  - ❑ setHighScore

  - ❑ unlockAchievement

  - ❑ uploadBlob—Not supported on Android

  - ❑ downloadBlob—Not supported on Android

- ◆ parms—Parameters used in the preceding OpenFeint commands:

  - ❑ setHighScore: { leaderboardID="123456", score=50 }

  - ❑ unlockAchievement: "achievementId"

  - ❑ uploadBlob: "uploadBlob", key, data

  - ❑ downloadBlob: key, [listener]—listener for "completion" event with "blob" key set

Example:

The following unlocks the specified achievement:

```
gameNetwork.request( "unlockAchievement", "achievementId" )
```

The following sets a high score on the leaderboard:

```
gameNetwork.request( "setHighScore", { leaderboardID="1234567",
score=50, displayText="50 points" } )
```

The preceding function takes a table as the parameter with the following elements:

◆ `leaderboardID`: String. The ID of the OpenFeint leaderboard where the high score should be posted.

◆ `score`: Number. The new high score value to post to the specified leaderboard.

◆ `displayText`: String. An optional string to display in place of the numeric score specified by the value assigned to the score parameter.

The following saves a blob of game data in the cloud, using OpenFeint's *Network Save Card* feature:

```
gameNetwork.request( "uploadBlob", key, data )
```

The following downloads data saved previously saved uploadBlob:

```
gameNetwork.request( "downloadBlob", key, listener ) -- listener for
"completion" event with "blob" key set.
```

OpenFeint in a jiffy

What better way to implement OpenFeint than by using a game we have already made in this book!

Time for action – setting up OpenFeint leaderboards and achievements in Egg Drop

We'll be incorporating our Egg Drop game with the OpenFeint features that we have discussed so far.

1. Create an account on the OpenFeint Developers site: `http://openfeint.com/` `developers`. You can use **Egg Drop** as the game name to test and then delete it later. You can choose to have it work for iOS or Android or both. The choice is up to you. Once you're logged in, click on the **Account Information** tab to view the **Product key**, **Product secret**, and **Client Application ID**. These will need to be added into your application.

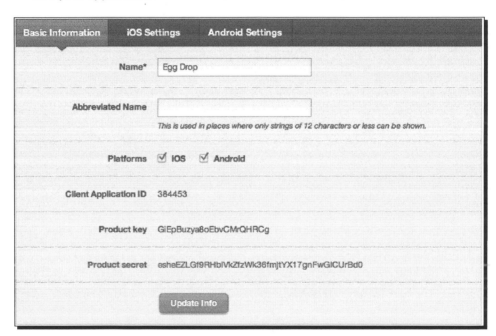

2. From the `Chapter 9` folder, copy the `Egg Drop with OF` project folder to your desktop. You can download the project files accompanying this book from the Packt website. Open up the `mainmenu.lua` file. Insert the game network features after the UI module and initialize it with information obtained from the OpenFeint developer account.

```
local gameNetwork = require("gameNetwork")

gameNetwork.init( "openfeint", "<OpenFeint Product Key>",
"<OpenFeint Product Secret>", "Display Name", "<App ID>" )
```

3. Underneath the chunk of code pertaining to `optBtn`, create a new UI button called `local ofBtn` that transitions from offscreen to y=280 in 500 milliseconds. Add in a local function called `onOFTouch()` with an `event` parameter. Upon an `event.phase == "release"` have the game network display the leaderboard. Save and close your file.

```
local ofBtn

local onOFTouch = function( event )
   if event.phase == "release" then

      audio.play( btnSound )
      gameNetwork.show( "leaderboards" )

   end
end

ofBtn = ui.newButton{
   defaultSrc = "ofbtn.png",
   defaultX = 60,
   defaultY = 60,
   overSrc = "ofbtn-over.png",
   overX = 60,
   overY = 60,
   onEvent = onOFTouch,
   id = "OFButton",
   text = "",
   font = "Helvetica",
   textColor = { 255, 255, 255, 255 },
   size = 16,
   emboss = false
}

ofBtn.x = 50; ofBtn.y = 440
screenGroup:insert( ofBtn )

btnAnim = transition.to( ofBtn, { time=500, y=280,
transition=easing.inOutExpo } )
```

4. Go back into the OpenFeint developer portal and click on the **Features** tab and then the **Achievements** tab. Click on the orange button that says **Add Achievement**.

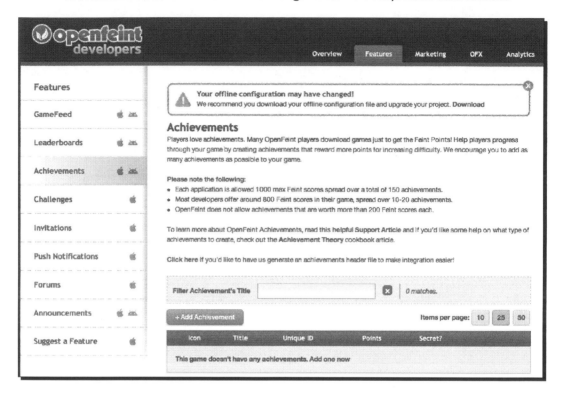

5. The particular achievement we will create is when the character catches his first egg. Create a title for the achievement, determine a point value you want to determine out of 1000 Feint points, and write a short subscription. You can add an achievement icon if you wish, but is not necessary for this tutorial. Click on **Save Achievement** when you have finished.

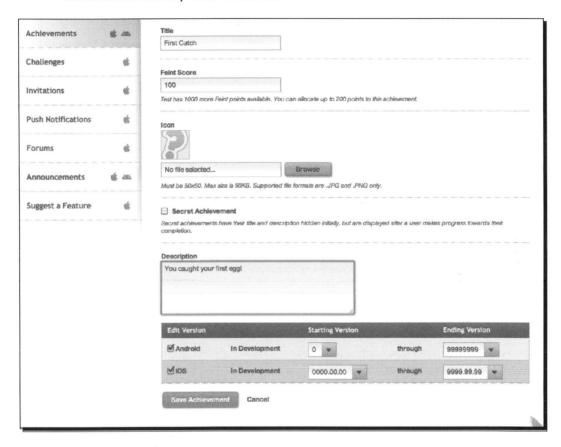

6. In the next screen, you will see the achievement added along with a **Unique ID**, which we'll be using to create an achievement in the game. You will be using your own Unique ID that is generated for you in OpenFeint unlike the one displayed in the following screenshot:

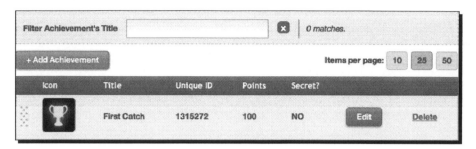

7. Open the `maingame.lua` file in the project folder. In the `onEggCollision()` function, locate the `if` statement containing `event.force > 1.0 and self.isHit == false`. Create another `if` statement near the bottom of the function that requests `gameNetwork()`, the achievement, and your own Unique ID when one egg has been caught.

```
if eggCount == 1 then
   gameNetwork.request( "unlockAchievement", "1315272" ) -- replace
the Unique ID with the one you created in OpenFeint
end
```

8. Go back to the OpenFeint developer portal and click on the **Leaderboards** tab. Click on the orange button that says **Add Leaderboard**. You can create any name that pertains to the level. You can keep the checkboxes as is. Click on the **Save Leaderboard** button.

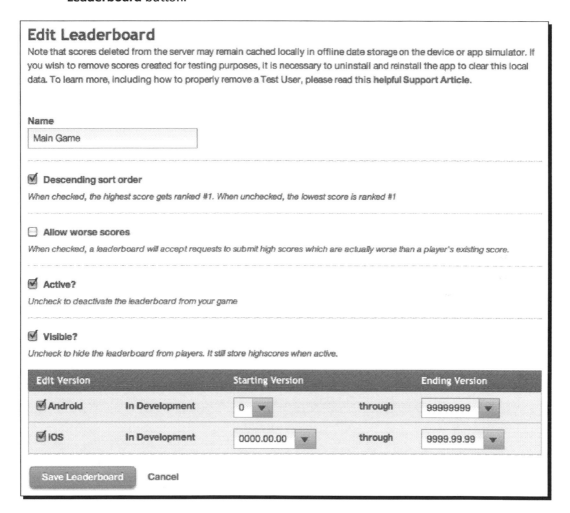

9. You will be greeted with your new Unique ID for the Leaderboard on the next screen.

10. In the `maingame.lua` file, locate the `callGameOver()` function. Within the `if` statement that says `gameScore > highScore`, add in the `gameNetwork()` request to post the highest score of the game to OpenFeint. Use the Unique ID to fill in the `Leaderboard ID`. You will be using your own Unique ID for the Leaderboard which was generated for you in OpenFeint to determine the high score, `score=gamescore`. Save your file.

```
gameNetwork.request( "setHighScore", { leaderboardID="957686",
score=gameScore } ) -- replace the Unique ID with the one you
created in OpenFeint
```

11. Adding achievements and leaderboards is done! OpenFeint capabilities cannot be run on the simulator. You'll have to load the game build to a device to view the results.

What just happened?

`gameNetwork.init()` initializes an app with the parameters (`"openfeint"`, `"<OpenFeint Product Key>"`, `"<OpenFeint Product Secret>"`, `"Display Name"`, `"<App ID>"`) required by the game network provider.

The main menu displays `ofBtn` and establishes the connection to `gameNetwork.show ( "leaderboards" )` and opens the user's Leaderboard dashboard.

When adding achievements, we added `if eggCount == 1 then gameNetwork. request( "unlockAchievement", "1315272" ) end` in the `onEggCollision()` function because we know that `eggCount` is tracked through every collision made by the main character. This will unlock the achievement in OpenFeint since we specified it through the unique ID we created.

Leaderboards keep track of the high scores implemented overall in each level. We added `gameNetwork.request( "setHighScore", { leaderboardID="957686", score=gameScore } )` within the `callGameOver()` function and inside the `if` statement that compares `gameScore` and `highScore`. If a high score is achieved for the level, it is sent to the leaderboard in OpenFeint under the unique ID set in the developer portal.

> Having an OpenFeint membership does not cost any money when you register under the developer portal. When you have completed your game, make sure to register it so it will have full access to OpenFeint features amongst the public.

Have a go hero – adding more OpenFeint achievements

By using the current game, try coming up with other achievements that can be unlocked and figure out how they can be accessed by OpenFeint. Here are some ideas to get you started:

- Reaching a certain amount of points
- Catching a certain amount of eggs
- Catching a certain amount of eggs with all three lives available

There are many possibilities that can be created. Give it a try!

Pop quiz – handling social networks

1. What is the specific API that scales down high-resolution sprite sheets?
    a. `object.xScale`
    b. `display.contentScaleX`
    c. `object.xReference`
    d. None of the above

2. What is the maximum amount of Feint points that can be given to a user in OpenFeint throughout the application?
    a. 200
    b. 750
    c. 10000
    d. 1000

3. Which of the following are valid parameters required for `gameNetwork.init()`?

    a. App ID

    b. Product Key

    c. Product Secret

    d. All of the above

Summary

We have covered several more areas on enhancing configuration settings and integrating three of the most popular social networks in today's media in our apps.

We took an in-depth look into:

- Build settings
- Dynamic content scaling and dynamic image resolution
- High-resolution sprite sheets
- Post message feeds to Twitter and Facebook
- Implement achievements and leaderboards in OpenFeint

In the next chapter, we will go over the process on how to submit our games to the App Store and Google Play Store. You don't want to miss this for the world!

10
Optimizing, Testing, and Shipping your Games

Developing a game to the point of completion is a great accomplishment. It's one step closer to sharing it with the rest of the world so other people can play your new app. The benefit of creating your game with Corona SDK is that you have the option to build for iOS and/or Android. You want to ensure your application is ready for submission so it can be distributed in the mobile platform you're developing in. We'll go over the process of what it takes to prepare your game for its release state.

In this chapter, we will learn the following topics:

- ◆ Improve performance of your application
- ◆ Set up a distribution provisioning profile for the App Store
- ◆ Manage application information in iTunes Connect
- ◆ Learn how to submit an application to application loader
- ◆ Sign applications for Android
- ◆ Learn how to submit an application to the Google Play Store

Understanding memory efficiency

As you develop your application, you should always consider how your design choices affect the performance of your application. Device memory still has its constraints even though there are improvements in computing power and memory. Performance and optimization within the device will not only achieve faster response times, but also help minimize memory usage and maximize battery life.

Memory is an important resource on mobile devices. When too much memory is being consumed, devices may force quit your application when you least expect it. Here are some things to be aware of while developing:

- **Eliminate memory leaks**: Allowing leaks to exist means extra used memory in your application that takes up valuable space. Even though Lua does automatic memory management, memory leaks can still occur in your code. For example, when you introduce global variables into your application, it is your job to tell Lua when they are not needed anymore so memory can be freed. This is done through using `nil` in your code (`myVariable = nil`).

- **Display images should be made as small as possible**: You may want to have many display images in your scene, but it may take up too much texture memory. Sprite sheets can take a toll on taking up a lot of memory in your apps. They should also be created at the smallest size as conveniently possible and have the appropriate amount of frames that demonstrate the animation clearly. For all items that you have displayed, plan out which elements are constantly in your background and foreground. If there is a way to combine several images together if they don't move, do so. It'll save some memory when adding multiple display images.

- **Do not load all your resources all at once**: Avoid loading resource files until they are actually needed. This will help save memory and keep your application from crashing while trying to load too many things at once.

- **Remove objects from the display hierarchy**: When a display object is created, it is implicitly added to a display hierarchy. When you no longer need a display object, you should remove it from the display hierarchy, especially when the objects contain images. This can be done by using `display.remove( myImage ); myImage = nil`.

  For example:

  ```
  local box = display.newRect( 0, 50, 100, 100)
  box:setFillColor( 255, 255, 255, 255 )
  box.alpha = 1

  local function removeBox()
    if box.alpha == 1 then
  ```

```
    print("box removed")
    display.remove( box )
    box = nil
  end
end
timer.performWithDelay( 1000, removeBox, 1 ) -- Runs timer to 1000
milliseconds before calling the block within removeBox()
```

- ◆ Sound files should be made as small as possible: use a free program like Audacity or your preferred audio software to compress music or sound effects and build for the device. It is best to compare untouched audio with compressed audio to hear the difference in quality. This will help you determine a good median between sound quality and file size.

Graphics

Display images have a way of taking up a lot of texture memory if you're not paying attention to the size and amount of images being used all at once.

Group objects

If a property of several objects is set to the same value, it's preferable to add the objects to a group and then modify the property of the group. It'll make it much easier for you to code and it optimizes your animation.

Turn off animations when they're not being used

It's easy to forget to stop animations from running in the background when they're not needed or when you simply have them invisible.

When you include a listener such as `"enterFrame"` and the objects registered under the listener have been set to `.isVisible = false`, it'll continue to run in the background even though it is not seen onscreen. Make sure that listeners are removed when they are not needed.

Optimizing image sizes

When you have large file sizes, especially full-screen images, the responsiveness of your application will slow down because of the time it takes to load and plus it uses up a lot of memory. When using large images, try compressing the file size as much as you can with an image-editing tool such as Photoshop or Pngcrush for example. It'll help reduce the file size and save you the pain on application lag. Compressing large image sizes will benefit you in the long run.

Distributing iOS applications

Once your game is finally debugged and completed, what's next? Assuming you're already registered in the iOS Developer Program, there are some guidelines that have to be followed before an application can be submitted to the App Store.

Prepping your app icons

There are various image sizes and naming conventions required for your app icon depending on which iOS devices your application is developed for. You can find the latest information in the **Application Icons** section of the iOS Human Interface Guidelines on the Apple Developer website: `https://developer.apple.com/library/ios/documentation/ UserExperience/Conceptual/MobileHIG/MobileHIG.pdf`.

The following are the app icon requirements, which also need to be in `.png` format:

◆ `iTunesArtwork`—512x512 px image. The .png extension needs to be removed for this image.

◆ `Icon.png`—57x57 px image. Used for the App Store and home screen on iPhone 3G/iPod Touch.

◆ `Icon@2x.png`—114x114 px image. Used for the iPhone 4/4S home screen.

◆ `Icon-72.png`—72x72 px image. Used for the iPad home screen.

◆ `Icon-72@2x.png`—144x144 px image. Used for the iPad (high resolution) home screen.

◆ `Icon-Small.png`—29x29 px image. Used for Spotlight and Settings.

◆ `Icon-Small@2x.png`—58x58 px image. Used for iPhone 4/4S Spotlight and Settings.

◆ `Icon-Small-50.png`—50x50 px image. Used for iPad Spotlight and Settings.

◆ `Icon-Small-50@2x.png`—100x100 px image. Used for iPad (high resolution) Spotlight and Settings.

In your `build.settings` file, you will need to include the icon references for all the devices you are building for in your application. The following is an example of how to set up your file if creating universal builds:

```
settings =
{
        orientation =
        {
                default = "landscapeRight",
```

```
            },

    iphone =
        {
                plist =
                {

                        CFBundleIconFile = "Icon.png",
                        CFBundleIconFiles = {
                        "Icon.png",
                        "Icon@2x.png",
                        "Icon-72.png",
            "Icon-72@2x.png",
                        "Icon-Small.png",
                        "Icon-Small@2x.png",
                        "Icon-Small-50.png",
                        "Icon-Small-50@2x.png",
                        },

                },
        },

    }
```

You do not need to include the iTunesArtwork image in the plist, but make sure that it's inserted to your build project folder.

Time for action – setting up your distribution certificate and provisioning profile for the App Store

We have focused on creating development certificates and provisioning profiles to test and debug our apps on a device. Now we have to create a distribution version of them in order to submit an iOS application. Please be aware that Apple can change the design of their website at any time. So don't get frustrated if the steps and screenshots do not match up.

1. Log in to your Apple Developer account and go to the iOS Provisioning Portal. Select App IDs. Create a new App ID that pertains to your application so you can identify it. If you have an existing App ID that you have been using during development, you can disregard this step. You can use an existing Bundle Seed ID if you choose to, otherwise select **Generate New** if this is your first in the bundle or if you simply want to create a new standalone application.

In the **Bundle Identifier (App ID Suffix)** field, specify a unique identifier for your app. It is recommended that you use the reverse-domain style string, that is, `com.domainname.appname`. You will need to replace **domainname** with your own domain name and **appname** with your own application name.

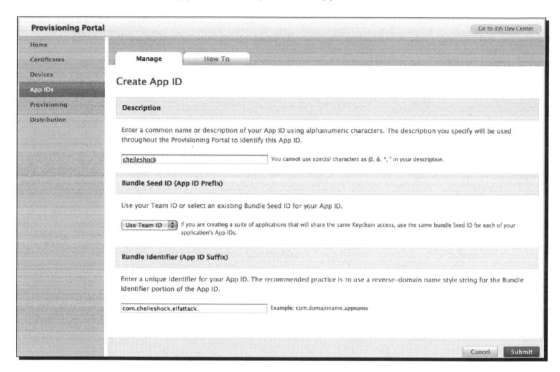

2. Navigate to the Provisioning section of the **Provisioning Portal** and select the **Distribution** tab. Select the **App Store** radio button next to **Distribution Method**. Create a **Distribution Provisioning Profile Name**. Check to make sure that your iOS **Distribution Certificate** is displayed. Lastly, select the **App ID** you plan to use to create your **Distribution Provisioning Profile**. Click on the **Submit** button.

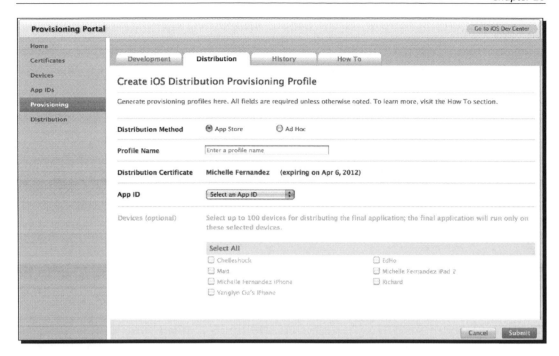

3. Refresh your browser and download your new **Distribution Provisioning Profile**.

4. Launch Xcode if it's not already open and press *Shift + Command + 2* on the
keyboard to open **Organizer**. Under **Library**, select the **Provisioning Profiles**
section. Drag your downloaded `.mobileprovision` file to the **Organizer**
window. This will automatically copy your `.mobileprovision` file to the
proper directory or double-click on the file to add it.

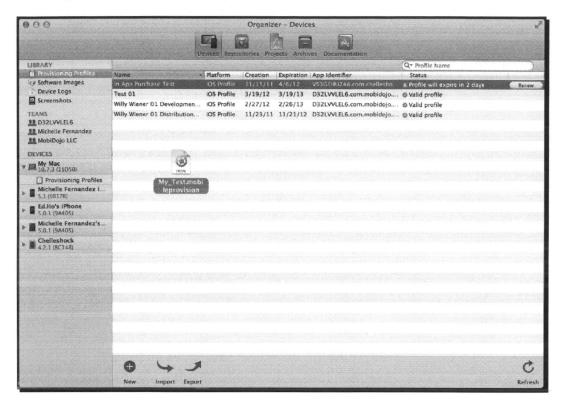

What just happened?

The **App ID** you use is imperative to identify your app that will be submitted. It is best to
have a unique reverse domain style string. As for your **Bundle Identifier** (**App ID Prefix**), you
can generate a new one as well or use an existing one. If you are implementing Game Center
or In App Purchase in your application, do not substitute a wild-card character (asterisk *).
The **Bundle ID** needs to be completely unique.

In order to distribute for the App Store, you need to create an App Store Distribution Provisioning Profile. Any other profile, whether development or ad-hoc will not be accepted. The process is similar to making a Development Provisioning Profile.

You can find more information on Distribution Provisioning Profiles on the Apple Developer site at: `https://developer.apple.com/ios/manage/distribution/index.action` (You will be asked to log in to your Apple Developer account if you haven't done so already). And Anscamobile's site at: `http://developer.anscamobile.com/content/building-devices-iphoneipad`.

iTunes Connect

iTunes Connect is a suite of web-based tools that allows you to submit and manage your applications for distribution on the App Store. In iTunes Connect, you will be able to check the status of your contracts, set up your tax and banking information, obtain sales and finance reports, request promotional codes, manage users, applications, metadata, and your In-App Purchase catalog.

Contracts, tax, and banking

If you plan on selling your app, you need to have a paid commercial agreement in place so that it can be posted to the App Store. You will have to request a contract pertaining to iOS Paid Applications. All this is done through iTunes Connect under the **Contracts**, **Tax**, and **Banking** link.

When requesting contracts, be advised of potential issues that can occur, such as delays when Apple processes your information for the first time and/or changing your current contact information in iTunes Connect (that is, change of address if you have moved to a different location). It is your responsibility to consistently contact Apple for support to make sure the information is always up to date in your contracts.

Time for action – managing your application in iTunes Connect

We are going to go over how to set up your application information in iTunes Connect. Any other information pertaining to user accounts, contracts, and banking that you would like to set up can be found at the following URL: `https://developer.apple.com/appstore/resources/submission/`.

1. Log in to iTunes Connect at: `http://itunesconnect.apple.com/`. Your login information is the same as your iOS Developer account. Once logged in, select **Manage Your Applications**. Click on the Add **New App** button. The **App Name** is the name of your application. The **SKU Number** is a unique alphanumeric identifier for the app. Your **Bundle ID** is the one you created in the iOS Provisioning Portal. Fill in the information and click **Continue**.

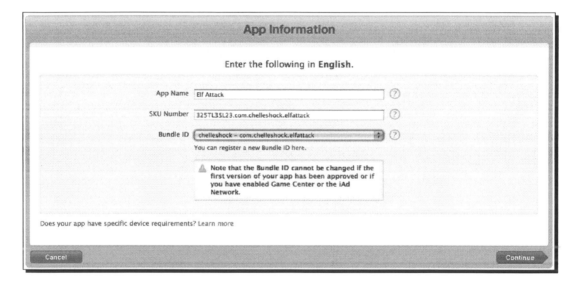

2. The next step is selecting the date you want your application to be live in the App Store and the **Price Tier** you want to charge. There is an optional checkbox for **Discount for Educational Institutions**. This is only if you want your app to be discounted for educational institutions that want to purchase multiple copies at the same time. Click **Continue** when done.

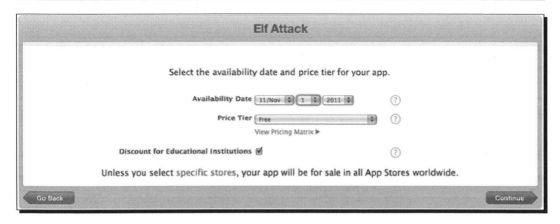

3. Next fill in the **Metadata** section about your application. This includes the version number, description of your game, categories, and keywords pertaining to your app, copyright, contact information, and support URL.

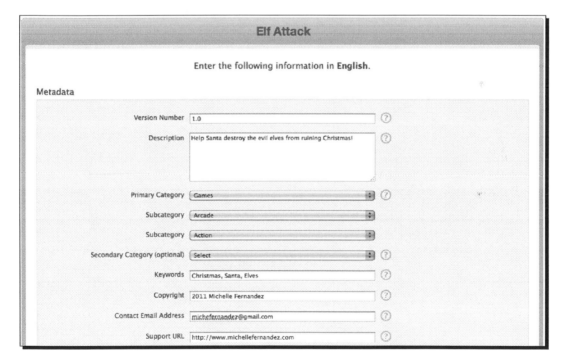

4. The **Rating** section is based on the content of your application. For each description, choose the level of frequency that best describes your app. There are certain content types that will result in automatic rejection such as realistic violence portrayed in your app or personal attacks to a target individual or group are a few examples. You can learn more about the **App Store Review Guidelines** at the following URL: `https://developer.apple.com/appstore/resources/approval/guidelines.html`.

Rating

For each content description, choose the level of frequency that best describes your app.

App Rating Details ▶

Apps must not contain any obscene, pornographic, offensive or defamatory content or materials of any kind (text, graphics, images, photographs, etc.), or other content or materials that in Apple's reasonable judgment may be found objectionable.

9⁺

App Rating

Apple Content Descriptions	None	Infrequent/Mild	Frequent/Intense
Cartoon or Fantasy Violence	○	◉	○
Realistic Violence	◉	○	○
Sexual Content or Nudity	◉	○	○
Profanity or Crude Humor	◉	○	○
Alcohol, Tobacco, or Drug Use or References	◉	○	○
Mature/Suggestive Themes	◉	○	○
Simulated Gambling	◉	○	○
Horror/Fear Themes	◉	○	○
Prolonged Graphic or Sadistic Realistic Violence	◉	○	○
Graphic Sexual Content and Nudity	○	○	○

5. As discussed earlier in the **Uploads** section, you will need a large version of your app icon, iPhone/iPod Touch screenshots and iPad screenshots (if your app runs on iPad) of the content in your application.

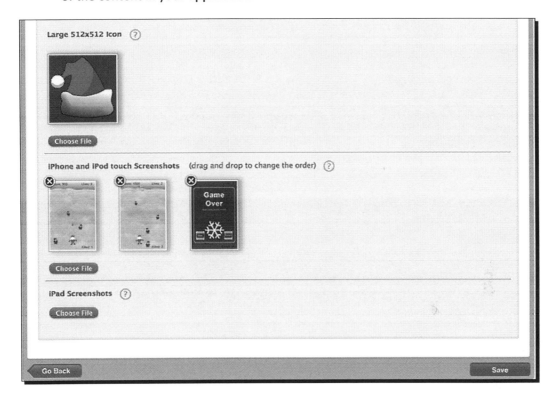

6. You will be greeted with a page summary of your application information. Check to make sure everything is displayed correctly and then click **Done**.

7. You will be sent back to your version details page. Notice a button that says **Ready to Upload Binary**. Click on the button and you will be required to answer a couple of questions about **Export Compliance**. Once completed, you will have the permission to upload your binary through **Application Loader**.

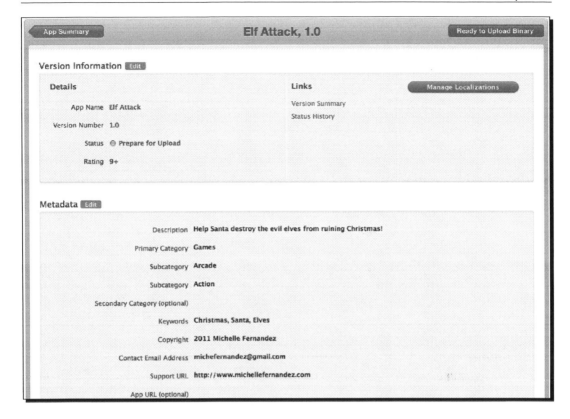

What just happened?

iTunes Connect is where you'll be managing your application from here on out when distributing to the App Store. Every single piece of information you want to display about your app is done in iTunes Connect.

Once you're in the section pertaining to **App Information**, make sure your **SKU Number** is unique and that it relates to your app so you can identify it later down the line. Also, make sure the **Bundle ID** you designated for your app is the correct one.

The app availability in the **Rights and Pricing** section controls when you want your app to go live once it's approved. It's good to set it at a date a couple of weeks in the future from when you submit it. It can take a couple of days to a couple of weeks for the review process to go from **Under Review** to **Ready for Sale** as long as there are no problems with the submission. The price tier is where you set the price for your app or it can be set to **Free**. You can click on **View Pricing Matrix** to determine the price thet you're aiming to sell your app for.

Filling out the information in the **Metadata** section is what the customer will see in the App Store. The **Rating** section pertains to Apple Content Descriptions. Make sure the level of frequency is checked off as close as possible to the content of your application.

The **Uploads** section is where your include your 512 x 512 px app icon and screenshots that best suit your app visually. Make sure you provide the correct image sizes. Once you have transitioned back to the **Application Information** screen, you'll notice the status says **Prepare for Upload**. When you click on the **Ready to Upload Binary** button on the Version Details page, you will answer questions about Export Compliance. Soon after, the status will change to **Waiting for Upload**.

More information relating to iTunes Connect can be found at the following URL: `https://itunesconnect.apple.com/docs/iTunesConnect_DeveloperGuide.pdf`.

Building an iOS application for distribution in Corona

We have come to the homestretch on getting your iOS application submitted to the App Store. Assuming you have already tested your application and debugged with your development provisioning profile, you're ready to create a distribution build that will create a binary ZIP file of your app.

Time for action – building your application and uploading to Application Loader

Time to create the final game build for iOS distribution and upload it to the Application Loader for review under Apple's board.

1. Launch the Corona simulator, navigate to application project folder, and run it. Go to the Corona simulator menu bar and select **File | Build | iOS**. Fill in all your application details. Make sure that your **Application Name** and **Version** match what is displayed in your iTunes Connect account. Choose **Device** to build an app bundle. Next, select the target device (iPhone or iPad) your app is created for from the **Supported Devices** drop-down menu.

Under the **Code Signing Identity** drop-down menu, choose the **Distribution Provisioning Profile** you created in the iOS Provisioning Portal. In the **Save to folder** section, click **Browse** and choose where you would like your application to be saved. Click on the **Build** button when done.

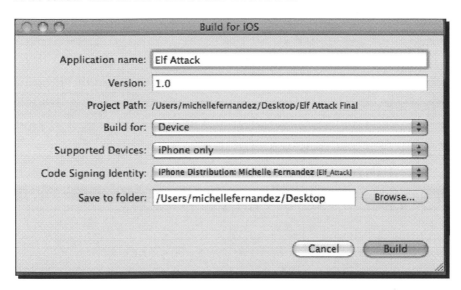

2. When the build has been compiled, you will be greeted with a display that your application is ready for distribution. Select the **Upload to App Store** button.

3. When the **Welcome to Application Loader** window pops up, log in with your iTunes Connect information. You will then be brought to another window with the option to **Deliver Your App** or **Create New Package**. Choose **Deliver Your App.** The next window displays a drop-down menu; choose the name of the application you will be submitting and then click on the **Next** button.

4. The available application information found in iTunes Connect is displayed. Verify that it is correct and then click on the **Choose** button.

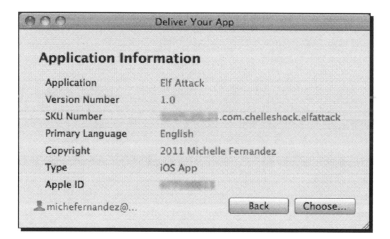

5. Click the ellipsis (...) button to replace the current file before submitting and then select the **Send** button.

6. The Application Loader will begin submitting your application binary file to the App Store.

7. You will get a confirmation that your binary was delivered to the App Store if it uploaded successfully. You can check on the status of your application in iTunes Connect when it goes to review, ready for sale, live, and so on. An e-mail will be sent to you upon every status change of your application. That's it! That's how you submit an app to the App Store!

8. When your application has been reviewed and approved in the App Store, you can go into iTunes Connect and adjust the availability date if it is approved before your proposed launch date. Your app will be live in the App Store instantly.

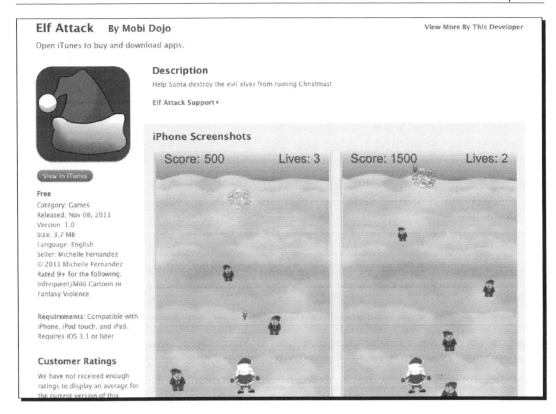

What just happened?

It's important that when you build your app that under **Code Signing Identity**, you select your Distribution Provisioning Profile that was created for your distribution build. Upon the compilation of your build, you can launch the Application Loader. Make sure that you have Xcode installed. Application Loader will launch readily after you select the **Upload to App Store** button.

While you're in Application Loader, the name of your app will be displayed in the drop down once you have completed loading the binary information to iTunes Connect. When you deliver your app, select the zipped up binary from the location you saved your file at.

As soon as the file is uploaded, a confirmation window will appear and an e-mail will be sent to the Apple ID assigned to your Apple account. Your binary will be shown with a status as **Waiting for Review** in iTunes Connect.

After all those steps, you officially know how to submit an iOS application to the App Store. Hooray!

Have a go hero – making a universal iOS build

If you developed an application for iPhone only, try implementing it as an iPad version as well so it can become a universal build. Take the lessons you learned from the previous chapters using your `build.settings` and `config.lua` to resize your application. Also, don't forget about what is required of your app icon as well. It's like hitting two birds with one stone!

The Google Play Store

The Google Play Store is a publishing platform that helps you publicize, sell, and distribute your Android applications to users around the world.

To register as an Google Play developer and get started with publishing, visit the Google Play Android Developer Console site publisher site. You can sign up for an account at the following URL: `https://play.google.com/apps/publish/`.

Creating launcher icons

A launcher icon is a graphic that represents your application. Launcher icons are used by applications and appear on the user's home screen. Launcher icons can also be used to represent shortcuts into your application. These are similar to the icons created for iOS applications. The following are the launcher icon requirements, which also need to be in 32-bit `.png` format:

- `Icon-ldpi.png`—36x36 px image. Needs to be at 120 dpi. Used for low-density screen.

- `Icon-mdpi.png`—48x48 px image. Needs to be at 160 dpi. Used for medium-density screen.

- `Icon-hdpi.png`—72x72 px image. Needs to be at 240 dpi. Used for high-density screen.

- `Icon-xhdpi.png`—96x96 px image. Needs to be at 320 dpi. Used for extra-high density screen.

Launcher icons need to be placed in your project folder at the time you build your application. The Google Play Store also requires you to have a 512 x 512 px version of your icon, which will be uploaded in the developer console at upload time of your build. For more information about launcher icons, visit: `http://developer.android.com/ guide/practices/ui_guidelines/icon_design_launcher.html`.

Time for action – signing your app for the Google Play Store

The Android system requires that all installed applications be digitally signed with a certificate whose private key is held by the application's developer. The Android system uses the certificate as a means of identifying the author of an application and establishing a relationship of trust between applications. The certificate is not used to control which applications the user can install. The certificate does not need to be signed by a certificate authority; it can be self-signed. Certificates can be signed on either Mac or Windows systems.

1. On the Mac, go to **Applications | Utilities | Terminal**. On Windows, go to **Start Menu | All Programs | Accessories | Command Prompt**. Using the Keytool command, add in the following lines and press *Enter*:

```
keytool -genkey -v -keystore my-release-key.keystore -alias
aliasname -keyalg RSA -validity 999999
```

 Replace `my-release-key` with the name of your application. Also, if you add any extra numbers past 999999 (that is, extra 9s) the application will appear broken.

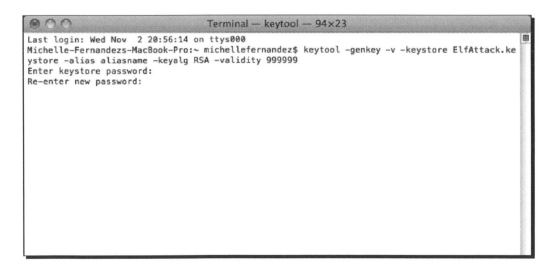

```
Last login: Wed Nov  2 20:56:14 on ttys000
Michelle-Fernandezs-MacBook-Pro:~ michellefernandez$ keytool -genkey -v -keystore ElfAttack.ke
ystore -alias aliasname -keyalg RSA -validity 999999
Enter keystore password:
Re-enter new password:
```

2. You will be asked to enter a keystore password. From here you will create a unique password that you as the developer must come up with. You will be asked to re-enter it once you've added it. The remaining other questions that will be asked pertains to your developer/company information, location, and so on. Fill it all in. Once you have completed the required information, you have generated a key to sign your Android build. For more information pertaining to app signing, visit: `http://developer.android.com/guide/publishing/app-signing.html`.

3. Launch the Corona simulator, navigate to the application project folder, and run it. Go to the Corona simulator menu bar and select **File | Build | Android**. Fill in the information for **Application Name** and **Version** pertaining to your app. Specify a **Package** name using the Java scheme. Under **Keystore**, select the **Browse** button to locate your signed private key and then from the pull-down, select your generated key for your release build. You will be prompted to enter your keystore password you used to sign your application in the Keytool command. Under **Key Alias**, choose **aliasname** from the pull-down and enter your password when prompted. Select the **Browse** button to choose a location for your app build. Choose the **Build** button when finished.

What just happened?

The Keytool generates the keystore as a file called `my-release-key.keystore`. The keystore and key are protected by the passwords you entered. The keystore contains a single key, valid for 999999 days. The alias is a name that you will use later, to refer to this keystore when signing your application.

Your keystore password is something you will create and must remember when you build your app in Corona. There will be an option if you want to use a different password for the aliasname. You can press *Enter* to use the same one while you're in the Terminal or Command Prompt.

When you create your build in Corona, make sure your version number is an integer with no special characters. Also, you will have to make sure your `build.settings` includes the `versionCode` as well. This will be the same number as your version number. Refer to *Chapter 9, Handling Multiple Devices and Networking your Apps for more information*.

The Java scheme in your build is the reverse of your domain name with the name of your product/company appended, and the name of your app. For example, `com.mycompany.games.mygame`.

When you have your app built using your private key and you have selected an alias name, the `.apk` file will be created and ready to publish on the Google Play Store.

Time for action – submitting an app to the Google Play Store

We'll be using the Developer Console. This is where your developer profile will be created to publish to the Google Play Store.

1. Once you're logged in to the Developer Console, click on the button that says **Upload Application**. You will be greeted with a pop-up window that will allow you to upload your build. Click on the **Choose File** button and locate the `.apk` file of your application. Select the **Upload** button. When your `.apk` file is uploaded, click on the **Save** button. Lastly, click on the **Close** button.

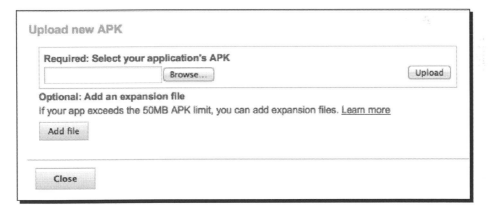

2. Select the **APK files** tab and press the **Activate** link on the right side of the screen to activate the `.apk` file.

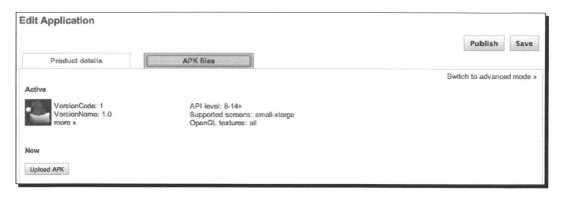

3. Now, select the **Product details** tab. In the **Upload assets** section, you will require a couple of screenshots from your application and a 512 x 512 px version of your app icon. There are optional graphics and videos you can include as well if you desire. Scroll down the page to the **Listing details** section. Fill out the information with the details of your app, including the application **Title**, **Description**, **Application Type**, and **Category**. The next section entails the **Publishing options**. Check off the information that pertains to your app. The pricing is defaulted at **Free**. If you want to make a paid version, you must set up a merchant account with Google Checkout. The next section is **Contact information**. Fill out the necessary information. The last section is **Consent**. Carefully acknowledge the requirements for publishing to the Google Play Store and check off the boxes.

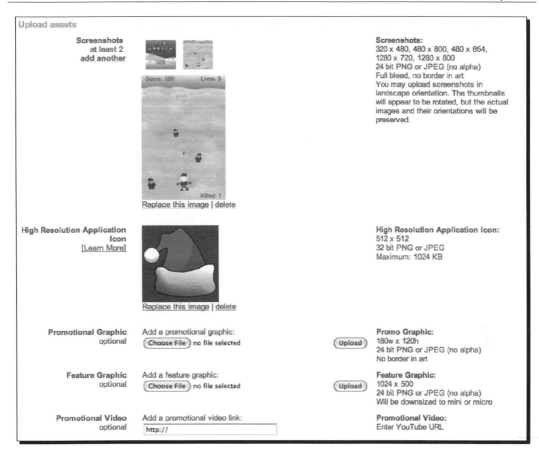

4. Once you have filled in the details in the **Product details** tab, click on the **Save** button so all your APK information is saved in the Developer Console.

5. Finally, click on the **Publish** button. You will be brought to the main screen of the Developer Console and your application status will display **Published**. Congratulations, you have published your app to the Google Play Store!

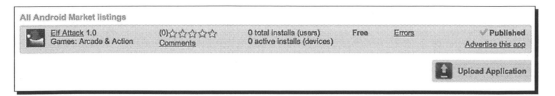

What just happened?

The Developer Console page displays a simple step-by-step process on how to publish your .apk file. While in the **APK files** tab, selecting the **Activate** link will allow the console to check which devices the build is compatible with.

The assets required to publish an app show the acceptable resolution and image types next to each section. It is optional to include a promotional graphic, feature graphic, and promotional video, but it would be in your best interest to add enough substance to your app page. This will make it appealing to potential customers.

After all the information related to your app is completed, make sure to save your progress. Once you click on the **Publish** button, you're done! You should be able to see your app in the Google Play Store within the hour you published it.

Have a go hero – adding more promos

The Google Play Store gives you many options on how to promote your application. Additional assets can be included from the Developer Console. Try the following:

◆ Add a promotional graphic.

◆ Add a feature graphic.

◆ Create a promotional video of your app. A website like YouTube is a good way to share a trailer of your game.

Pop quiz – publishing applications

1. When creating an iOS Distribution Provisioning file, what distribution method do you need to use?

    a. Development

    b. App Store

    c.   Ad-hoc

    d.   None of the above

2. Where do you refer to for the status of submitted iOS applications?

    a.   iTunes Connect

    b.   iOS Provisioning Portal

    c.   Application Loader

    d.   None of the above

3. What is required to build an app for the Google Play Store?

    a.   Create a private key under Keytool command

    b.   Sign your application with a debug key

    c.   Sign your application with your private key

    d.   a and c

Summary

We have accomplished a huge milestone with this chapter. Not only do we know how to submit to one major app market, but two! Publishing your applications to the App Store and Google Play Store is not a scary place after all.

We have covered the following topics:

◆ The importance of memory efficiency

◆ Creating Provision Profiles for Distribution to the App Store

◆ Managing iTunes Connect

◆ Submitting a binary to the Application Loader

◆ Signing a release build for Android applications

◆ Submitting `.apk` files to the Google Play Store

In the next and final chapter, we will discuss everything about applying in-app purchases to your applications. We'll dive into Corona's store module and learn how to make purchases, transactions, and more! You don't want to miss this exciting chapter.

11

Implementing In-App Purchases

In-App Purchase is an optional feature, which developers can use to embed a store directly within an app. Sometimes you may want to extend more features in your current game to keep your consumers interested in playing. Here's your chance and possibly more revenue in your pocket!

This chapter only concerns with In-App Purchases in the Apple iTunes Store for the iOS platform. If you are a paid Corona SDK subscriber, In-App Purchase support for Android via Google's Google Play Store (not available on Kindle Fire and Nook) is available in the Daily Builds page starting with build 2012.760. The Daily Builds can be found at: `http://developer.anscamobile.com/ downloads/daily-builds.` *Android developers who want to implement In-App Purchases in their apps can use this as an alternative.*

We'll cover the following in this chapter:

- ◆ Consumable, non-consumable, and subscription purchases
- ◆ Making transactions
- ◆ Restoring purchased items
- ◆ Initializing Corona's store module
- ◆ Creating and testing In-App Purchases on a device

Ready, set, go!

The wonders of In-App Purchase

The purpose of implementing In-App Purchase is to add an in-app payment functionality to collect payment for enhanced functionality or additional content usable in your game. The following are options of incorporating this feature:

♦ A game that offers new level packs to play outside of the default content

♦ A freemium game that allows you to purchase virtual currency to create/build new assets during gameplay

♦ Adding additional characters or special power ups to enhance game elements

These are some examples that can be done with In-App Purchases.

In-App Purchases allow users to purchase additional content within an application. The App Store manages transaction information only. Developers cannot use the App Store to deliver content. So, either you bundle content with your app when you ship it waiting to be unlocked upon purchase, or you have to work out your own system to download the data if you wish to deliver content.

Types of In-App Purchases

There are several In-App Purchase types you can apply in your apps. They are as follows:

♦ **Consumable**: These are products that must be purchased each time the user needs that item. They're typically a one-time service, such as money in an app where you need to pay for supplies to build structures.

♦ **Non-consumable**: These are products that only need to be purchased once by the user. This could be additional level packs in a game.

♦ **Auto-renewable subscription**: These are products that allow the user to purchase in-app content for a set duration of time. An example of an auto-renewable subscription would be a magazine or newspaper that takes advantage of the auto-renewing functionality built into iOS.

♦ **Free subscriptions**: These are used to put free subscription content in newsstands. Once a user signs up for a free subscription, it will be available on all devices associated with the user's Apple ID. Note that free subscriptions do not expire and can only be offered in newsstand-enabled apps.

♦ **Non-renewing subscriptions**: Similar to auto-renewable subscriptions, this is a non-renewing subscription that requires a user to renew each time the subscription is due to expire. Your app must contain code that recognizes when the expiration occurs. It must also prompt the user to purchase a new subscription. An auto-renewable subscription eliminates these steps.

Corona's store module

Applying In-App Purchases in your application can be a little mind-boggling and a tedious process. Integrating it with Corona requires calling the `store` module:

```
store = require("store")
```

The `store` module is already incorporated into the Corona API, similar to Facebook and Game Network. You can find more information on Corona's `store` module at the following URL: `http://developer.anscamobile.com/reference/in-app-purchases`.

store.init()

This must be called when handling store transactions to your app. It activates In-App Purchases and allows you to receive callbacks with the listener function you specify.

Syntax:

```
store.init( listener )
```

Parameters:

`listener`—This function that will handle transaction callback events.

Example:

The following blocks determine the transaction states that can occur during an In-App Purchase. The four different states are: purchased, restored, cancelled, and failed.

```
function transactionCallback( event )
      local transaction = event.transaction
      if transaction.state == "purchased" then
            print("Transaction successful!")
            print("productIdentifier", transaction.
productIdentifier)
            print("receipt", transaction.receipt)
            print("transactionIdentifier", transaction.identifier)
            print("date", transaction.date)

      elseif  transaction.state == "restored" then
            print("Transaction restored (from previous session)")
            print("productIdentifier", transaction.
productIdentifier)
            print("receipt", transaction.receipt)
            print("transactionIdentifier", transaction.identifier)
            print("date", transaction.date)
```

```
                print("originalReceipt", transaction.originalReceipt)
                print("originalTransactionIdentifier", transaction.
        originalIdentifier)
                print("originalDate", transaction.originalDate)

        elseif transaction.state == "cancelled" then
                print("User cancelled transaction")

        elseif transaction.state == "failed" then
                print("Transaction failed, type:", transaction.
        errorType, transaction.errorString)

        else
                print("unknown event")
        end

        -- Once we are done with a transaction, call this to tell the
        store
        -- we are done with the transaction.
        -- If you are providing downloadable content, wait to call
        this until
        -- after the download completes.
        store.finishTransaction( transaction )
        end

        store.init( transactionCallback )
```

event.transaction

The object containing the transaction.

The transaction object supports the following read-only properties:

- `state`—A string containing the state of the transaction. Valid values are `"purchased"`, `"restored"`, `"cancelled"`, and `"failed"`.

- `productIdentifier`—The product identifier associated with the transaction.

- `receipt`—A unique receipt returned from the store. It is returned as a hexadecimal string.

- `identifier`—A unique transaction identifier returned from the store. It is a string.

- `date`—The date of when the transaction occurred.

- `originalReceipt`—A unique receipt returned from the store from the original purchase attempt. This is mostly relevant in a case of a restore. It is returned as a hexadecimal string.

- `originalIdentifier`—A unique transaction identifier returned from the store from the original purchase attempt. This is mostly relevant in a case of a restore. It is a string.

- `originalDate`—The date of when the original transaction occurred. This is mostly relevant in a case of a restore.

- `errorType`—The type of error that occurred when the state is `"failed"` (a string).

- `errorString`—A descriptive error message of what went wrong in the `"failed"` case.

store.loadProducts()

This method retrieves information about items available for sale. This includes the price of each item, a name, and a description.

Syntax:

```
store.loadProducts( arrayOfProductIdentifiers, listener )
```

Parameters:

- `arrayOfProductIdentifiers`—An array with each element containing a string of the Product ID of the In-App product you want to know about.

- `listener`—A callback function that is invoked when the store finishes retrieving the product information.

Example:

The following block displays the list of products that are available in the app. Information about the product can be retrieved from the `loadProductsCallback()` function and determines whether it is valid or invalid.

```
-- Contains your Product ID's set in iTunes Connect
local listOfProducts =
{
        "com.mycompany.InAppPurchaseExample.Consumable",
        "com.mycompany.InAppPurchaseExample.NonConsumable",
        "com.mycompany.InAppPurchaseExample.Subscription",
}

function loadProductsCallback ( event )
        print("showing valid products", #event.products)
        for i=1, #event.products do
                print(event.products[i].title)
                print(event.products[i].description)
```

```
                    print(event.products[i].price)
                    print(event.products[i].productIdentifier)
            end

            print("showing invalidProducts", #event.invalidProducts)
            for i=1, #event.invalidProducts do
                    print(event.invalidProducts[i])
            end
    end

    store.loadProducts( listOfProducts, loadProductsCallback )
```

event.products

When `store.loadProducts()` returns its requested list of products, you can access the array of product information through the `event.products` property.

Product information such as title, description, price, and the product identifier is contained in a table.

Syntax:

```
event.products
```

Each entry in the `event.products` array supports the following fields:

◆ `title`—The localized name of the item

◆ `description`—The localized description of the item

◆ `price`—The price of an item (as a number)

◆ `productIdentifier`—The product identifier

event.invalidProducts

When `store.loadProducts()` returns its requested list of products, any products you requested that are not available for sale will be returned in an array. Access the array of invalid products through the `event.invalidProducts` property.

It is a Lua array containing the product identifier string requested from `store.loadProducts()`.

Syntax:

```
event.invalidProducts
```

store.canMakePurchases

This returns true if purchases are allowed, false otherwise. Corona's API can check if purchasing is possible. iOS devices provide a setting that disables purchasing. This can be used to avoid purchasing apps accidentally.

Example:

```
if store.canMakePurchases then
        store.purchase( listOfProducts )
else
        print("Store purchases are not available")
end
```

store.purchase()

`store.purchase()` Initiates a purchase transaction on a provided list of products.

This function will send out purchase requests to the store. The listener specified in `store.init()` will be invoked when the store finishes processing the transaction.

Syntax:

```
store.purchase( arrayOfProducts )
```

Parameters:

`arrayOfProducts`—An array specifying the products you want to buy.

Example:

```
store.purchase{ "com.mycompany.InAppPurchaseExample.Consumable"

}
```

store.finishTransaction()

This method notifies the App Store that a transaction is complete.

After you finish handling a transaction, you must call `store.finishTransaction()` on the transaction object. If you don't do this, the App Store will think your transaction was interrupted and will attempt to resume it on the next application launch.

Syntax:

```
store.finishTransaction( transaction )
```

Parameters:

`transaction` - The transaction object belonging to the transaction you want to mark as finished.

Example:

```
store.finishTransaction( transaction )
```

store.restore()

Any previously purchased items that have been wiped clean from a device or upgraded to a new device can be restored on the users account without paying for the product again. The `store.restore()` API initiates this process. Transactions can be restored by the `transactionCallback` listener, which is registered with `store.init()`. Transaction state will be `"restored"` and your app may then make use of the `"originalReceipt"`, `"originalIdentifier"`, and `"originalDate"` fields of the transaction object.

Syntax:

```
store.restore()
```

Example:

The block will run through the `transactionCallback()` function and determine if a product has been previously purchased from the application. If the result is true, `store. restore()` will initiate the process of retrieving the product without asking the user to pay for it again.

```
function transactionCallback( event )
        local transaction = event.transaction
        if transaction.state == "purchased" then
                print("Transaction successful!")
                print("productIdentifier", transaction.
productIdentifier)
                print("receipt", transaction.receipt)
                print("transactionIdentifier", transaction.identifier)
                print("date", transaction.date)

        elseif  transaction.state == "restored" then
                print("Transaction restored (from previous session)")
                print("productIdentifier", transaction.
productIdentifier)
                print("receipt", transaction.receipt)
                print("transactionIdentifier", transaction.identifier)
```

```
                print("date", transaction.date)
                print("originalReceipt", transaction.originalReceipt)
                print("originalTransactionIdentifier", transaction.
originalIdentifier)
                print("originalDate", transaction.originalDate)

        elseif transaction.state == "cancelled" then
                print("User cancelled transaction")

        elseif transaction.state == "failed" then
                print("Transaction failed, type:", transaction.
errorType, transaction.errorString)

        else
                print("unknown event")
        end


        -- Once we are done with a transaction, call this to tell the
store
        -- we are done with the transaction.
        -- If you are providing downloadable content, wait to call
this until
        -- after the download completes.
        store.finishTransaction( transaction )
end

store.init( transactionCallback )
store.restore()
```

Create an In-App Purchase

Before reading on, make sure you know how to create an App ID and Distribution Provisioning Profile from the iOS Provisioning Portal. Also, make sure you already know how to manage new applications in iTunes Connect. If you're unsure, please refer to *Chapter 10, Optimizing, Testing, and Shipping your Games*, for more information. The following are the things that need to be ready in your app before creating an In-App Purchase:

◆ A Distribution Certificate already made for your app.

◆ An explicit App ID for your application that is, `com.companyname.appname`. Do not substitute a wild-card character (asterisk *). The **Bundle ID** needs to be completely unique to use the In-App Purchase function.

◆ An ad-hoc Distribution Provisioning Profile (used for testing In-App Purchases). When you're ready to submit an app with In-App Purchase, an App Store Distribution Provisioning Profile is required.

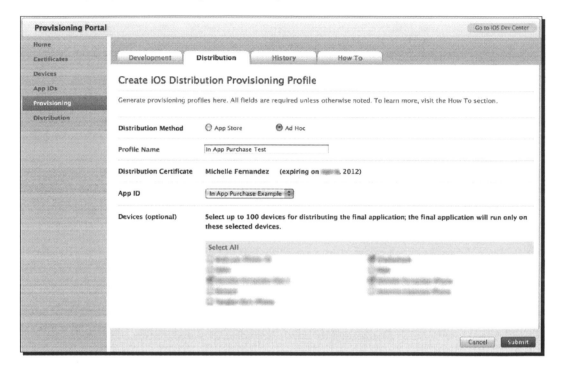

◆ Have your application information set up in iTunes Connect. You do not have to have your binary uploaded to create or test In-App Purchases.

◆ Make sure that you already have an iOS Paid Applications contract in effect with Apple. If you don't have, you'll need to request one in **Contracts, Tax, and Banking** located on the iTunes Connect home page. You will need to provide your banking and tax information in order to offer In-App Purchases in your apps.

Time for action – creating the In-App Purchase in iTunes Connect

We'll be implementing an In-App Purchase through iTunes Connect and create a scenario in a sample application that will call a transaction. Let's create the Product ID that will use in our In-App Purchase.

1. Log in to iTunes Connect. On the home page, select **Manage Your Applications**. Select the application you plan to add an In-App Purchase to.

2. Once you're on the app summary page, click on the **Manage In-App Purchases** button and then click on the **Create New** button on the top-left corner.

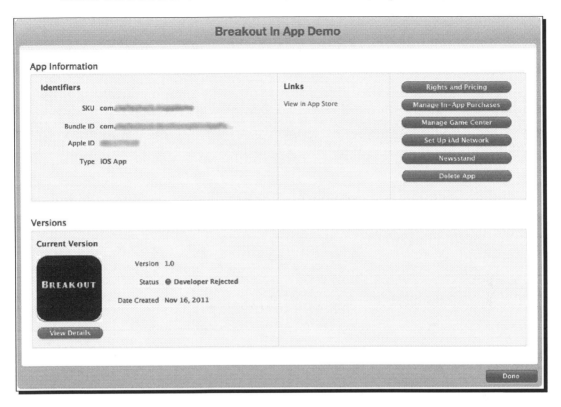

3. You will be brought to a page that shows you a summary of the type of In-App Purchases you can create. For this example, **Non-Consumable** is selected. We'll be creating a product that only needs to be purchased once.

4. In the next page is the area you fill in the information about the product. The information applies to consumable, non-consumable, and non-renewing Subscription In-App Purchases. Fill out the **Reference Name** and **Product ID** for your product. The **Product ID** needs to be a unique identifier and can be any alphanumeric sequence of letters and numbers (that is, `com.companyname.appname.productid`).

Auto-Renewable subscriptions require you to generate a shared secret. If you are to use Auto-Renewable Subscriptions in your app, then on the **Manage in-App Purchases** page, click on the **View or generate a shared secret** link. You will be brought to a page to generate the shared secret. Click on the **Generate** button. The shared secret will display a string of 32 randomly generated alphanumeric characters. When you choose Auto-Renewable Subscriptions, the difference from the other In-App Purchase types is that you have to choose the duration between auto-renewals of your product. For more information on Auto-Renewable Subscriptions, go to: `https://itunesconnect.apple.com/docs/iTunesConnect_DeveloperGuide.pdf`.

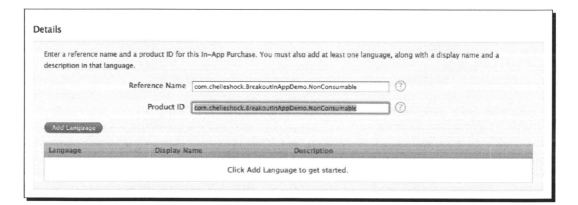

5. Click on the **Add Language** button. Select the language that will be used for the In-App Purchase. Add a **Display Name** for your product and a short description about it. When you're done, click on the **Save** button.

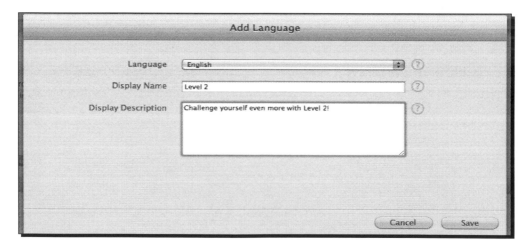

6. In **Pricing and Availability**, make sure that **Yes** is selected for **Cleared for Sale**. In the **Price Tier** drop-down menu, select the price you plan to sell your In-App Purchase. In this example, **Tier 1** is selected. In **Screenshot for Review**, you'll need to upload a screenshot of your In-App Purchase. If you're testing on an ad-hoc build, the screenshot is not necessary. Once you're ready for distribution, the screenshot is required so the In-App Purchase can be reviewed upon submittal. Click on the **Save** button when done.

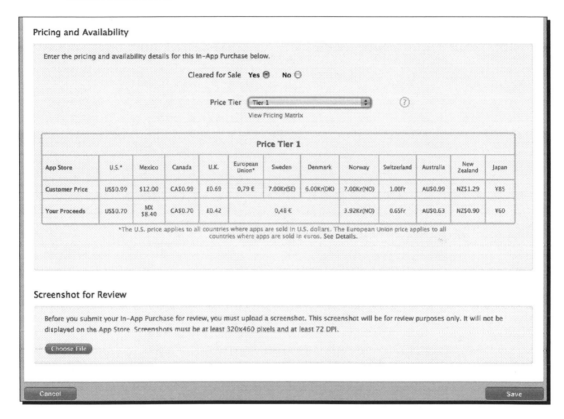

Pricing and Availability

Enter the pricing and availability details for this In-App Purchase below.

Cleared for Sale Yes ◉   No ○

Price Tier [Tier 1 ⏷]   ⑦

View Pricing Matrix

Price Tier 1												
App Store	U.S.*	Mexico	Canada	U.K.	European Union*	Sweden	Denmark	Norway	Switzerland	Australia	New Zealand	Japan
Customer Price	US$0.99	$12.00	CA$0.99	£0.69	0,79 €	7.00Kr(SE)	6.00Kr(DK)	7.00Kr(NO)	1.00Fr	AU$0.99	NZ$1.29	¥85
Your Proceeds	US$0.70	MX $8.40	CA$0.70	£0.42	0,48 €			3.92Kr(NO)	0.65Fr	AU$0.63	NZ$0.90	¥60

*The U.S. price applies to all countries where apps are sold in U.S. dollars. The European Union price applies to all countries where apps are sold in euros. See Details.

Screenshot for Review

Before you submit your In-App Purchase for review, you must upload a screenshot. This screenshot will be for review purposes only. It will not be displayed on the App Store. Screenshots must be at least 320x460 pixels and at least 72 DPI.

(Choose File)

Cancel   Save

7. You will see a summary of the In-App Purchase you created on the next page. Click on the **Done** button if all the information looks correct.

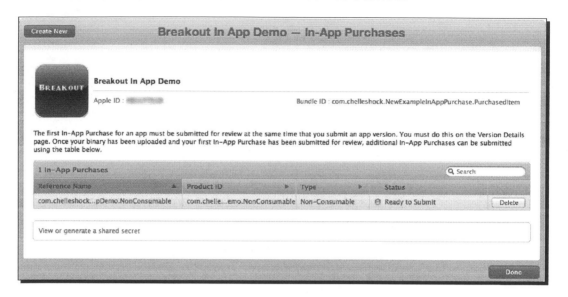

What just happened?

Adding a new In-App Purchase is a rather simple process. The information contained in the **Product ID** is what will be called upon during a transaction. Managing the type of In-App Purchase is entirely up to what type of product you want to sell in your game. This example demonstrates the purpose of taking a non-consumable product that represents purchasing/unlocking a new level in a game. It's a common scenario for users that want to sell level packs.

Your application does not have to be completed to test In-App Purchases. All that is required is to have your application information set up in iTunes Connect so you can manage In-App Purchase features.

Time for action – using the Corona store module to create an In-App Purchase

Now that we have set up our Product ID for our In-App Purchase in iTunes Connect, we can implement it into our app to purchase the product we're going to sell. A sample menu app of **Breakout** was created to demonstrate how to purchase levels within an application. The app contains two levels in the level select screen. The first one is available by default and the second one is locked and can only be unlocked by purchasing it for $0.99. We're going to create a level select screen so it acts in that manner.

1. In the `Chapter 11` folder, copy the `Breakout In-App Purchase Demo` project folder to your desktop. You can download the project files accompanying this book from the Packt website. You will notice that the configuration, libraries, assets and `.lua` files needed are included.

2. Create a new levelselect.lua file and save it to the project folder.

3. Set up the scene with the following variables and saving/loading functions. The most important variable of all is `local store = require("store")` which calls the `store` module for In-App Purchases.

```
local storyboard = require( "storyboard" )
local scene = storyboard.newScene()

local ui = require("ui")
local movieclip = require( "movieclip" )
local store = require("store")


------------------------------------------------------------------
----------------
-- BEGINNING OF YOUR IMPLEMENTATION
------------------------------------------------------------------
----------------


local menuTimer

-- AUDIO
local tapSound = audio.loadSound( "tapsound.wav" )


--*************************************************

-- saveValue() --> used for saving high score, etc.

--*************************************************
local saveValue = function( strFilename, strValue )
  -- will save specified value to specified file
  local theFile = strFilename
  local theValue = strValue

  local path = system.pathForFile( theFile, system.
DocumentsDirectory )

  -- io.open opens a file at path. returns nil if no file found
  local file = io.open( path, "w+" )
```

```
      if file then
         -- write game score to the text file
         file:write( theValue )
         io.close( file )
      end
   end


--***************************************************

-- loadValue() --> load saved value from file (returns loaded
value as string)

--***************************************************
local loadValue = function( strFilename )
   -- will load specified file, or create new file if it doesn't
exist

   local theFile = strFilename

   local path = system.pathForFile( theFile, system.
DocumentsDirectory )

   -- io.open opens a file at path. returns nil if no file found
   local file = io.open( path, "r" )
   if file then
      -- read all contents of file into a string
      local contents = file:read( "*a" )
      io.close( file )
      return contents
   else
      -- create file b/c it doesn't exist yet
      file = io.open( path, "w" )
      file:write( "0" )
      io.close( file )
      return "0"
   end
end

-- DATA SAVING
local level2Unlocked = 1
local level2Filename = "level2.data"
local loadedLevel2Unlocked = loadValue( level2Filename )
```

4. Create the `createScene()` event and remove the `"mainmenu"`, `"level1"`, and `"level2"` scenes.

```
-- Called when the scene's view does not exist:
function scene:createScene( event )
  local screenGroup = self.view

    -- completely remove maingame and options
    storyboard.removeScene( "mainmenu" )
    storyboard.removeScene( "level1" )
    storyboard.removeScene( "level2" )

    print( "\nlevelselect: createScene event" )
end
```

5. Next, create the `enterScene()` event and an array that contains a string of the **Product ID** set as an In-App Purchase in iTunes Connect.

```
function scene:enterScene( event )
  local screenGroup = self.view

    print( "levelselect: enterScene event" )

    local listOfProducts =
    {
        -- These Product IDs must already be set up in your store
        -- Replace Product ID with a valid one from iTunes Connect
      "com.companyname.appname.NonConsumable", -- Non Consumable In-
App Purchase
    }
```

6. Add a local blank table for `validProducts` and `invalidProducts`. Create a local function called `unpackValidProducts()` that checks valid and invalid Product IDs.

```
local validProducts = {}
  local invalidProducts = {}

    local unpackValidProducts = function()
        print ("Loading product list")
        if not validProducts then
            native.showAlert( "In-App features not available",
"initStore() failed", { "OK" } )
        else
            print( "Found " .. #validProducts .. " valid items ")
```

```
                    for i=1, #invalidProducts do
                        -- Debug:  display the product info
                            native.showAlert( "Item " .. invalidProducts[i] ..
    " is invalid.",{ "OK" } )
                            print("Item " .. invalidProducts[i] .. " is
    invalid.")
                    end

            end
        end
```

7. Create a local function called `loadProductsCallback()` with an `event` parameter. Set up the handler to receive product information with `print` statements.

```
local loadProductsCallback = function( event )
    -- Debug info for testing
    print("loadProductsCallback()")
    print("event, event.name", event, event.name)
    print(event.products)
    print("#event.products", #event.products)

    validProducts = event.products
    invalidProducts = event.invalidProducts
    unpackValidProducts ()
end
```

8. Create a local function called `transactionCallback()` with an `event` parameter. Add in several cases of results that are supposed to occur for every `transaction.state`. When the store is done with the transaction, call `store.finishTransaction(event.transaction)` before the end of the function. Set up another local function called `setUpStore()` with an `event` parameter to call `store.loadProducts(listOfProducts, loadProductsCallback)`.

```
local transactionCallback = function( event )
    if event.transaction.state == "purchased" then
        print("Transaction successful!")
    saveValue( level2Filename, tostring(level2Unlocked) )
    elseif event.transcation.state == "restored" then
    print("productIdentifier", event.transaction.
productIdentifier)
    print("receipt", event.transaction.receipt)
    print("transactionIdentifier", event.transaction.
transactionIdentifier)
```

```
                print("date", event.transaction.date)
                print("originalReceipt", event.transaction.originalReceipt)
            elseif event.transaction.state == "cancelled" then
                    print("Transaction cancelled by user.")
            elseif event.transaction.state == "failed" then
                  print("Transaction failed, type: ", event.transaction.
        errorType, event.transaction.errorString)
                    local alert = native.showAlert("Failed ", infoString,{
        "OK" })
            else
                  print("Unknown event")
                local alert = native.showAlert("Unknown ", infoString,{ "OK"
        })
                end
            -- Tell the store we are done with the transaction.
            store.finishTransaction( event.transaction )
            end

            local setupMyStore = function(event)
              store.loadProducts( listOfProducts, loadProductsCallback )
              print ("After store.loadProducts(), waiting for callback")
            end
```

9. Set up the display objects for the background and level 1 button.

```
    local backgroundImage = display.newImageRect(
"levelSelectScreen.png", 480, 320 )
    backgroundImage.x = 240; backgroundImage.y = 160
    screenGroup:insert( backgroundImage )

    local level1Btn = movieclip.newAnim({"level1btn.png"}, 200, 60)
    level1Btn.x = 240; level1Btn.y = 100
    screenGroup:insert( level1Btn )

    local function level1touch( event )
      if event.phase == "ended" then
            audio.play( tapSound )
          storyboard.gotoScene( "loadlevel1", "fade", 300  )
      end
    end
    level1Btn:addEventListener( "touch", level1touch )
    level1Btn:stopAtFrame(1)
```

10. Set up the level 2 button placement.

```
-- LEVEL 2
local level2Btn = movieclip.newAnim({"levelLocked.
png","level2btn.png"}, 200, 60)
level2Btn.x = 240; level2Btn.y = 180
screenGroup:insert( level2Btn )
```

11. Use the local `onBuyLevel2Touch(event)` **function and create an** `if` **statement to check when** `event.phase == ended` and `level2Unlocked ~= tonumber(loadedLevel2Unlocked)` **so the scene changes to** `mainmenu.lua`.

```
local onBuyLevel2Touch = function( event )
    if event.phase == "ended" and level2Unlocked ~=
tonumber(loadedLevel2Unlocked) then
    audio.play( tapSound )
    storyboard.gotoScene( "mainmenu", "fade", 300  )
```

12. Within the same `if` statement, create a local function called `buyLevel2()` **with a** `product` **parameter to call the** `store.purchase()` **function.**

```
local buyLevel2 = function ( product )
    print ("Congrats! Purchasing " ..product)

    -- Purchase the item
        if store.canMakePurchases then
            store.purchase( {validProducts[1]} )
    else
            native.showAlert("Store purchases are not
available, please try again later",  { "OK" } ) - Will occur only
due to phone setting/account restrictions
            end
        end
        -- Enter your product ID here
    -- Replace Product ID with a valid one from iTunes Connect

                        buyLevel2("com.companyname.appname.
NonConsumable")
```

13. Add in an `elseif` statement to check when level 2 has been purchased and unlocked once the transaction has been completed.

```
    elseif event.phase == "ended" and level2Unlocked ==
tonumber(loadedLevel2Unlocked) then
    audio.play( tapSound )
      storyboard.gotoScene( "loadlevel2", "fade", 300  )
    end
```

```
end
level2Btn:addEventListener( "touch", onBuyLevel2Touch )

if level2Unlocked == tonumber(loadedLevel2Unlocked) then
  level2Btn:stopAtFrame(2)
end
```

14. Activate the In-App Purchase with `store.init()` and call `transactionCallback()` as the parameter. Also call `setupMyStore()` with a timer set at 500 milliseconds.

```
store.init(transactionCallback)
  timer.performWithDelay (500, setupMyStore)
```

15. Create the close UI button and a local function called `onCloseTouch()` with an event parameter. Set the function transition scenes to `loadmainmenu.lua` upon release of the close button. Close the `enterScene()` event with `end`.

```
local closeBtn

local onCloseTouch = function( event )
  if event.phase == "release" then

    audio.play( tapSound )
    storyboard.gotoScene( "loadmainmenu", "fade", 300  )

  end
end


closeBtn = ui.newButton{
  defaultSrc = "closebtn.png",
  defaultX = 100,
  defaultY = 30,
  overSrc = "closebtn.png",
  overX = 105,
  overY = 35,
  onEvent = onCloseTouch,
  id = "CloseButton",
  text = "",
  font = "Helvetica",
  textColor = { 255, 255, 255, 255 },
  size = 16,
  emboss = false
}
```

```
closeBtn.x = 80; closeBtn.y = 280
closeBtn.isVisible = false
screenGroup:insert( closeBtn )

menuTimer = timer.performWithDelay( 200, function() closeBtn.
isVisible = true; end, 1 )
```

```
end
```

16. Create the `exitScene()` and `destroyScene()` events. Within the `exitScene()` event, cancel the `menuTimer` timer. Add in all the event listeners to the scene events and `return scene`.

```
-- Called when scene is about to move offscreen:
function scene:exitScene()

    if menuTimer then timer.cancel( menuTimer ); end

    print( "levelselect: exitScene event" )

end

-- Called prior to the removal of scene's "view" (display group)
function scene:destroyScene( event )

    print( "((destroying levelselect's view))" )
end

-- "createScene" event is dispatched if scene's view does not
exist
scene:addEventListener( "createScene", scene )

-- "enterScene" event is dispatched whenever scene transition has
finished
scene:addEventListener( "enterScene", scene )

-- "exitScene" event is dispatched before next scene's transition
begins
scene:addEventListener( "exitScene", scene )

-- "destroyScene" event is dispatched before view is unloaded,
which can be
scene:addEventListener( "destroyScene", scene )

return scene
```

17. Save the file and run the project in the Corona simulator. When you select the **Play** button, you will notice a **1** button and a **Locked** button on the level select screen. By pressing the **Locked** button it calls the store to make a transaction. You will notice a `print` statement in the terminal that displays what **Product ID** is being referred to for purchase. The full In-App Purchase features cannot be tested in the simulator. You will have to create a distribution build and upload it to an iOS device to instigate a purchase in the store.

What just happened?

In this example, we used the `saveValue()` and `loadValue()` functions from the `BeebeGames` class to implement how our locked level will go from locked to unlocked using movieclips as buttons. The array in `local listOfProducts` displays a Product ID in a string format. The **Product ID** in this example needs to be a non-consumable In-App Purchase type and has to be an existing one in iTunes Connect.

The `unpackValidProducts()` function checks how many valid and invalid items are in the In-App Purchase. The `loadProductsCallback()` function receives the product information in the store. The `transactionCallback(event)` function checks every state—`"purchased"`, `"restored"`, `"cancelled"`, and `"failed"`. When a `"purchased"` state is achieved within the In-App Purchase, the `saveValue()` function is called to change the value of `level2.data`. When the transaction is completed, `store.finishTransaction(event.transaction)` needs to be called to tell the store you are done with your purchase.

The `setupMyStore(event)` function calls `store.loadProducts(listOfProducts, loadProductsCallback)` and checks the available Product ID(s) in the application. The event is handled once `store.init(transactionCallback)` is initialized and `setupMyStore()` is called.

The onBuyLevel2Touch(event) function allows us to check when an In-App Purchase has been made for the locked level. When the user is able to purchase and accepts the In-App Purchase, the transaction is processed and the value of level2Unlocked will match that of tonumber(loadedLevel2Unlocked). The buyLevel2(product) function validates the purchased item with store.purchase() once the Product ID returns valid.

After the In-App Purchase, the screen transitions to the main menu to allow the **Locked** button to change to the level **2** button. Once the button has changed to frame 2, level 2 is accessible.

Have a go hero – handling multiple product IDs

Now that you know how to create an In-App Purchase for one product, try adding more than one in the same application. The scenarios are open-ended.

You can add the following:

◆ More levels for purchases

◆ New characters the user can play as if your game has a feature user character.

◆ New background scenes for your application

How you handle new products for your store is up to you.

Testing In-App Purchases

You want to make sure that purchases work correctly. Apple provides a sandbox environment that allows you to test your app In-App Purchases. The sandbox environment uses the same model as the App Store, but does not process actual payments. Transactions return as if payments were processed successfully. It is a requirement to test In-App Purchases in a sandbox environment before submitting them for review by Apple.

When testing in the sandbox environment, you'll need to create a separate user test account that is different from your current iTunes Connect account. Using your current account is not allowed to test your store in the sandbox.

User test accounts

While logged into your iTunes Connect account, you'll have to select the **Manage Users** link from the home page. Select **Test User** on the **Select User Type** page. Add a new user and make sure that the test account uses an e-mail address that is not associated with any other Apple account. All test accounts should only be used in the test environment when testing In-App Purchases. Click on the **Save** button when all the information is filled in.

Once your user test account is created, you'll have to make sure that you're signed out of your Apple account in the **Store** settings of your device. This will keep non-test accounts from being used when testing In-App Purchases. You're only allowed to sign in to your user test account when prompted in the In-App Purchase sandbox when testing your application. Do not sign in to your test account before the application is launched. This will prevent it from invalidating your test account.

Time for action – testing the In-App Purchase with the Breakout In-App Purchase demo

Before you can test an In-App Purchase on an iOS device, make sure that you have a test user account already made in iTunes Connect. Also, make sure that you created a distribution build using an ad-hoc Distribution Provisioning Profile for the app to test In-App Purchase features. If you followed all the earlier steps in this chapter, testing a purchase through the store will work accordingly.

1. In the Corona simulator, create a distribution build of the Breakout In-App Purchase Demo. Once the build has been compiled, upload the build to your iOS device.

2. Keep your device connected to your machine and launch Xcode. In the toolbar, select **Windows | Organizer**. Once you're in **Organizer**, select the device that is connected in the **Devices** section and then select **Console**. This will allow you to check the console output of your device to catch debug messages from your code, (that is, `print` statements) and any application crashes.

3. Before launching the application, you'll need to select the **Settings** icon on your device. Scroll up until you see the **Store** icon and select it.

4. Sign out of your iTunes Store account if you're logged in so you can test In-App Purchases in the sandbox environment.

5. Launch the Breakout In-App Purchase demo from your device. Select the **Play** button and then select the **Locked** button. The screen will transition back to the main menu and a window will pop up to confirm your In-App Purchase. Click on **OK** to continue with the purchase.

6. Next you will be greeted with another window to sign in with your Apple ID. This is where you will log in with your test user account you created in iTunes Connect. Do not sign in with your actual Apple account ID used to log in to iTunes Connect.

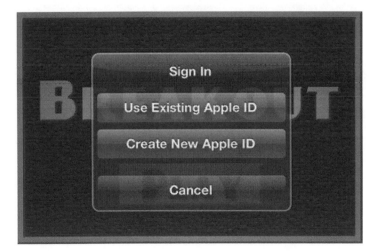

7. Once you're logged in, select the **Play** button again. You will notice that the **2** button has been unlocked. When you select it, you will have access to that scene.

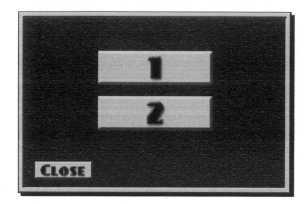

8. Exit out of the app and refer to the console. You will notice the output from the device and some familiar `print` statements from our code. The console log displays the **Product ID** used for the In-App Purchase and informs you if it is valid and if the transaction was successful.

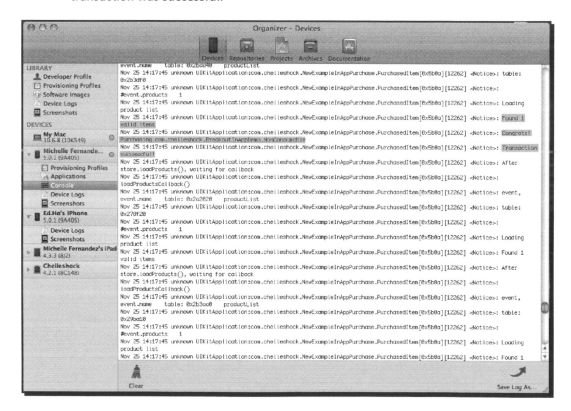

9. If you want to make sure that the In-App Purchase actually worked, delete the application from your device and log out of your user test account. Upload the same build to your device. No need to create a new one. Launch the application and run the In-App Purchase again. Log in using the same user test account. You should receive a pop-up window that mentions you already purchased the product and asks you if you want to download it again for free. Receiving a notification means your In-App Purchase was successful!

What just happened?

It is important to follow the In-App Purchase test steps accordingly. To make sure you're getting accurate results in the sandbox environment, signing out of your Apple account from the **Store** settings is the key to this whole process.

Once you launch the application and call the store function by clicking on the **Locked** button, you will notice the display name and price of the In-App Purchase. It should match what you created in iTunes Connect if you implemented it correctly.

When you log in using the test user account you created in iTunes Connect, the transaction should go through without any errors assuming there are no server issues on Apple's side or connection problems on the device. **Level 2** on the level select screen will be unlocked and accessible. Congratulations! You have created an In-App Purchase!

Have a go hero – using other In-App Purchase types

In the Breakout In-App Purchase demo, we focused more on non-consumable In-App Purchases. Try integrating consumable, auto-renewable subscriptions, or non-renewing subscriptions to your own apps.

Apps that feature consumable products are games that require currency to buy or build things in a free-to-play environment. Subscription products can be focused towards games that are never-ending and are constantly updated with new levels or may require an online server to interact in a multiplayer environment. See what you can come up with!

Pop quiz – all about In-App Purchases

1. What are non-consumable purchases?
   a. Products that only need to be purchased once by the user.
   b. Products that need to be purchased each time the user needs the item.
   c. Products that allow the user to purchase content for a set duration of time.
   d. A subscription that requires a user to renew it each time it expires.

2. What is true about testing In-App Purchases?
   a. You need to be logged in to your account at all times.
   b. Your Apple account is used to test In-App Purchases.
   c. Log in to your user test account when prompted in In-App Purchase sandbox.
   d. None of the above.

3. What type of Provisioning Profile must be used to test In-App Purchases?
   a. Development Provisioning Profile.
   b. Ad-hoc Distribution Provisioning Profile.
   c. App Store Distribution Provisioning Profile.
   d. None of the above.

Summary

We can finally see the light at the end of the tunnel. By now, you should have an idea on how to implement In-App Purchases in to your games. It is a very lengthy process to organize, set up the code, and testing accurate purchases in the sandbox environment.

The following were discussed in this chapter:

◆ Setting up Product IDs for In-App Purchases in iTunes Connect

◆ Implementing purchase items using Corona's `store` module

◆ Adding test user accounts in iTunes Connect

◆ Testing In-App Purchases on a device

Grasping the concept of In-App Purchasing can take some time. It is best to study the sample code and review the functions pertaining to Corona's `store` module.

Check out Apple's In-App Purchase Programming Guide at: `https://developer.` `apple.com/library/ios/documentation/NetworkingInternet/Conceptual/` `StoreKitGuide/StoreKitGuide.pdf` and the In-App Purchases in the API Reference section of Anscamobile's site: `http://developer.anscamobile.com/reference/` `index/app-purchases` for more references pertaining to this topic.

After 11 chapters, we have reached the end of this book. You now have obtained enough knowledge to create your own applications to sell in the App Store or Google Play Store. Hopefully all the information you have acquired has been helpful. I look forward to hearing about the games you have developed using Corona SDK!

Pop Quiz Answers

Chapter 1, Getting Started With Corona SDK

Pop quiz – understanding Corona

1	a
2	d
3	b

Chapter 2, Lua Crash Course and the Corona Framework

Pop quiz – basics of Lua

1	d
2	c
3	d

Chapter 3, Building our First Game: Breakout

Pop quiz – building a game

1	d
2	d
3	a

Chapter 4, Game Controls

Pop quiz – working with game controls

1	c
2	c
3	d

Chapter 5, Animating our Game

Pop quiz – animating graphics

1	a
2	c
3	c

Chapter 6, Playing Sounds and Music

Pop Quiz – all about audio

1	c
2	d
3	a

Chapter 7, Physics: Falling Objects

Pop quiz – animating the graphics

1	a
2	c
3	a

Chapter 8, Operation Storyboard

Pop quiz – game transitions and scenes

1	b
2	a
3	c
4	b

Chapter 9, Handling Multiple Devices and Networking your Apps

Pop quiz – handling social networks

1	b
2	d
3	d

Chapter 10, Optimizing, Testing, and Shipping your Games

Pop quiz – publishing applications

1	b
2	a
3	d

Chapter 11, Implementing In-App Purchases

Pop quiz – all about In-App Purchases

1	a
2	c
3	b

Index

Thank you for buying
Corona SDK Mobile Game Development
Beginner's Guide

About Packt Publishing

Packt, pronounced 'packed', published its first book "Mastering phpMyAdmin for Effective MySQL Management" in April 2004 and subsequently continued to specialize in publishing highly focused books on specific technologies and solutions.

Our books and publications share the experiences of your fellow IT professionals in adapting and customizing today's systems, applications, and frameworks. Our solution-based books give you the knowledge and power to customize the software and technologies you're using to get the job done. Packt books are more specific and less general than the IT books you have seen in the past. Our unique business model allows us to bring you more focused information, giving you more of what you need to know, and less of what you don't.

Packt is a modern, yet unique publishing company, which focuses on producing quality, cutting-edge books for communities of developers, administrators, and newbies alike. For more information, please visit our website: www.PacktPub.com.

Writing for Packt

We welcome all inquiries from people who are interested in authoring. Book proposals should be sent to author@packtpub.com. If your book idea is still at an early stage and you would like to discuss it first before writing a formal book proposal, contact us; one of our commissioning editors will get in touch with you.

We're not just looking for published authors; if you have strong technical skills but no writing experience, our experienced editors can help you develop a writing career, or simply get some additional reward for your expertise.

Cocos2d for iPhone 0.99 Beginner's Guide

ISBN: 978-1-84951-316-6   Paperback:368 pages

Make mind-blowing 2D games for iPhone with this fast, flexible, and easy-to-use framework!

1. A cool guide to learning cocos2d with iPhone to get you into the iPhone game industry quickly

2. Learn all the aspects of cocos2d while building three different games

3. Add a lot of trendy features such as particles and tilemaps to your games to captivate your players

4. Full of illustrations, diagrams, and tips for building iPhone games, with clear step-by-step instructions and practical examples

Cocos2d for iPhone 1 Game Development Cookbook

ISBN: 978-1-84951-400-2   Paperback: 446 pages

Over 90 recipes for iOS 2D game development using cocos2d

1. Discover advanced Cocos2d, OpenGL ES, and iOS techniques spanning all areas of the game development process

2. Learn how to create top-down isometric games, side-scrolling platformers, and games with realistic lighting

3. Full of fun and engaging recipes with modular libraries that can be plugged into your project

Please check **www.PacktPub.com** for information on our titles

Unity iOS Game Development Beginners Guide

ISBN: 978-1-84969-040-9   Paperback: 314 pages

Develop iOS games from concept to cash flow using

1. Dive straight into game development with no previous Unity or iOS experience

2. Work through the entire lifecycle of developing games for iOS

3. Add multiplayer, input controls, debugging, in app and micro payments to your game

4. Implement the different business models that will enable you to make money on iOS games

Unity iOS Essentials

ISBN: 978-1-84969-182-6   Paperback: 358 pages

Develop high performance, fun iOS games using Unity 3D

1. Learn key strategies and follow practical guidelines for creating Unity 3D games for iOS devices.

2. Learn how to plan your game levels to optimize performance on iOS devices using advanced game concepts.

3. Full of tips, scripts, shaders, and complete Unity 3D projects to guide you through game creation on iOS from start to finish.

Please check **www.PacktPub.com** for information on our titles

Made in the USA
Lexington, KY
02 September 2012